SBC

Start Your Own

Must See

Home Business

...In No Time

OPEN

Carol Anne Carroll

que

800 East 96th Street,
Indianapolis, Indiana 46240

Start Your Own Home Business In No Time

International Standard Book Number: 0-7897-3224-6

Library of Congress Catalog Card Number: 2004107641

Printed in the United States of America

First Printing: August 2004

07   06   05   04   4   3   2   1

Trademarks

Warning and Disclaimer

Bulk Sales

Que Publishing offers excellent discounts on this book when ordered in quantity for bulk purchases or special sales. For more information, please contact

U.S. Corporate and Government Sales
1-800-382-3419
corpsales@pearsontechgroup.com

For sales outside of the U.S., please contact:

International Sales
international@pearsoned.com

Executive Editor
Candace Hall

Development Editor
Lorna Gentry

Managing Editor
Charlotte Clapp

Project Editors
Sheila Schroeder
George Nedeff

Copy Editor
Rhonda Tinch-Mize

Indexer
Mandie Frank

Proofreader
Juli Cook

Technical Editor
Gina Woods

Publishing Coordinator
Cindy Teeters

Designer
Anne Jones

Cover Illustrator
Nathan Clement, Stickman Studio

Page Layout
Julie Parks

Table of Contents

I Getting Ready

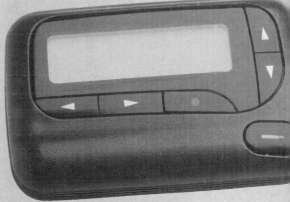

III Appendix

Small Business Troubleshooting Toolkit

About the Author

Carol Anne Carroll runs a highly successful one-woman writing business from her home office in Northern California. With clients ranging from individuals to large corporations, she specializes in writing effectively—and teaching others to do the same. Her published works include hundreds of articles and more than a dozen courses, as well as business and marketing materials. For more information, please visit her website, www.carolannecarroll.com.

Dedication

This book is dedicated to Alice, my steadfast and loving partner.

Acknowledgments

Writing a book does indeed take a village. Although my name appears as the author, I simply could not have made this book a reality without many other people who were more than willing to help me achieve the final product you now hold in your hands.

Special thanks to Candace Hall, who discovered me and my self-published tome and saw a better, future version of that work; to Lorna Gentry, whose patience and expertise during the editing process has been a lifesaver; to Gina Woods, who provided excellent technical advice; and to all the staff at Que. This book is better, wiser, more complete, and more helpful because of their contributions.

Tell Us What You Think!

As the reader of this book, *you* are the most important critic and commentator. We value your opinion and want to know what we're doing right, what we could do better, what areas you'd like to see us publish in, and any other words of wisdom you're willing to pass our way.

You can email or write me directly to let me know what you did or didn't like about this book, as well as what we can do to make our books stronger.

Please note that I cannot help you with technical problems related to the topic of this book, and due to the high volume of mail I receive, I might not be able to reply to every message.

When you write, please be sure to include this book's title and author as well as your name, email address, and phone number. I will carefully review your comments and share them with the author and editors who worked on the book.

Email: feedback@quepublishing.com

Mail: Executive Editor
Candace Hall
Que Publishing
800 East 96th Street,
Indianapolis, IN 46290 USA

For more information about this book or another Que Publishing title, visit our website at www.quepublishing.com. Type the ISBN (excluding hyphens) or the title of a book in the Search field to find the page you're looking for.

Introduction

Welcome to a Better Way of Living and Working!

That claim sounds fishy, doesn't it? Yet the facts backing up that claim are all around us.

Starting your own home business is one of the best ways to balance your checkbook and your life simultaneously. Have you ever noticed

- Most people on lists of the wealthiest individuals made money through self-employment?

- Thanks to technology, fewer and fewer jobs need to be performed at a single, central location (usually an expensive, dreary office)?

- Employers often think of their employees as commodities, rather than people?

There has never been a better time to start a home business. If you are reading this book, you might have noticed that many people are aware of this trend and are wildly writing about home business opportunities.

This book is different. Instead of writing about home business, this book shows you (yes, you) how to start and operate one.

Instead of insisting that a specific type of business is "perfect" for you, it acknowledges that you know—better than anyone—the business you are best suited to own and operate. Instead of worrying about degrees or pedigrees, this book focuses on the tools you need to give your business the best chance of success. Instead of dwelling on shortcomings (which we all have), this book will start with the assets you have—then help you develop the resources you need. Instead of theories and dry citations, this book provides you with reality-based exercises and guidance.

This book speaks to you for who you are: a future home business owner; an intelligent adult; an employee whose humanity, intelligence, and abilities are routinely overlooked; a person who wants a life in which he enjoys his work—but also wants to knock off at 3 p.m., once in awhile, to catch his kid's soccer game.

By the end of this book, you will know what you need to do in order to

- Own a fully operating home business.
- Use a workable business plan, a realistic budget, and a sound marketing plan.
- Live a life that not only reflects *what* you want to be doing, but *how* you want to do it.

Who Should Read This Book

If you are ready to start your own home business, this is the book for you. You want real information about starting a home business—not home business scams, not snooty theory, but real information you can use in your own, real world. You have definitely opened the best book on the subject.

But if you aren't sure whether you want to own a home business, read the book anyway. Because this book covers most of the decisions and dilemmas home business owners face, you will have a realistic picture of what owning your home business will be like. And as you will read in Chapter 1, "Exposing Myths of Self-Employment," many of us make such decisions based on myth, not fact. Gird yourself with the facts, and a more realistic picture of what owning a home business will be like, by reading this book. That one act will make your decision as well-informed as possible.

If you want to start a business, but aren't sure whether to base it at home, read this book. This book provides specific details about a home business, so you will learn more about the unique advantages and challenges of a home business within these pages than you will anywhere else. (In fact, a special icon alerts you to these variations.) You will also learn what is involved in expanding a home business to a more traditional setting, as well as how to make that decision.

Career changers or recently unemployed readers will also benefit greatly from this book. While you are scanning the Want Ads, posting resume after resume on one

Internet site after another, this book will provide you with another option. (And unlike some of the job offers you might receive, this book will actually be honest with you.)

How This Book Is Organized

If you have given your home business some thought—and at this point, you probably have—the process can seem overwhelming. That sleek, new office furniture would be the ideal addition to your home office. But maybe you should have a phone line or two added first. And does your office give you enough space for a new computer, as well as space to meet clients? Or will you meet clients in your home? In fact, can you do so—or is it forbidden? Suddenly, what seemed like a simple furniture purchase results in questions that put you right into overload.

This book is organized to avoid that paralyzing sense of confusion. Taking things in a logical order, step by step, you will be answering the most important questions first. Then, by dividing your larger goal into smaller, manageable tasks, you'll avoid inaction, and meet your goal of starting your home business.

How the Information Is Organized

This book is divided into two parts, which reflect the major stages of running your home business:

- Part I: "Getting Ready," covers all the planning and preparation necessary to launch your home-based business. Because this is a life changing endeavor that is also risky, the planning section is quite long. But don't let that discourage you. Success is often based on how well prepared you are. (Just think about how much planning you put in to any important, life changing endeavor, such as moving your home, having a child, or graduating from school.)

- Part II: "Putting Your Plan to Work," covers issues that frequently arise after your business is open. It will make sure that you know how to get your phone ringing and help you avoid customers who will cost you more than they are worth. And, real home business owners weigh in on their own experiences, providing you with additional help in starting and running your own successful home business.

The Small Business Troubleshooting Toolkit

After you have your home business up and running, of course, you face a whole new series of challenges. How do you prepare for and avoid work slowdowns resulting from computer or equipment problems? How do you keep your business running when you become ill? How do you manage problems when they arise, and what can you do to avoid angry clients? And what happens when you don't have enough work to meet your financial obligations, or when you have too much work to do before deadlines arrive? To help you answer these and a number of other important questions, we've provided a downloadable Small Business Troubleshooting Toolkit. This series of value-added chapters is available as downloadable text from our website at www.quepublishing.com. Type the ISBN of the book (10-digit number listed next to the bar code on the back of your book) into the Search field. On the book's web page you'll find a More Information box listing the Toolkit. The chapters in the Toolkit include:

- When Your Business is Well—But You Aren't
- Houston, We Have a Problem: Preventing Disasters During Equipment Failure
- Managing Angry Clients
- Surviving Lean Times: No Work, No Money
- Keeping Up When You Have Too Much Work

Basic Tools and Special Elements

To help you keep track of what you want within your home business, you will be creating several documents throughout the course of this book. Those documents are

- **A business plan.** This plan is written for your own reference, but later on, it can also be a document submitted to financial institutions when applying for a loan. As your business grows and changes, so will this document.
- **A business budget**. These are the numbers that back up the words in your business plan. Without the budget, your business plan is just a nice idea.

These two documents will be your constant companions. They are "living documents"—that is, they will constantly be changing. It's a good idea to put them on your computer, if you are comfortable doing so. Treat them with care. They are the blueprints for your new life.

Throughout the book, you will be creating, adding, and changing both the business plan and the budget. Most of this work will take place in Part I, with some changes and additional work with these documents taking place in Part II and in the downloadable Small Business Troubleshooting ToolKit.

In addition, special icons point out particularly important items and related information. Here are the special icons you'll find in this book, and what they represent:

The Resource icon marks text that provides you with contact or order information for a company, book, or other item that can help you.

The Watch Out icon alerts you to text that describes situations or items that require extra care.

The Budget icon alerts you to items you should include in your budget.

The Business Plan icon alerts you to items you should consider or discuss in your business plan.

The Walk the Walk icon marks information that suggests ways to get into the business owner mindset. These items include exercises you might want to try, as they can help you improve the skills you need to run your home business.

In most chapters, you'll see a number of lists. To Do lists outline major tasks you'll accomplish within the associated section of the chapter. You'll Need lists provide a fast checklist of all the materials, tools, and supplies you'll need in order to accomplish the tasks described in the associated section. The book also contains a number of notes, tips, cautions, and sidebars—all containing useful information that will help you make the most of the skills you're learning.

Recommendations for Using This Book

If your hobbies include woodworking, home improvement, or sewing, you have probably heard the adage, "Measure twice, cut once." The idea is simple: Plan what you are going to do. Then, check your plan before implementing it.

If there was ever a time when this adage should be adhered to, it is now. Starting your home business will change your life, most likely for the better. But the process involves risk, and you might risk quite a bit, including your income and your home.

Because so much is at risk, it is particularly important that every item in this book is considered and, if applicable, acted upon.

Right now, you are probably thinking, "But wait. I can't keep track of everything. I'll miss something! Yikes! I'm human, remember?!?" Or, "Gosh, I'm so excited! Can't I just get going? C'mon! Let's go. Let's open the doors of the business tomorrow!"

We're all human. We overlook things. We forget something we read. It happens. But that doesn't have to mean you fail to do something important when starting your home business.

Read the book all the way through, and follow the instructions. Then, skim through it a second time. During the first few months of your home business, scan the pages again, making sure that you are taking care of everything you need to do in order to give yourself the best possible chance of business success.

Last, work through the book at your own pace. If you feel comfortable completing the book in one week, good for you. If you complete the book in three months, that is equally good. This is not a race. There is no prize for finishing first. There is great reward in finishing best.

Make the book yours. Mark up the book. Highlight key points. Write in the margins. Put colored tabs at key passages. This isn't school. You aren't expected to turn in your book at the end of the year, and no one is going to call your mom to complain. Keeping your book "clean" is not important. Keeping your business running successfully is.

Part 1

Getting Ready

Exposing Myths
of Self-Employment

Think you know the truth about self-employment? Think again. Your day job might be a much riskier proposition. But don't view owning your home business through rose-colored glasses, either—they'll be shattered by stark reality.

Risk is part of starting a home business or any type of self-employment. Depending on your current job, you might be risking more at a seemingly steady, seemingly stable, nine-to-five job.

In this chapter, we'll look at the risks and costs associated with regular employment and compare those with the risks you will assume as someone starting and running a home business as your sole source of income.

You will calculate the cost of your current employment and use this information when you formulate your business plan and budget in Chapters 3, "Creating Your Business Plan, Part 1: What, Where, When, and How," and 4, "Creating Your Business Plan, Part 2: The Money Pages."

In fact, while reading this chapter, it is important to remember that we take only this one chapter to discuss the risks and costs of your probable current situation (regular employment). The rest of the book deals with the risks and costs of running your own business—and whether such a business is right for you.

In this chapter:

* Understanding the costs and risks of regular employment

* Understanding the costs and risks of being self-employed

* Comparing employment and self-employment, and beginning to collect the information you will need to intelligently begin your home business

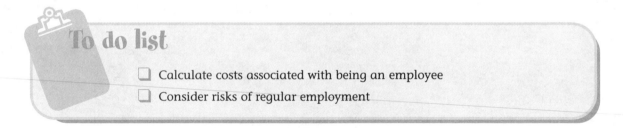

To do list

- ☐ Calculate costs associated with being an employee
- ☐ Consider risks of regular employment

Calculating the Costs and Risks of a Nine-to-Five Job

Think a home business means taking on a lot of risk? Chances are, if you are currently employed in the United States, you are taking on more risk than you realize.

As an employee, you expect to give up your ability to call all the shots and control your workflow and schedule in exchange for security. Most of us like to believe that if we do good work, we will always have a job. For most Americans who are not self-employed, the control that they give up to attain that security is substantial. Here are some basic realities of being an employee:

- You are told when to come in to the office and when to leave.
- You are told what to do and (in many cases) when to do it.
- You are told who to work with—whether you consider them to be qualified to do the job or not.
- You will be held responsible for the job you do, even if you are asked to perform a task that provides no real benefit to the company (and even if you must work with people you would not hire).
- You might frequently be asked to do all of this in a time frame that allows you little or no personal life—with no additional compensation.
- You will be told if you can take time off, when you can take the time, and how long you can be away. If you disagree with any of those decisions—well, too bad. Your choices are to accept the decision or to leave.

With so much control being sacrificed, we should be the most secure workers in the world.

But ask yourself these questions:

- How many times have you rewritten your resume? How many times have you switched jobs?
- How many times have you or your co-workers been laid off—and not known you were "getting the ax" until you were shown the door?

- How many times have you been told you would not be laid off, and then been assigned the workloads of those who just left?
- How many hours have you worked without additional compensation, only to be told you cannot take time off, either?

Table 1.1 shows a comparison of the risk involved in being an employee as opposed to being a business owner.

Table 1.1   The Risk of Self-Employment Versus the Risk of Being an Employee

Self-Employment	Employee
Customers might not use you, so money does not come in.	Customers might not use company, but you might not know it until company closes or lays off employees.
If cash flow slows down, you are the first to know. You have the capability of changing a slow cash flow to a steady cash flow, making your future more secure.	If cash flow slows down, you might be the last to know. Cash flow problems often lead to benefit or salary cuts, layoffs, or even company closure. And because you aren't aware of what is coming, you could find yourself forfeiting expected raises or losing your job entirely—with no notice and no time to plan.
You can choose to cut expenses in order to preserve cash flow.	You have no say over expenses, even if salary might be at risk.
You can plan personally for buyouts, mergers, and business succession.	You cannot plan personally for buyouts, mergers, and business succession because knowledge of these actions is limited.
You receive direct feedback from customers and bank account regarding the health of the business.	You receive no direct feedback; you are provided only with the feedback that is approved (and perhaps edited) by the company.
Business will not relocate unless you choose to make it happen.	Business might relocate with little or no notice; relocation can be across the country or across the world.
You control your retirement contributions and plan.	You have little to no control over retirement contributions and plan. (Remember Enron?)
If your work results in additional income, you receive that income directly.	If work results in additional income, you continue to receive salary. You might or might not receive a bonus. And if you do receive a bonus, it might or might not compensate you for additional hours you contributed.
Ability to earn more is largely under your control.	Ability to earn more is controlled by one or more bosses and might hinge more on office politics than your actual contribution.
The business is run to make you money. You earn as much as you possibly can.	The business is run to make executives and shareholders money. You are paid as little as possible.

JOB HOPPER, LOYAL EMPLOYEE, OR SAVVY BUSINESS OWNER?

Many people need to change jobs at least once every two to three years. If they do not, their salary usually stagnates, while the salaries of their job-hopping peers increase substantially. Often, the job market values job hoppers and penalizes loyal employees. Too many people have found themselves, after 10 years or more with one employer, cast adrift. Whether the reason was downsizing, office politics, or something else, it makes little difference. Job hunting then becomes extremely difficult, as a long-term employee frequently appears to be "branded" with his former employer's name, as if he were company property.

If the former long-term employee is more than 35 years old, prospects are generally even worse, thanks to society's ingrained ageism. Yet, if that same person launches his or her own business, what was once viewed as "baggage" is now considered wisdom and experience.

But many costs of being an employee aren't readily apparent. Table 1.2 shows some of the more common hidden costs.

Table 1.2   The Hidden Costs of Being an Employee

Item	Employee Cost	Business Owner Cost
Commuting	Employee pays; almost never tax deductible	Business owner chooses cost by choosing location of business; home business owner has no cost
Lunch	Might have to eat out; employer might might or might not provide kitchen facilities; almost never tax deductible	Chooses whether to eat out; home business owner has kitchen nearby; eating out usually means entertaining a client and thus, is a business expense
Dry cleaning	Little control over cost because employer dictates dress code; can only deduct as itemized expense in special circumstances (uniforms)	Although you still must consider clients' expectations, you probably won't need as much "professional" clothing, no matter what style of business you do
Resumes and other expenses to find work	Usually a constant expense; can only deduct from taxes if itemizing	Finding work is called marketing, directly deducted as a business expense

Table 1.2   Continued

Item	Employee Cost	Business Owner Cost
Home office (including computers and other equipment)	Might have to bear some or all the expense; even though work is done there, employer says location of work is the office	Business owner decides whether to have a home office; as a home business owner, costs are deductible as a business expense

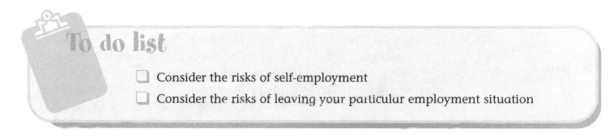

To do list

- ☐ Consider the risks of self-employment
- ☐ Consider the risks of leaving your particular employment situation

Calculating the Costs and Risks of Self-Employment

Before you give notice, however, it is important to realize that you are taking on a whole new set of risks when you launch your own business. And along with those risks comes a set of costs your employer currently subsidizes or pays outright. Anyone who is considering starting a home business has to stop and weigh these costs and risks in order to understand the challenges he or she is facing. This risk and cost assessment shouldn't discourage you from striking out on your own; but it should *prepare* you for the road ahead. View this information as part of your decision-making tool kit as you consider leaving your current employment and starting your own business.

Considering the Risks

The most threatening risk of self-employment is simply put. If you don't work, you won't have any money. You could go bankrupt. You could go homeless and hungry.

The feedback that leads to these consequences is equally, brutally abrupt. The phone will go silent. The mailbox will be empty. There will be no performance reviews, no "warnings," no closed-door meetings offering a second chance.

And the risk is very real. Approximately 500,000 small businesses (10% of all businesses in operation) closed in 2003. A roughly similar number started the same year.

Of the business closures, a little more than 35,000 went bankrupt—meaning that they couldn't pay their bills. (For additional information on these statistics, visit the Office of Advocacy website of the Small Business Administration, http://app1.sba.gov/faqs/faqIndexAll.cfm?areaid=24.)

Perhaps 10% of all businesses doesn't seem like a high percentage to you. But when you consider the hard work, money, and risk assumed by someone starting a business, you quickly realize it is a high stakes gamble. If another 10% of all businesses fail the following year, too, and the year after that, and the year after that (as the historical data cited previously suggests), perhaps very few small businesses succeed for very long.

But it's the gaps in information that speak the loudest. We don't know who fails, really—which industries, or which small businesses. Nor do we know why. Even the methodology is open to question. Search for "small business failures" on the Internet, and you are more likely to find arguments about why some statistics are misleading than you are to find the statistics the debates are actually referring to.

So it is pretty much up to you to figure out if the risk is worth it—with at least some indication of a pretty high chance of failure.

Assessing the Costs

In addition to the possibility of failure, however, you are also taking on considerable cost. In essence, you are gambling that you can make enough money in your home business to provide you with adequate income and cover the additional costs you'll assume.

Here are just some of the many expenses you'll take on when you become self-employed:

- All of your Social Security contributions—15.3% of everything you make over $400. Right off the top, you'll pay $3,060 for earning a modest $20,000.

- Estimates of your income tax payments—with penalties and interest if you under pay.

- All of your retirement contributions, medical and dental insurance, disability insurance, life insurance, and child care. Kiss your "matching funds" goodbye. Remember your employer's cafeteria plan? Well, the cafeteria is closed now.

- Vacation pay, holiday pay, sick pay, bereavement leave. Call it whatever you want (hey, you're the boss now), but no one is going to pay you for these days. This is now coming out of your earnings.

This isn't even a complete list—just the start of a long list of risks and responsibilities you are now going to fully accept. You'll also be responsible, for example, for purchasing and maintaining all of your equipment and supplies, providing utilities, paying for your business postage, and doing without the services of the mailroom, tech support group, and cleaning staff.

Take a moment to compile your own list of the complete costs and benefits you'll be assuming when you start your own business. Then, compare it to the costs and benefits of regular employment that you assessed in the preceding section. By comparing the two assessments, you'll have a better feel for the demands and rewards of the road ahead.

Summary

In this chapter, you took a moment to calculate the benefits and costs of leaving your current job and becoming your own employer. By objectively calculating the cost of regular employment, you have a list of realistic, actual costs you are currently incurring. By comparing these against the costs you will now need to assume as you start your home business, you will gain a realistic sense of the financial advantages and disadvantages when you compare the two situations.

As you learned in this chapter, however, assessing the risks is a bit more difficult. How much did risk impact your employment? It's tough to calculate that, particularly if you were "almost" laid off or "nearly" part of a merger. Likewise, business risks aren't always easy to pin down. Putting a price tag on months and months of worry over what "almost" happened can be tough to do as well.

The better suited you are to self-employment, the less risk such an undertaking represents. In the next chapter, we will look at the qualities needed for self-employment and to what extent you have those qualities. Then, in Chapters 3 and 4, we'll look closely at everything you need to begin your home business—and how much that will cost.

Assessing Your
Home-Business Readiness

In this chapter, we will go over a brief, true/false quiz and 10 key questions to assess your home business readiness.

By examining your responses to the first quiz, you'll get a good picture of how well prepared you are for the realities of starting and running a home business.

The results of the 10-question quiz will also help you understand your basic preparedness for running your own business. And, by examining your responses in detail, you will gain valuable information that can help you determine what to include in your budget and business plan in Chapters 3, "Creating Your Business Plan, Part 1: What, Where, When, and How," and 4, "Creating Your Business Plan, Part 2: The Money Pages," respectively.

Understanding the Basics:
True or False

Let's get you started thinking on your feet. (Okay, for this test, you are allowed to sit down—but answer quickly.) The following quick quiz will tell you how realistic your current approach to a home business actually is.

Each question is true or false. Provide your first answer, and take no more than 60 seconds per question.

The Questions

Answer each of these questions true or false:

1. A home business should turn a reasonable profit within the first year—otherwise, there's a problem.

2. A home business' success depends heavily on starting it correctly.

3. Most home businesses follow the same general business plan and pattern and can succeed if owners adopt a few standard rules and practices.

4. You need money to make money, so you shouldn't try to start a home business unless you've already accumulated some wealth.

5. A college degree is a key indicator of whether you can start and successfully run a home business.

The Results

All the answers are false. Surprised? Unfortunately, owning and running a home business has as many myths surrounding it as regular employment. Fortunately, even if you got all of the answers wrong, you might still be able to run your own home business. You just need to know the truth. Here it is:

1. **A home business might not show a profit for three to five years—but that doesn't necessarily mean it's a bad idea**. If you have expressed any interest in starting your own home business, you have probably received mountains of advertisements promising great riches for little or no work. Those who take their businesses seriously put in a lot of hard work and effort. If you do the same, there is a good chance you will make enough money to pay your bills—after a few weeks, a few months, or a few years. Being rich might happen much later—or not at all. Some businesses (such as printing) are pretty straightforward and therefore might require very little lead time. (By "lead time," I mean the amount of time from when a prospective client first expresses interest to the time when a business owner has done the work and is paid.) Think about it—you walk in to your local print shop, the employee runs 100 copies, and you walk out again. The lead time is short, and the exchange of money for services is straightforward because you pay a set amount in exchange for a set number of copies.

Yet other businesses requiring trust—such as securities dealing or selling homes—might require months (or years), where most of your time is spent marketing. Eventually, clients expect a good return on their investment, or to own (or sell) a home. But how that happens isn't always clear. For instance, a realtor might show dozens or hundreds of homes to possible buyers before they see what they want and decide to make an offer. It might be several years before a securities dealer builds the trust of wealthy clients to make a sufficient profit.

You'll need to know the expected lead time for your particular business before you can say whether a lack of profit is normal or indicative of problems. You'll also need to have sufficient funding—both for business expenses and for your own essential living expenses. (If you don't know what typical lead times are in your chosen field, you need to think carefully whether you know the profession well enough to launch a business.)

2. **Home businesses can survive with some minor mistakes at the beginning— but will certainly fail if owners expect the business to "run itself."** Home business owners work hard, day after day. Depending on whether your home business is a full- or part-time venture, you can expect it to take more than 40 hours per week to run, and it could consume every spare moment you have. This is especially true during the first three years. Yes, you will be able to attend your children's soccer games on a Tuesday afternoon, or attend a matinee on the occasional Wednesday—but that will probably mean working more hours some other day. Do not confuse a *flexible* schedule with the *lack* of a schedule.

In this sense, owning your home business is much like driving a car. There are a few big mistakes that might hinder your journey (such as not having a full gas tank, or, in the case of a business, not being fully funded to meet business and living expenses). But when you're on the road, you can't stop looking out the windshield! In fact, as you drive, you are constantly adjusting your car's speed, direction, and position on the road to keep it heading in the right direction and moving safely through changing road and traffic conditions.

Owning your business is just like that. After you get the business moving, you will need to adjust and revise a host of issues, from pricing and marketing to customer expectations to file storage. And, everything changes. Your customers change. The economy changes. Seasons change. Technology introduces changes to your particular industry or market sector. Just as you should never take your eyes off the road, you should never take your eyes off your business.

3. **A home business is not a "one size fits all" venture.** Much of owning and operating a home business is personal and really all about you: who you are, what skills you bring, what you enjoy doing, and what your goals are. Deciding what business to own and operate and how to go about doing so, is a process as unique as your fingerprints. The business model your brother-in-law swears is an infallible income magnet might require skills, experience, or chutzpah that you simply do not have. Or you might simply be bored to tears at the thought of operating such a business—even if you could do it well. The business that makes you blissfully happy will drive another person crazy. (And that is a good thing because the person who would be driven crazy by your business is more willing to hire you to do the very task he hates!)

For this reason, your home business should be what makes you happy, what will motivate you to work long hours (besides avoiding bankruptcy), and what will make you happy to do day after day.

The business you choose must be directly tied to you—not only to your skills and experience, but also to your own likes and dislikes, enjoyment, dreams and goals. Whether a particular business is suitable for you can *only* be answered by you.

4. **You can get wealthy by operating a home business, but you do not have to be wealthy already.** How much startup money you need depends on your acceptable risk level, the other resources you have available to you, and the type of business you start.

In Chapters 3 and 4, you will form your draft business plan—and the budget that goes with it. Because home businesses vary widely, so too do the funds required to start one. Most home businesses require the savings of at least two to six months of living expenses. Additional funding sources are available, too, for small-business startups, particularly if you are in a Redevelopment Zone.

Redevelopment Zones and Enterprise Zones are undeveloped or poverty-stricken areas the government is hoping to improve. The government will provide you with loans or other assistance in exchange for you establishing a business there. Other criteria are also sometimes required, such as hiring local help. Check with your local (city or county) government for more information about these zones in your area.

For possible funding sources beyond your local bank, check with your local Small Business Administration office (or go online at www.sba.gov). Enterprise Zones can be found by contacting your state or local government offices.

5. **Results count. Paper gets recycled.** Learning comes in many, many forms. Experience in the real world, trying something new, independent reading and study, travel, volunteering, raising kids, and many other activities all offer opportunities for learning valuable skills. Don't get me wrong—college degrees are very valuable. But running your own business is a highly pragmatic endeavor. For someone who holds any type of formal academic diploma, the actual degree is usually not as important as what you have learned to get it.

In some professions, licensing is required, often in a process that includes coursework, experience, and a college degree. But if you are considering being an accountant, for example, you should already be aware of the requirements and possess any licensing you need. If you are in a field in which licensing is key, and you don't have it, you might want to wait (or consider a line of business in which licensing is not required).

And if you have not had the opportunity to obtain a college degree, don't sweat it. Did you know that Bill Gates dropped out of college? Dave Thomas, who started the Wendy's fast food chain, never made it to high school. Some studies have shown that college graduates earn more, but these studies have, overwhelmingly, focused on people who are employees, not business owners.

To do list

- ❑ Determine whether you're financially and psychologically ready to start a home business.
- ❑ Examine your skills in self-discipline, organization, and perseverance.
- ❑ Explore your abilities in customer-relations, creative thinking, and leadership.
- ❑ Think about your interest in ongoing professional growth and development.
- ❑ Determine where and how you can achieve improvements in your business-readiness.

Ten Questions to Assess Your Home Business Potential

These 10 questions probe your possession of, or ability to implement, the most important qualities of a home business owner. So, pull out your resume, gather your financial records (including income and expense records) for the previous year, think about your experiences, and answer all the questions completely and truthfully. Record the answers to these questions in your business planning journal so that you can keep them for later reference.

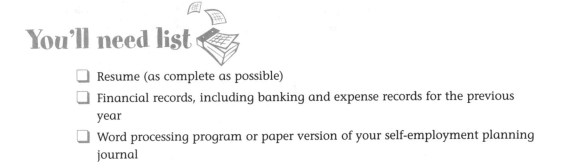

You'll need list

☐ Resume (as complete as possible)

☐ Financial records, including banking and expense records for the previous year

☐ Word processing program or paper version of your self-employment planning journal

The Questions

1. If you were laid off today, how long could you live on the cash in your checking and savings accounts? (Do not count retirement, stocks, or bonds.)

2. What marketable skills do you have, and how do they apply to the home business you've chosen to launch? If you ran in to someone who could refer 100 ideal customers to you right now, how would you describe your business—in 30 seconds or less?

3. How do businesses similar to the one you propose to launch gain customers? Be specific. How much do you know about the industry or profession you're entering in to?

> **tip** Recording your answers to this quiz in your business planning journal gives you a valuable record of the ideas, skills, and weaknesses you possessed when you launched your business. You might want to periodically review your answers and retest yourself on the first anniversary of your business opening.

4. What happens on days when you just don't feel like working, but things have to get done? Do you accomplish the tasks before you, or do you spend your time trying to avoid them?

5. Have you ever worked toward a goal that took six months or more to complete? How did you motivate yourself to sacrifice time, money, and other resources?

6. Can you give an example of a time you said, "No" to someone regarding a business request, while still maintaining a strong business relationship? Are you able to speak up for your own needs and wants—politely (at first, anyway)?

7. Can you locate last year's utility bills? How much money was in your checking account one year ago today?

8. Why do you learn new things—because you want to, because someone else told you it was a good idea, or a little bit of both? When was the last time you learned a new skill or took a class regarding some aspect of your line of work?

9. You must go to another city, 300 miles away, for a business meeting. All flights are booked. Your car is in the shop for repairs. What do you do?

10. Do you serve on a nonprofit board? Have you ever organized an event for your favorite charity? Do you currently supervise others? Are you responsible for another person's welfare? How do you handle being in charge? Can you admit your mistakes—even when you are in a leadership position?

Assessing Your Responses

In this section of the chapter, you learn what your answers to the preceding questions tell you about your likelihood of success in launching your own home business. For each of the preceding questions, the following assessment indicates the basic skill set the question tests and the criteria for scoring your response. Based on your answers and the evaluation criteria listed in this section of the chapter, you will award yourself one of three scores for each of the questions you just answered:

A plus + for answers that fully meet or exceed the criteria

A check √ for answers that adequately (though not completely) meet the criteria

A minus – for answers that fail to meet the criteria and indicate that you need improvement.

Any question that receives a minus is likely to indicate issues that will add to your budget in the next chapter. Note the "How To Improve" solution, and plan for meeting these additional costs.

> **note** Some questions have no middle ground, so the scoring is a simple plus or minus.

1. **Asset: Financial Resources**

   Scoring:

   + Give yourself extra credit if you have 6 to 12 months' worth of living expenses in the bank.

   √ You pass if you have at least three months' worth of living expenses in the bank.

   > **tip** No matter what score you receive, read the "How To Improve" information for every question. This information provides valuable tips for improving your chances of business success.

   – You fail this question if you have less than three months' worth of living expenses in the bank, or if you cannot tell what you spend over an average month.

You also fail this question if you have more than 12 months' savings in your account. Why? Because the extra money should be earning a higher yield for you than what you get on your savings account. Plus, having all that money at your disposal increases the chance that you will waste it.

How To Improve:

- If you have less than three months' worth of living expenses in the bank, you need to work on saving money right now. Although it is risky to start a business with such a small amount in the bank, having an inadequate financial cushion is just as risky when you work for someone else. As you work through this book, you will probably find that you need at least six months' worth of living expenses (at a minimum) in order to start your business, and possibly as much as one year's worth.

> **caution** When calculating your current financial assets/resources, be sure that you do not include money specifically saved and earmarked in anticipation of a large bill in the near future, such as your annual car insurance payment. If money in your savings account is really set aside for a balloon payment on your mortgage, for example, do not count this as true savings.

- You can either a) accept the higher level of risk, b) cut back on spending and wait to start your business until you save more, or c) start your business on the side while maintaining a regular job.

- If you have more than 12 months' savings in your account, consider moving the additional money in to your retirement fund or investment accounts.

2. Asset: Marketable Skills

+ Give yourself extra credit for up to five skills.

√ If you have two to four skills, you pass this question nicely.

− If you have fewer than two skills, you fail this question.

caution

Watch Out

If you cannot ascertain how much you spend each month, slow down. Hire a bookkeeper or accountant to help you, if you need it, and figure out your monthly household budget.

note What are the most likely places of waste in your budget? Cable television, cell phones, eating out, vacations, and clothing.

Resources

Must bee

If you have more than five skills listed in your description of the services or products you provide in your business, you probably should whittle them down to no more than four skills (or just those skills that can be marketed seamlessly). You're allowed to go back and rethink the skills you would use in your business. You can undermine your credibility by offering services or products based on too many different types of skills.

So how do you know whether your skills can be "marketed seamlessly"?

Let's say that you want to start a home business as a marketing consultant. You have a background in sales that provides credibility to your advice in this area. But you have also been tinkering with computers, and you'd like to offer tech support, too.

Most people won't go to the same source for assistance with both technical support and marketing expertise. These seem like unrelated skill sets, and potential customers might assume that if you've developed worthwhile expertise in one, you probably haven't had the time and energy to develop equally professional skills in the other. Marketing this combination would be a challenge, as well. It would be difficult to seamlessly transition from discussing your marketing services to discussing your technical support services.

However, let's say that you are starting a marketing consulting business, based on the same sales background. You have also had experience with television production and video editing. So, you would also like to offer television production services, and plan to sell these services to many of your clients.

After all, many clients who are revamping their marketing plans (and seeking your advice as a consultant) might also choose to use your company to produce a television advertisement.

How To Improve:

- If you don't have at least two marketable skills that are directly applicable to your home business, you need to gain the necessary training or experience to obtain them.

- If you have too many skills, and they don't mesh nicely, prioritize them. Which services would you most like to offer in your home business? In the preceding example, the business owner would probably need to choose between marketing and technical support—perhaps growing the business in to a "one stop" service center. If the decision is tough, work through the business plan and budget for each separate business.

3. Asset: Industry Knowledge

+ You easily pass this question if you have at least three to five years' experience providing the service or product you plan to offer through your business, and you know the industry well. But demote yourself to a check score if all of your experience is with only one employer.

√ If you have less than three years' experience, but know the industry well, you still pass.

– If you have less than three years' experience and do not know the industry well, you fail the question.

How To Improve:

- You really need industry knowledge. By that, I mean that you have some understanding of issues such as these, as they affect your business:

    Are there slow and busy times within the industry?

    What professional organizations are important to belong to? How is your profession or industry structured? What divisions exist for entry level, mid-career, and advanced levels?

What happens during the normal course of business? For instance, if your industry is publishing, what happens in order for a book to be published? Can you name all the steps? Which steps would a customer expect you to perform, and which would be referred elsewhere?

What is the jargon used in your industry or profession? What words will you need to know in order to communicate with people while doing your work?

How is the industry segmented? Using publishing as an example again, do you know that the industry is segmented in to small publishers, specialty publishers, large publishers with multiple imprints, and so on?

What rules govern your industry or profession? What licensing is required? Which government agencies regulate the industry/ profession?

If you don't have industry knowledge appropriate to the business you're planning to launch, there are two things you can do: a) Stay in the work force and gain the knowledge you need, or b) Choose an industry in which you have more experience and knowledge. This is one positive aspect of regular employment. Employers provide great on-the-job training—the results of which are tough (and expensive) to replicate. It is much more cost-effective to gain experience (and make mistakes) on someone else's dime.

4. Asset: Self-Discipline

+ If you currently perform your work without supervision, or work on long-term projects at home without supervision, you easily pass this question.

− If you are supervised constantly at work and never accomplish anything on your own at home, you fail this question.

How To Improve:

• Coaches and psychologists might help you uncover why you have a tough time getting moving without a taskmaster.

• Check with your doctor to see if undiagnosed learning disabilities might also be the culprit. (See Appendix A for resources.)

• If you would like to improve your self-discipline, try keeping track of your goals versus what you do on a typical day. What distracts you?

How do you spend your time? Write down what you do, every day, for two weeks. (You can use increments as small as five minutes.) A lot of self-discipline is getting rid of the time-wasting activities (or at least limiting them so that they're the occasional reward, not the daily habit).

5. **Asset: Long-Term Thinking**

+ If you have completed a project that took six months or more to finish, and you fully understand how you maintained your motivation during that time, you easily pass this question.

√ If you completed a project of six months or more, but don't really know or can't explain what kept you motivated, or if your motivation included nagging from others, you pass this question—but barely.

− A no answer, indicates that you have not finished a long-term project, so you fail this question.

How To Improve:

- Tackle a project requiring multiple steps, but with less riding on it than running your own business. You might learn woodworking and build your own furniture. Or, you might try to increase your education—taking an evening class or obtaining professional certification will tell you a lot about your ability to sacrifice now for future gain.

tip   Always remember that when you are self-employed, the 16 hour day you work today will have rewards weeks or months from now. You get paid today because you planned last year, marketed last season, and worked last month.

WHAT'S YOUR DEFINITION OF LONG-TERM?

Americans are known to have a tough time with the concept of "long term." I once lived in Europe. Before leaving the United States, I was listening to an American newscast that talked about a company's future "long term." The news story then went on to say that, by long term, it meant the company's performance over the next five quarters—barely more than one year! Several months later, while in Europe, I was introduced to some people by my Dutch colleagues. While doing the introduction, they explained that I was in the country "tijdelijk"—meaning temporarily. I was scheduled to stay for three years. I thought back to the American newscast and wondered how they would take that comment from my Dutch acquaintances.

6. **Asset: Assertiveness**

+ If you can provide examples of times when, in the course of business, you stood up for your own needs politely and maintained your relationship with your boss, co-worker, or client, you easily pass this question.

√ If standing up for your own needs usually means alienating others, or you can recall when you lost a client or damaged a working relationship as a result of asserting yourself, you fail this question.

− A no answer also means that you fail this question.

How To Improve:

- Whether you cannot stand up for yourself, or alienate others when you do, some introspection is clearly in order. Psychologists and coaches are professionals who can help uncover why you are so afraid to stand up for yourself—or why you are so threatened when you must do so.

- Remember, too, that the way we do something is sometimes at least as important as *what* we do. Choose your words carefully when a situation becomes tense. The idea is to de-escalate the situation, and keep things as calm as possible. Don't use words that would inflame the situation.

7. **Asset: Organization**

+ If you located the information requested in fewer than five minutes, you easily passed this question.

√ If it took you fewer than 20 minutes (but more than five), you pass—but barely.

− If it took you more than 20 minutes to find the information (or if you just gave up), you failed the question.

How To Improve:

- Make the time to organize your paperwork. If you have difficulty doing this, a professional organizer can help you set up a system that works. When your system is in place, try it for several months before you open your business. You want to be sure that the system works.

note Are your computer and paper files well organized? Don't forget—both are important! Your organizational style and technique don't have to match a single "gold standard," either, as long as it works. Starting a business means that you need to keep track of potential customers, expenses, income, and other details. Because this is your home business, if the system works for you, we'll consider you organized.

8. **Asset: Constant Learning**

+ If you have learned about three or more subjects on your own, and not at the behest of your employer, you pass this question readily.

√ If you have learned about one or two subjects independently, you pass—but barely.

– If you have never learned about a particular subject on your own, you fail this question.

How To Improve:

- Take a class.
- Learn how to perform some repair job around the home.
- Take up a foreign language.

> **tip**
> What do you do when you read a book and come across an unfamiliar word? How often do you read? What subjects do you read about? Opportunities to learn are all around you. It doesn't matter what you learn, but rather, how well you learn and how eager you are to do so.

9. **Asset: Creativity Coupled With Perseverance**

+ You pass this question easily if you took the train (or at least checked train schedules), rented a car, or borrowed a car. In fact, if you got to the appointment by any practical means (such as getting a spouse, partner, or friend to drive you), you did well.

√ You pass this question (barely) if you called the client and rescheduled the appointment.

– If you couldn't think of what to do, or gave up, you failed this question.

> **note**
> Part of owning your home business is knowing when "no" is not the answer, as well as knowing how to resolve problems that appear insurmountable. Your creativity and resourcefulness will determine how successful your business will be at weathering the events and market changes over time. What worked yesterday might be disastrous if you try it today. And learning to attack the impossible might be what sets you apart from your competition.

How To Improve:

- Try to break old patterns and learn to think beyond your typical way of doing things. A coach might be able to help you build your creativity if you find this difficult.

- Try to do as many things differently as you can for one entire week. How many different ways can you commute to work? How many meals can you fix that you have never made before? How many routes can you take to and from your home or office? What if you watched something other than your regular television shows—or turned off the television altogether?

10. Asset: Responsibility

+ The responsibility that will really help you pass this question is the kind that is above and beyond the minimum requirements of daily life. Try to think of responsible roles you willingly took, yet weren't necessarily expected of you. If you can identify at least one major responsible role that you currently fulfill or have fulfilled in the past, and can easily admit making mistakes in this role, you pass this question.

√ If you have started a business before, and can honestly state why it failed (or why you closed it), you automatically pass this question with a plus.

– Those with no responsible roles, or those who have responsible roles but have never admitted making a mistake as part of that role, fail the question.

note If your only responsible role is "parent," the scoring becomes a bit tricky. Did you plan for the child? Are you the primary caregiver? Those are good indications of responsibility. And admittedly, a home business will certainly feel like your "baby" in some respects.

How To Improve:

- If you have trouble admitting your mistakes, practice admitting them. We are all human, and no one is perfect. When you own your business, sooner or later you will have to admit a mistake to a client. If you hide the mistake, the situation will only get worse—and it can harm an otherwise impeccable reputation.

- If you have not had responsible roles, volunteer. Start with a small commitment—say, once a month. Increase that commitment, both in time and responsibility, after 6 to 12 months. When a position on a nonprofit board becomes available, willingly take on the role. (Of course, this should be a nonprofit you are excited about helping.)

- If you can't find responsible and interesting volunteer roles, ask yourself: "If I could do anything to improve the world, what would I do?" Then see what you might be able to do to make that happen. You might not want to start your own nonprofit organization (after all, you're going to be busy running a business), but you might be able to make a difference and assume a leadership role in the process.

See Appendix A for suggestions on coaches, psychologists, and other professionals who can help you with this topic.

To do list

- ☐ Assess your self-employment strengths and weaknesses.
- ☐ Consider how you might address weaknesses.
- ☐ Keep what you have written for Chapters 3 and 4.

Evaluating Your Overall Score

This section discusses how you should interpret the number of plusses, minuses, and check marks you scored in the preceding quiz. Note that, because all 10 qualities are important, plusses won't automatically "even out" the minuses. It is truly important to be fully prepared in all areas. Here's how to read your results:

- **Minuses:** If you have one or two minuses, you have some work to do, but you can probably take care of these issues and continue working toward starting your business.

  If you have more than two minuses, you might want to delay starting your business until you've improved in these areas. All 10 of these qualities are vital to starting your home business, and trying to create or greatly enhance 30% of them is going to be too overwhelming while you are also trying to start a business. Take 6 to 12 months, at least, and then retake the test.

- **Check Marks:** These are the "barely passing," or C- grades in this quiz. If you have up to four check marks, you have a lot of work to do, but you should still be able to start your business. If you have five or more check marks, put off the start of your business. Address the issues, and retake the test when you are ready.

- **Plusses:** If you have all 10 plusses—stop. Are you really being honest with yourself? Please be sure that you really deserve a plus next to all 10 questions. If you have six to nine plusses, good for you! Depending on the answers to your other questions, you probably passed this test. If you have fewer than six plusses, but have enough check marks to pass, you might still want to delay the start of your business. In this situation, it's really a judgment call.

Overall, any areas needing improvement should be addressed. The more areas of improvement you have, the riskier it will be for you to start your home business.

Summary

A home business reflects the business owner—both our good and bad traits show up in our home business. For that reason, it is very important to know our strengths and weaknesses and to try and correct those that will be detrimental to the operation of a business.

Such assessment is not easy. It requires a raw, unvarnished honesty that is rarely called on elsewhere in life. Get used to it. If you can keep that unflinching ability to continually assess yourself, warts and all it will help you resolve conflicts and correct small mistakes before they become big mistakes.

Now that you've assessed your business readiness, you're ready to get started creating the backbone of your new home business—your business plan and budget. In Chapter 3 you begin that process by putting together your business plan.

Creating Your Business Plan, Part 1: What, Where, When, and How

3

In this chapter:

* Reviewing your current employment contract, calculating insurance costs, checking zoning restrictions, and eliminating major obstacles to your home business

* Drafting your home business plan

Okay, you now know that you can do this. But where do you start? This chapter takes you through the biggest obstacles first—those half dozen "deal breakers" that might make you seriously rethink starting your home business. Then, step by step, we will outline a business plan for your home business. You will describe your business and its structure, document who your customers are, and define what services you provide and how you get business. Your business plan must also outline the financial plan and structure of your home business; in Chapter 4, "Creating Your Business Plan, Part 2: The Money Pages," we will complete that aspect of your business plan. Do not proceed beyond Chapter 4 until you have completed the business plan and are satisfied with the results.

However, you should also have some idea of where we're headed—and if you're a "big picture" kind of person, plowing in to the details can be confusing. Figure 3.1 is an overview of what we will be doing for the rest of the book. There's no "you are here" arrow because it's simple—we're at the very beginning.

FIGURE 3.1
An overview of the
home business
process.

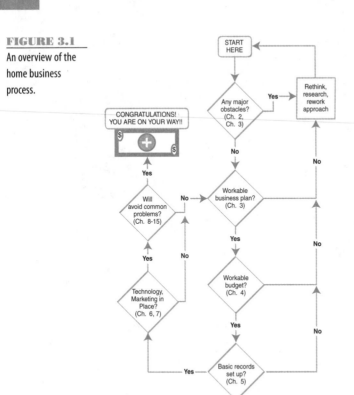

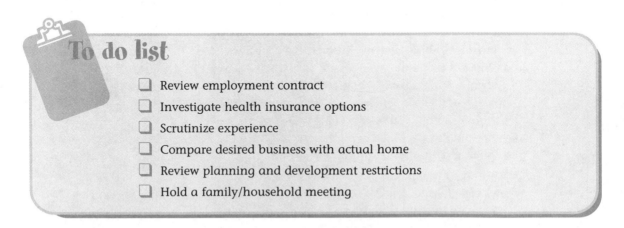

To do list

- ☐ Review employment contract
- ☐ Investigate health insurance options
- ☐ Scrutinize experience
- ☐ Compare desired business with actual home
- ☐ Review planning and development restrictions
- ☐ Hold a family/household meeting

Eliminating the Biggest Obstacles

There are six major obstacles to your home business—what business negotiators
would call "deal killers." These obstacles include limitations imposed by your existing employment contract, any outstanding legal issues you might be facing, your

health insurance costs, inexperience in your chosen field, neighborhood restrictions, and family objections to the home business.

Most of these obstacles can be resolved. But before you consider the cost of a new computer or give notice at your current job, you need to determine whether any of these issues present insurmountable barriers to the success of your new business.

You'll need list

- ☐ Self-employment journal
- ☐ Notes from Chapters 1 and 2
- ☐ Current employment contract and related communications
- ☐ Copies of all current rental or homeowners' restrictions/guidelines

Review Your Employment Contract

Before you put the first word on your business plan, take out your current employment contract and read it carefully, word for word. If you have emails, letters, or other documents instead of, or in addition to, a formal contract, read those, too.

Don't assume that stipulations agreed to in email are not binding because you "didn't sign anything." In many instances, such emails can be considered evidence of what is called an oral contract, and therefore legally binding. If you are unsure whether you would be held to the terms, consult an attorney.

Did you agree not to contact customers about your impending departure from the company or for a given period of time after leaving the company's employment? Are you required to provide a certain amount of notice? Are you allowed to pursue a business that competes with your current employer? Employment contracts often include language that restricts or prohibits direct competition, taking customers, and similar activities. Be sure that you know what limitations you must abide by prior to starting your business.

But what do these limitations mean, in terms of your business? It depends:

- If you are planning to start a business in direct competition with your employer, and your employment contract forbids it, your home business plans might be thwarted. However, if the noncompetition language seems broad, you might want to have an attorney review it to determine whether it is enforceable. But bear in mind that you might have to fight your employer in court to prove how unenforceable it is.

- If you are not allowed to take current customers with you, you might have to allow for a higher marketing budget in Chapter 4. Check whether your contract allows you to have any contact with these customers at all—even if they cannot be your customers, perhaps they would be willing to refer others, thus partially circumventing this restriction.

As your excitement about your business escalates, you will want to tell the world. Don't do it (not yet, anyway). Although you might be very excited about your new venture, your co-workers might have very different feelings. They might be jealous, longing for the courage you have and envying your ability to make such a transition. Meanwhile, your boss could become suspicious, wondering if you are stealing supplies or customers, wooing other employees to be part of your new venture, or just not being as loyal as he expects you to be. Depending on your company's policy and your current job, you could even be escorted out the door as soon as you announce your plans. Keep quiet until you give notice with a specific plan in mind.

Clear Up Outstanding Legal Issues

Is there a student loan that you "forgot" about? Do you need to attend traffic school—but haven't, even though the ticket was five years ago? Are you in the middle of a divorce, or waiting for the divorce to be finalized? Are you aware of any outstanding arrest warrants? Is the IRS trying to collect money from you? Do you have a lien against your house or other property? Do you owe property, state, or local taxes?

These issues will come back to haunt you, especially when you begin the process of launching a home business. Starting a business means that you will be filling out paperwork—and that paperwork will enable many government entities to find you. What's more, your marketing efforts will be telling everyone about you and your new business. The entire world will know about you, so if you have to clean up some neglected legal or tax issues, now is the time to do it.

When you take care of the problem, be sure that you know how long any such delinquency will appear on your credit report or criminal record. Credit problems, once fixed, might remain on your record for as long as 7 to 10 years. Criminal matters might stay on your record indefinitely. Be sure that you know what consequences are likely as a result of tax or legal issues. Most problems won't necessarily prohibit you from owning a business, but you will need to know, for example, that a bankruptcy on your credit report means that you won't be able to get a business loan for quite some time.

IS MOONLIGHTING THE BEST OPTION?

Normally, starting your business on the side (also known as "moonlighting") can be frustrating. You are usually restricted from competing with your employer, and have to figure out how to meet your own clients' needs while putting in a full day for your full-time employer. And, although your income from a side business will typically be less than that of a full-time business, your business expenses might not be proportionately less. After all, you still have to have a desk and computer (or whatever equipment your business requires), whether you use it 4 hours a week or 40. And, because you are not working at the effort full time, your ability to deduct some business expenses might be limited. Nevertheless, you might want to consider moonlighting if

* You need to hang on to your job for health insurance or other benefits.

* You are still gaining experience, but want to begin your business anyway.

* You have the energy to devote sufficient time to both your full-time employer and your side business.

At times, moonlighting can also resolve the problem of insufficient startup funding. However, this is not always the case. If you are concerned about money, be sure to read Chapter 4 before making a decision to start your business on the side.

For criminal matters, enlist the help of an attorney. (You can usually obtain a referral from your local bar association.) Tax and financial matters can be resolved with the help of an accountant or credit counselor. If you need a credit counselor, be sure to use a nonprofit agency. Avoid scams that offer to clean up your credit for a price.

Calculate the Cost of Health Insurance

Pick up any newspaper, visit any news site on the Internet, and the current health insurance situation screams from the headlines. Health insurance can be expensive, tough to get, and insufficient when it comes to covering chronic illnesses or prescription drugs.

Is the need for health insurance a deal killer? Perhaps not. Consider these options:

- Check whether your spouse or partner's employer can cover you.

- Join a group offering health insurance. Check with your local chamber of commerce or professional industry group. These plans often allow participation without minimal restrictions on prior conditions, and are less likely to require a physical or reject you for a health condition.

- Choose to form a partnership or corporation, which might qualify you for group rates. Talk to a benefits specialist about the minimum requirements for obtaining group insurance and the difference in pricing between an individual and group policy.

- Continue your employer's coverage via COBRA (Consolidated Omnibus Budget Reconciliation Act), national legislation enacted that allows an employee to continue health insurance through his or her employer, even after leaving. There are a number of restrictions and requirements—for example, you must be working for an employer with at least 20 employees or more and be currently enrolled in the health plan. If eligible, you (and possibly dependents you also covered via your employer's health plan) would be able to continue this coverage for 18–36 months, depending on your circumstances. However, this does not mean that you will pay the same amount currently deducted from your paycheck—you will be paying your employer's contributions to your health premiums as well, making the total cost higher, and often prohibitive. (For more information, visit www.dol.gov/dol/topic/health-plans/cobra.htm and www.dol.gov/ebsa/faqs/faq_consumer_cobra.html.)

Not sure who to contact as a benefits specialist? My recommendation is Maria Poroy, Access Business Services, Inc. She can be reached at 415–986–7726 or visit www.accessbenefitsgroup.com. Based in California, she is licensed in some other states as well. Maria has been invaluable to me when assessing health insurance options.

Or, you might want to check with the National Association of Professional Insurance Agents (www.pianet.com) or the Independent Insurance Agents and Brokers of America (www.iiaa.org). See Appendix A, "References and Resources," for more insurance resources.

Overcome Your Inexperience

Earlier in the book, I noted that ageism actually works in your favor when you strike out on your own. Owning your own business remakes you from an employee who seems "too old" into a consultant who is wise and experienced.

Conversely, if you are on the opposite end of the experience ladder, you might struggle gaining the confidence of potential clients. If you don't have at least three to five years of experience in your chosen line of work, you will need to prove to prospective customers that you have what it takes to work for them. (And no, a college degree, in and of itself, won't cut it.)

For those with little or no experience, you might have the necessary credibility if you

- Started a business (and operated it successfully) earlier in your life
- Worked at a job in your chosen field while attending school
- Have a solid background in business in general and possess sufficient basic business and interpersonal skills (often called "transferable skills")

In all three cases, however, you will be working harder than other business owners, who have the experience you don't. Seriously consider this. The average 12-hour day of a new business owner might be 14 or 16 hours for you, as you gain experience others already possess.

Determine That Your Business "Fits" As a Home Business

Is your business suitable as a home business? To make that determination, ask yourself how well your situation matches these descriptions:

- Almost no clients will visit your office. When they do, it will be rare and will be one car/one person at a time. Someone viewing your home from the outside would not know that a business is being run inside.
- You will rely heavily on phone, fax, email, and regular or "snail mail," and you will frequently visit clients at their offices or meet them at a coffee house or restaurant—if you have to visit them at all.
- You are probably offering a service. If you are offering a product, it is either solely offered over the Internet or through mail order; or it is in conjunction with, or resulting from, your service business.(For example, as a writer, I offer both a service and products (books), but people don't come to my house to buy them.
- You regularly employ only yourself and can run the business without permanent, full-time employees. (Occasional or temporary help is fine. More on this later in the chapter.)
- Your business does not require exterior signage or equipment that's too large or otherwise incompatible with in-home use.
- It would be virtually impossible for someone passing by your home on foot to know that you are conducting business.

- Your home can accommodate any special needs the business will require—such as adequate space for activities and necessary equipment (copiers or printers for a small printing business, room for temporarily holding dogs for a dog-walking business, space for producing soap and bath salts for a small toiletries business, and so on).

The less your business fits the preceding profile, the more difficult (but not necessarily impossible) it might be to actually operate your business from home. Two important factors might give you the setting you need even if your business differs radically from what is detailed previously: the specifications of your own home and your local area's planning guidelines.

If your home is a studio apartment, you will be much more limited than if your home is a 10-room house with one or two acres of land. Setting aside a storage room, or setting up a shed, for your business is much easier if you have the space for it.

The long-term development goals of your community—as expressed by your city or county's planning department in the form of building codes, use regulations, and other rules—will also greatly determine how close your business must fit the previous description. Which leads us to our next "make or break" consideration.

Studying Relevant Planning and Development Restrictions

How will you use your home to operate your home business? That question is a big one—and one you will have to answer to the satisfaction of your local planning commission, as well as your landlord if you rent. Those living in condominiums or other planned developments will need to review their CC&Rs (Covenants, Conditions, and Restrictions), which might restrict or forbid a home business.

Whether you need to speak to a city planner, your homeowners association, or your landlord, their concerns will be the same: They do not want you doing anything that will create noise, traffic, or eyesores that will in any way interfere with the quality of life in your neighborhood. Homeowners and planners will particularly be concerned with a possible decrease in property values. The following sections discuss specific ways you can track down and familiarize yourself with the relevant rules and restrictions governing small businesses in your neighborhood.

Renters and Condo or Planned Development Homeowners

You will need to review your lease/CC&Rs and talk to your landlord/condo association, respectively. There is a very good chance your lease or CC&Rs out-and-out forbids business activity. However, if you have a decent relationship with your landlord, approach him or her and ask for a change to that stipulation. Condominium owners might be in a more difficult bind—although you own your own condominium, changing CC&Rs usually requires great effort, as you often must convince the majority of owners in your complex to go along with the change. How to go about getting such a change should be covered in CC&Rs or other paperwork relating to your condominium owners' association.

Whether you need to renegotiate your lease or get your co-owners' permission, try to couch your discussion in terms that avoid the phrase "running a business" out of your home. This has the connotation that you want to start a nightclub, trucking company, or department store from your humble abode—and you definitely do not want your landlord or neighbors to think in those terms!

When you approach your landlord, start off with a comment such as, "I don't know if you remember, but I do quite a bit of writing." Continue by saying that you would like to do this kind of work for yourself instead of others. You have now placed the activity into the category of something that is already happening, with no adverse consequences. Your landlord might worry about your ability to pay the rent, and might ask for additional money in your deposit or verification of money in the bank. Before you talk to your landlord, be sure that you have several reassuring things to tell her, such as, "I've been doing this for other companies for 15 years, and I already have 10 clients interested in my services," or, "As you know, my partner's salary alone is sufficient to pay our rent." If you know of people in your complex who work from home for their employer, who are students, or who are retired and home during the day, be sure to compare yourself to these people as favorably as you can. After all, if your next door neighbor is doing work from his home for ABC Corporation, why should your landlord refuse to grant you a modification on your lease so that you can do similar work for yourself?

Condominium and planned development homeowners can try a similar approach, but again, changing the rules governing your condo might be difficult. Although renters usually have one person—a landlord or apartment manager—to convince, you might have to persuade the entire complex.

What do you do if your landlord/condo association won't budge? If you really want to start your business, move. Every region in the United States has plenty of apartment and condominium complexes that will not mind if you are running a home business. Look especially in up-and-coming areas of your city or areas that are struggling a bit.

Zoning Issues

Whether you rent or own your home, you must comply with your city or county's zoning laws. Finding out the laws in your area should be fairly simple. If you have a computer, look up your city's web page on the Internet. Go to the section of the planning department, and look for information on running a home business. If you cannot find the information that way, stop by your city's planning department and ask for regulations governing home businesses.

As with landlords and homeowner associations, most planning departments will be concerned about noise, traffic, and eyesores. They don't want a big sign reading, "Al's Junkyard" in a quiet, residential neighborhood, and they don't want traffic rivaling Macy's on a busy Saturday. If your planning department hits you with regulations that might be problematic, ask if there is a workaround or if you can receive a variance.

Don't hesitate to ask the planning department how many home businesses it has licensed. Chances are, the more it has allowed, the more routine your visit will be, and the less hassle involved. If your planning department has not experienced very many home businesses, set up a second meeting. Bring as much research as you can find about your type of home business, and educate your planning department.

Don't let all those scary stories about the planning department put you off—yes, planning departments can give big developers a hard time, and often for very good reasons. But you're a very, very small and very quiet fish. Many planning departments will be relieved that someone like you is waiting to see them. With a check and a completed form in my hand, I was in the Planning Department offices for 30 seconds! The planner on duty said something along the lines of, "Writer—can't get less controversial than that," signed off on my home permit, and shooed me out of the planning office.

Will the Business Fit Your Physical Home?

Perform a thorough, visual walk-through of your home. No matter how crazy, briefly consider the possibility of each room in your home being used as your home office or workshop. List your top three possibilities.

Of the top three options, which room is best suited for this purpose? Will you need to repaint or switch bedrooms or other uses? Is the wiring "iffy"? Is your home prone to leaks? They can damage costly equipment, so address the problem before you move in costly furniture and computers. Is the area out of the traffic flow of your home? Will it be sufficiently quiet, so you can work? Is it separate enough, so you can avoid entering the work area when you are on personal time, such as evenings and weekends?

If you don't have a separate room, don't worry. Can you divide a larger room with panels or room dividers? Or mark an area by the use of a different carpet and/or creation of "walls" using bookcases?

Not only does this break up the space and encourage a better work-life balance, but it also helps meet the IRS provisions of having a separate space dedicated to business activity. Unless you provide day care, you will have to be sure that the space is set aside solely for business purposes, and not used for any other reason, if you want to deduct related expenses. For more information, see the IRS website: http://www.irs.gov/taxtopics/tc509.html.

Making Sure That Your Family Is On Board

Unless you are single and childless, you will need to convene one or more family meetings to be sure that everyone is comfortable with your home business. After all, one of the key words in home business is "home"—and you are going to be changing the way that your family's home operates somewhat. Although you could, technically, start a home business with no input from your household, it is not recommended. Other members of the household will need to honor your requests to work undisturbed, your need to work weekends or evenings, and perhaps give up some space currently used for other things.

Don't forget that there is a huge difference between telling your spouse or partner, "I'd like to start a business some day," and saying, "I am starting my own home business. Please look over my business plan." You are serious now, and setting aside a separate time to discuss the matter is a clear indication that you are no longer merely dreaming.

Here is how to talk about your ideas with the most important people in your life:

- First, sit down alone with your spouse or partner and discuss your desire to have a home business. You don't have specifics right now, but you do have dreams—share those with him or her!

- Be willing to address reasonable concerns. For example, if your partner objects because you have no savings (a very legitimate reason), discuss what an acceptable level of risk might be. If he or she simply says, "It's too risky," and clams up, try to discuss the perceived risks. Ask for the specifics.

- Although you will be in charge of how the business is run, your family should have a say in how the business affects home life. Will you need to alter the quantity or quality of your time together? Your partner might be fine with that, but will insist that Sundays are "family day," and no work will be done on that day of the week. One or two of these commitments should be

DO YOU NEED TO MOVE?

If you were discouraged by your planning department, or shot down by your landlord, you might want to consider relocating to a more home-business–friendly area.

When considering whether your current geographical area is adequate for your home business, consider your client base. If you live in a rural area and rely on customers who are accessible within a reasonable traveling distance from your home, you might be okay. If your business requires that you work and frequently meet with medium or large business, however, your location will determine whether you can afford the time and expense necessary to have those meetings. Being a freelance graphic artist in New York City or other major urban area, for example, seems logical. Starting your own business as a graphic artist in a remote, rural area could be problematic.

Also, consider the cost and availability of services in your geographic area. Can you

* Get a high-speed Internet connection if needed? Have access to a local dial-up number, 24 hours a day, 7 days a week?

* Send and receive packages by overnight courier?

* Have reasonable access to necessary services, such as copying and printing at a nearby office center?

* Get a second phone line installed in less than 30 days?

* Easily visit a library and other resources, or conduct necessary research online?

* Purchase office and other supplies close by, or pay the added expense of having them delivered within 48 hours?

Most, if not all, of these amenities should be readily available to you. If they are not, you can count on spending extra money and taking extra time to gain access to less readily available services or risking a loss of business because you cannot provide services to your clients within a reasonable time frame. It might be cheaper to live in an isolated area, but those savings might be offset by a reduced income because of the lack of access to clients or services.

Finally, do not assume that you can do all of your business online. Unless your business is a retail website, the Internet is much more likely to be a means of communication, and at most, you might be dealing with 10–20% of your clients from outside your initial area, especially when just starting your business. As the downslide in Internet-based businesses indicates, businesses with no local customer base are very difficult to build and take quite a bit of time, planning, and capital to succeed.

okay, but if you are presented with a long list, explain that much of the business is unknown; then, ask for the one or two commitments that are most important.

- Starting and running a business is a 40-hour–plus endeavor for most people. Your spouse or partner needs to understand the time involved and respect your decision enough to work with you on issues such as who does the housework, who chauffeurs the kids, and so on. If you are currently a stay-at-home mom or dad, be sure that your spouse or partner clearly understands that housework and children are no longer your sole priorities and that you expect them to pitch in regularly, without being asked.

- Work through the rest of the information in this book with your spouse or partner. Most people who are starting a home business find that their spouse or partner can be a valuable built-in sounding board. Your partner is usually close enough to be concerned with your business success, yet far enough removed from daily business activities to offer an objective opinion.

- If the discussion becomes heated, don't be afraid to seek couples counseling. As difficult as starting a business can be, it will be almost impossible if you are going through a breakup at the same time.

> **caution**   *Watch Out*
>
> In fact, if you are contemplating any major change in your household, you might want to consider putting off beginning your business. Juggling the beginning of a home business with other major events (even good ones, such as getting married or having a baby) can make an already stressful situation impossible.

Your children need to be prepared for changes resulting from your home business, too. If you are a single parent, sit down and talk with your child(ren) about what you are planning to do, and what it means to them. (If you have a spouse or partner, do this together.) Just be as honest as you can, and don't be afraid to say, "I don't know." If you approach the upcoming changes as a wonderful adventure, chances are your children will be more at ease than if you talk about how scary it is going to be.

At the same time, be realistic in your discussion. Although you will want to let your children know about the positive aspects (such as a more flexible schedule), be sure that they know not to volunteer you for a class field trip right away! Provide them with examples of what this venture will mean in terms of your time, your availability, and any additional chores they might need to do.

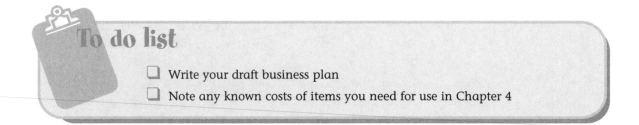

Creating the Framework of Your Business Plan

Now, you're ready to begin creating your business plan. From this point forward, your business plan will be one of the most important documents in your life.

Your business plan is your road map. As you might have noticed by now, starting a business requires the coordination of hundreds and hundreds of details. Every item has to be thought through and planned for intelligently—or your business will suffer. A logical, written plan ensures that you make the necessary arrangements, while at the same time, preventing or minimizing the feelings of being overwhelmed.

After your business starts, the business plan acts as your company handbook. What are your plans for the future? How will business be maintained? What terms do you offer clients? All of these questions are answered in your business plan, thus showing that your business is well thought out and consistent.

Rather than immediately writing your business plan from start to finish, you begin by constructing the framework, and then finish building the plan as you get the information you need to fill in the sections. You might need to rewrite some sections several times, as your plan becomes more precise and your assessment of business more realistic.

In this section, you learn how to begin building your plan by outlining a basic business plan "form" that lists all the necessary information and components of your business plan. Your business plan will be divided into sections; within each section, you will answer a series of questions that provide necessary information about your financial, logistical, and legal plans for your business. The basic format of the plan is shown in Figure 3.2.

These are the major headings that make up the framework of your business plan:

- Introduction/Overview
- The Basics
- Business Overview
- Marketing

FIGURE 3.2

FIGURE 3.2

This is the basic format I recommend for your business plan. You can create it in a word processing program or on paper.

Business Plan Form

1. **Introduction/Overview**
2. **The Basics**
   A. What is the business name? Is it a sole proprietorship, partnership, or corporation?
   B. Where will the business be located? (Presumably, you have answered this, and the answer is in your home.) Is there a Post Office Box?
   C. Will the business have a web presence? What is the domain name(s)?
   D. Who is the proprietor(s)? What is it about the proprietor(s) that makes him/her/them the right person(s) to run this business?
   E. What needs or wants of customers are being met? (Give a brief overview of who you are serving and why.)
3. **Business Overview**
   A. What does the business do or provide?
   B. Who or what does the business provide these service(s)/product(s) to? Are there specific industries or geographic locations services are provided to, or are they offered to the public? Is the entity business to business, business to consumer, or both?
4. **Marketing**
   A. How does the business reach customers? What need or desire is being fulfilled?
   B. What are the unique features this business offers that competitors do not?
   C. How will the business interact with and retain customers?
   D. How is pricing structured in your line of work? What is the going rate for the service you provide? Section
5. **Logistics**
   A. Where is the business located? How much space is rented/allocated?
   B. What equipment is purchased/needs to be purchased?
   C. What arrangements have been/need to be made with other businesses in order to provide the product(s) and/or service(s) offered by the business?
6. **Financials**
   A. How much money do you need to start this business (Day 1)?
   B. How much money do you need, monthly, to operate the business?
   C. How much money do you need, monthly, to live on, regardless of what the business brings in? Will this come from savings, partner's/spouse's income, part-time job, or other source?
   D. How much money can you reasonably expect to make from the business initially? (Take the going rates from the Marketing section of your business plan and expand them here.) What variables exist in pricing? What is the maximum income you can generate?
   E. What can you reasonably expect to earn from the business during the first year? Second? Third? Fourth, Fifth? Years Six through Ten?
7. **Assumptions, Expansion, and Exits**
   A. What assumptions have you made in order for your financial projections to work? What happens if those assumptions are incorrect?
   B. What assumptions have you made in your marketing and logistics? What happens if those assumptions are incorrect?
   C. At what point would it be impractical (financially and/or logistically) to run the business?
   D. At what point would it be impractical (financially and/or logistically) to run the business from your home? At what point financially? Logistics-wise?

- Logistics
- Financials
- Assumptions, Expansion, and Exits

Within each of these sections, you'll add information that answers a number of questions, as shown in Figure 3.2. The following sections detail these questions and discuss how to go about answering them within each of these important areas of your business plan.

As you fill in your business plan, create a list of any equipment, supplies, or other items you'll need to begin and run your business. If you know how much an item will cost, note that directly on your list. Save this list of items for the next chapter when you formulate a budget.

tip For additional help, check the many free publications available from the Small Business Administration. Much of the information can be downloaded from the website, http://www.sba.gov/library/pubs.html. Booklets and other informational pieces include a home business overview, how to determine if you are ready for business, and a wide variety of general and specific business plans. If you do not have Internet access, look up the nearest Small Business Administration (SBA) office in your phone book under the blue pages/government listings section.

You'll need list

- ☐ Self-employment journal
- ☐ Notes from Chapters 1 and 2
- ☐ Calculator

Introduction/Overview and Goals

Though it appears first in your business plan, the introduction and overview are written last; these elements offer a summary of the rest of the business plan. Return to the introduction and write it *only* after you have completed the rest of the business plan.

A written listing of your goals should be included in the introduction to your plan. Naturally, one of your goals is to make money. But how much per year? $100,000? $500,000? More? Less? Be specific.

What other goals do you have? Most people considering a home business want to make money, but they also might want to

MONEYMAKING BUSINESS, OR NONPROFIT ORGANIZATION?

Review your goals carefully. Your venture might be better suited to a nonprofit organization, as opposed to a business. For instance, you might set up a small publishing company as a home business. But if the goal of that company is to dispense information about a particular cause (for example, drug prevention, safety, or some other social cause), making money (beyond meeting your expenses and paying yourself a salary) might not be as important. Or, you might set up an insurance agency. But what is the goal of the agency—to make money, or to provide health insurance to as many people as possible? If you mention the latter, you will be better suited to a nonprofit organization. If this is the case, your process will be somewhat similar—but you will have donors who pay and clients who use your services, and your marketing will be called fundraising (or development).

Also, your business form will be that of a nonprofit organization—check with your state offices to determine what is required, and visit the IRS website pertaining to 501(c)3 (nonprofit) organizations at www.irs.gov/charities/index.html.

- Have more control over scheduling, particularly family or child commitments (for example, attending a child's soccer game)
- Do something they enjoy
- Minimize commuting
- Build a business to eventually sell at a profit or pass on to their children

Be sure that you are specific about your financial goals, but include your nonmonetary goals as well.

Outlining the Basics

In this section, you will outline the basic information regarding your business. The information you add here will answer these questions:

- What is the business name? Is it a sole proprietorship, partnership, or corporation?

- Where will the business be located? (Presumably, you have answered this, and the answer is in your home.) Is there a post office box?
- Will the business have a web presence? What is the domain name(s)?
- Who is the proprietor(s)? What is it about the proprietor(s) that makes him/her/them the right person(s) to run this business?
- What needs or wants of customers are being met? (Give a brief overview of who you are serving and why.)

Read on to learn about answering these questions within your business plan.

Business Name

As your first task in this section, you need to state the business name. When naming your business, be sure to choose a name that does not conflict with an existing business. If your name is truly unique, consider making it a trademark.

Visit the website of the Patent and Trademark Office, www.uspto.gov. A visit to this website will not only provide information about the trademark process, but also help you make a decision whether you need the help of a lawyer. If you decide to hire a lawyer, contact your local bar association and ask for a referral to an intellectual property (IP) attorney.

Whether you choose to trademark your business name or not, check business licenses filed with your local government, Fictitious Business Name statements filed with your local or state clerk's offices, as well as phone directories and other public sources for existing businesses in your area. Avoid any name that might be confused with another business.

In most instances, you will need to file a Fictitious Business Name Statement.

To verify the Fictitious Business Name requirements where you live, check with your city or county planning and development offices. In most cases, your city or county government will provide you with a consolidated checklist of all local requirements for a business. These checklists can be very helpful, and often provide additional information, such as how to do business with the city, county, or state.

Business Form

You also must state whether your business will be a sole proprietorship, partnership, or corporation.

A *sole proprietorship* is you, by yourself, owning and running the business. This is the simplest and most common form of business organization. Your income and expenses from the business are reported as part of your federal tax return on Schedule C, and you don't need to file incorporation papers to "form" your business.

The simplicity of this form of business is a distinct advantage, but it offers some disadvantages, as well. The chief disadvantage is that liability flows directly to you. This means that a customer can sue you directly for failing to perform the services you agreed to provide. Your home and other assets could be at risk. You can mitigate this risk by purchasing liability insurance (or errors and omissions insurance). If you own few assets (and rent, rather than own, your home), the liability issues might not be as important.

The more assets you have, and the more people who know you have liability insurance, the more likely you are to be sued.

The nature of your business is also a key factor. Are you offering services in which safety could be a factor, such as a building contractor who has to be sure that a staircase doesn't fail? Are you offering services that could greatly impact someone's life if done incorrectly, such as accounting or legal advice? What happens if you don't perform as promised? The greater the potential fallout to the client, the more likely someone could be injured or killed, and the more likely someone could be financially ruined, the more likely you are to be sued.

A *partnership* is a formal partnering of you with at least one other person. Forming a partnership generally requires an attorney.

As a home business, you might not be allowed to form a partnership unless it is with your spouse or domestic partner (depending on regulations of home businesses in your area). But this could make a partnership the ideal business structure. If you and your significant other are going to share in the work and expenses anyway, this might be a way to formalize that agreement.

Forming a partnership with someone not living with you is a bit trickier. But this is the twenty-first century—the era of the virtual company. If this is someone you know you can trust, and zoning regulations allow it, there's no reason why two people in different cities—or even different states or countries—can't use this business form. (With more than one state or country, however, bear in mind that you might have to report income or file forms twice—once in each jurisdiction.)

Whether your partner is in the next room or the next country, however, always consider such an arrangement carefully. Ask yourself whether you really know the person you are partnering with for this business. And no matter how well you think you know him or her, treat it as any other professional transaction. This means that

- All partners are willing to disclose their current financial positions and ability to contribute to the partnership financially.

- All partners are willing to fully disclose the skills and experience they bring to the partnership, as well as any potential liability.

- All partners are willing to provide other partners with a credit report, background check, or other documentation supporting their viability to be involved in the business.

- All partners are willing to formalize who does what, when they do it, and why, in a partnership agreement.

Why is this so important? Business partners generally all agree to pay the debts of the partnership. So, if one partner runs up debt and disappears, the remaining partner(s) is left repairing the financial situation and the reputation of the business. Having a partner is a great way to split the risk and the work, but it can be a headache if you don't know the other partner(s) well.

> **tip**
>
> If you choose to form your business as a partnership, be sure to discuss how the partnership will work and draft an agreement prior to engaging an attorney. This will save you time, money, and the embarrassment of trying to negotiate partnership terms in front of a third party.

A *corporation* is an entity that is completely separate from any person. In fact, corporations file their own taxes and have many rights and obligations, just as individuals do. Corporations offer some distance between you (an officer in the corporation) and the entity itself, which might be helpful when dealing with liability. (However, these rules have changed in response to scandal, and vary from state to state, so you will need to talk to an attorney to understand any benefits and limitations.) There are many types of corporations, and an attorney will be needed to advise you on the best corporation type for your business. Some forms of corporation can be one person, so check the corporation laws in your state to determine if this is the best organization for you.

As with partnerships, your city or county might restrict or forbid this type of business from operating from a private residence.

There are also some hybrid forms of business, which are not truly and entirely like a typical partnership or standard corporation. Those include

- A **Limited Liability Company (LLC)**, which mixes the decreased direct liability of a partnership with tax advantages more common to a corporation.

- A **Professional Corporation**, again, mixing some aspects of a partnership and a corporation. This corporation type is usually available only to certain types of businesses, however, and often limited to high-risk occupations such as doctors, lawyers, and accountants.

- An **S Corporation** is a corporation that has formed a standard corporation (as described previously) but filed proper forms with the IRS to have the business' profit taxed as if the business were a sole proprietorship. (Standard corporations are often also referred to as "C" corporations.)

For more information on business structures and considerations, visit www.AllLaw.com.

If you are uncertain which business entity is the right type for you and your business, check with an attorney. It is not unusual to start a business as a sole proprietorship and expand it to a partnership or corporation as the business grows, or as liability and other issues become more serious. Incorporating is an additional expense that, as a new business owner, you might not be able to justify until your income from the business can easily cover such costs.

note After choosing a business entity and registering it with the appropriate state agency, you might need to obtain an Employer Identification Number (EIN), also called a Federal ID number or Tax ID number. Visit http://www.irs.gov/formspubs/index.html for more information on whether you need or would benefit from obtaining this number for your business. For state tax information, contact the Department of Revenue in your state.

Your Business Location, Address, Web Presence, and Domain Name

Next in this section, you must describe where your business will be located and whether it has a post office box.

Presumably, your business will be located in your home. This might not mean, however, that your business will share your home's mailing address.

Using a post office box is one way to separate your personal mail from your business mail. It also affords you some privacy, as you do not have to provide your home address to as many people. Because most boxes are modestly priced, this is a relatively inexpensive way to help separate your business from your personal life.

Within this section of the business plan, you also must answer the questions, "Will the business have a web presence?" and "What is the domain name(s)?"

The answer to the first question, in almost all cases, should most certainly be "yes." As with business names, domain names should be researched carefully to avoid confusion and possible trademark violations.

Check for existing domain names on an Internet registration site, such as www.Register.com. This website provides information on whether a name is in use, and if so, who owns it and when the registration is set to expire.

Describing the Proprietor

Within this section, you need to name the proprietor(s) of your business and describe what makes that person (or those people) capable of running the business.

Thinking through the answer to this question is an important part of preparing your business plan because it helps you understand your business' strengths and weaknesses in the marketplace. It is highly unlikely you are beginning a business that is truly unique. If a prospective customer knows 30 plumbers, or 40 graphic artists, why should he choose you? What makes you stand out from the crowd of your competition? Address these issues as you answer the questions in this section of the business plan, and be specific.

Describing What Need Your Business Fulfills

The final question in this section of the business plan asks, "What needs or wants of customers are being met?" (Give a brief overview of who you are serving and why.)

The information you add here should flow directly from the information you offer to the previous question in this section. If your unique ability to perform graphics work and provide printing services distinguishes you, for example, your target customers might be people who want "one-stop shopping" and want to save time and money by using you for both services.

Business Overview

The Business Overview section of your plan will include answers to these questions, as described in the subsections that follow:

- What does the business do or provide?
- Who or what does the business provide these service(s)/product(s) to? Are there specific industries or geographic locations that services are provided to, or are they offered to the public? Is the entity Business to Business (B2B), Business to Consumer (B2C), or both?

Describing What the Business Does or Provides

To answer the first question in the Business Overview section, list all the services your business will provide. Be specific. For example, if you are starting a bookkeeping business, you might be providing bookkeeping, tax preparation, audit assistance, and financial records organization services.

Offering more than one service provides your business with an advantage. You will draw more customers, and you can often cross sell services—originally gaining a customer because of one service and selling him others as your relationship grows.

However, you will want to refrain from offering too many services. Aim for three to five separate services. Fewer than three, and customers are less likely to come to you. More than five, and prospective customers might not believe that you can do everything you say, or might feel that you do so many things because you do nothing well.

As an example, let's say that you offer sales consulting. Now, if you also offer computer repair, writing, and graphic design, you will be sending a message to clients that you aren't focused—these services don't mesh well together, and there appears to be too many of them.

In the preceding example, it would be wise to jettison the computer repair. You could then recast the writing, graphic design, and sales consulting as a "one-stop marketing shop," or a sales-boosting business. The writing and design continue to be offered, but only for sales-related materials for your clients. This pulls your business in to a cohesive offering. Instead of four disparate, unfocused services, you are now offering one, cohesive, inclusive service—building credibility and attracting more clients.

Defining Your Customer Base

The second question in this section of the business plan asks "Who or what does the business provide these service(s)/product(s) to? Are there specific industries or geographic locations services are provided to, or are they offered to the public? Is the entity Business to Business, Business to Consumer, or both?"

Using the final two questions from the previous section, as well as the description of services you wrote for this section, provide a detailed description of your ideal customer. This doesn't mean that you cannot have customers who don't fit this description, but you should have some idea of your target market.

You will probably have more than one target customer (or market segment), and it is important to provide details for each segment. For instance, as an attorney, you might provide services to individual clients as well as small businesses. Your individual clients might be people specifically concerned with estate planning, whereas your small business clients might have a need for succession planning (for example, who buys, operates, or inherits a business).

Creating Your Marketing Plan

You might think that cash is the lifeblood of your business. You are wrong. It is marketing.

It is the one activity (well actually, an entire group of activities) that will make or break your business. The day you aren't marketing is the day that your business stagnates.

In this section of your business plan, you'll answer these questions:

- How does the business reach customers?
- What are the unique features this business offers that competitors do not?
- How will the business interact with and retain customers?
- How is pricing structured in your line of work? What is the going rate for the service you provide?

Read on to learn about the information you'll enter to answer these questions.

Describing How Your Business Will Reach Customers

Pulling together the information you'll use to answer these questions might be quite simple. If you are offering surfing lessons, for example, you are probably reaching your customers on or near a beach. You are fulfilling their desire to learn how to surf and have fun in the water.

Of course, most answers to these questions are more complex because determining how to market to the right audience can be a complex task. You want to insert information about you and your business right in front of the people most likely to hire you. Where are they located?

If you are having difficulty answering this, visualize the target customer(s) you described in the previous section. Imagine one composite person who represents an entire target customer segment. When does this person get out of bed in the morning? What kind of home does he or she live in? Sketch an imaginary day in the life of Carl or Connie Customer. At what point in the day is their desire for your product or service at its high point? That is where and when your marketing should take place!

Describing the Unique Features of Your Business

Also in this section, you must answer the question, "What unique features does this business offer that competitors do not?"

In an earlier section of the business plan, you discussed your unique skills. The information you'll enter here is similar to that information, but here, you describe those skills in the third person—as a quality of your business, not as a personal quality.

So you might say, "Carol Anne Carroll Communications offers one-stop shopping, from conception to printed product, for a wide variety of documents." Or, it could be your location: "We're the only full-service bookkeeping business in the tri-county area." Or perhaps your equipment makes you stand out: "We are the only photographers with a fully-digital photo development process in the area."

Here, too, you will need to do some competitive analysis. What does your competition offer, and how is your business better?

Stating How Your Business Will Interact with and Retain Customers

You already know *when* your prospective customer most wants your services. *How* will he learn of you *at the right time*? If he wants to surf, and you offer lessons, will he receive a flyer as he arrives on the boardwalk? Will he hear your ad on the radio as he drives to or lays on the beach?

And how will you respond to customer contact? How will you work with them and follow up on their interest? What information will you provide over the phone? Do you send customers a brochure or price list? You should plan for a clear exchange of information, so your customers know how you will provide the services offered.

Describing Pricing Structure and Rates

I will talk more about pricing in the next chapter. But for now, be aware that you should know the going rate for the services you provide. If you are providing services to customers in more than one geographic area, be sure that you know the going rate for each location. Then, in this section of the business plan, you'll need to list and describe the pricing structure you intend to use for your business and the going rate for similar businesses in your market.

Describing the Physical Logistics of Your Business

Your business plan needs to include a full description of the physical location, size, and layout of your business. In this section of the plan, you'll answer these questions:

- Where is the business located? How much space is rented/allocated?
- What necessary equipment do you own, and what remains to be purchased? See Chapter 6, "Getting Technology You Really Need (and Only What You Need)," for more tips on purchasing technology.

- What arrangements have been/need to be made with other businesses in order to provide the product(s) and/or service(s) offered by the business?

The following sections explain how to answer these questions.

Describing the Geographic Area and Allocated Space

You must first answer the question, "Where is the business located? How much space is rented/allocated?"

You've already stated that the business will be in your home, but here, you should describe your home's location. What is your neighborhood like? Will clients be able to take public transportation (and will you)? Are coffee shops, restaurants, and other amenities nearby? Is there something you wish were close by, but isn't? How does that affect your business?

Next, describe where your office will be located within your home. Do you need a separate workshop space, too; if so, where is that? (Ideally, a workshop and office would be located right next to each other, but the layout of many homes would make this impractical.)

Outlining Equipment Needs

In this section of the business plan, list what equipment your business will need and whether you currently own or must purchase that equipment. Many home businesses require a computer, printer, fax machine, business phone line, and office supplies, as well as letterhead (including envelopes) and business cards. Your business might have other equipment needs, as well.

Also in this section, describe the necessary supplies you'll use in your business. Imagine the complete cycle of meeting your ideal customer, convincing him to hire you, performing work for him, and being paid. What supplies do you need at each step? What about software? Beyond word processing and spreadsheets, you will probably need software to store and manage client contact information, invoices, and orders. You might also need special software to perform the services you offer, such as database, graphic design, and/or presentation software.

caution   *Watch Out!*

Don't try to save money by using your home phone for work. The cost of your work phone is usually a deductible expense and allows you to further separate your business and home life. Imagine picking up a call because you are expecting a lucrative deal to come through, and instead, a chatty former co-worker is calling "just to see how things are going"? Of course, high-speed Internet or cable options will allow you to maintain multiple lines on one infrastructure. (See Chapter 6 for more discussion on this topic.)

Defining Relationships with Outside Vendors

Finally, within this section, answer the question, "What arrangements have been/need to be made with other businesses in order to provide the product(s) and/or service(s) offered by the business?"

Particularly if you offer "one-stop" shopping, you might need to subcontract with other businesses. For instance, if you are a writer and offer finished newsletters, you will need to work closely with a printer. Have you made that connection? Talk with any potential subcontractors and discuss how you will do business. Will you need to advance them a deposit when work is ordered, or will they bill for their services? Will you include the cost of their services on your invoice to the end client, or will they send a bill to the end customer separately?

Come to a formal, written agreement, involving an attorney to finalize the contract.

Planning the Financials of Your Business

This section will largely be completed in Chapter 4, but here is the information it will contain:

- How much money do you need to start this business (Day 1)?
- How much money do you need, monthly, to operate the business?
- How much money do you need, monthly, to live on? Where will this money come from during times of little or no business (such as during startup or down times)? Will this come from savings, partner's/spouse's income, part-time job, or other source?
- How much money can you reasonably expect to make from the business initially? (Take the going rates from the Marketing section of your business plan and expand them here.) What variables exist in pricing? What is the maximum income you can generate?
- What can you reasonably expect to earn from the business during the first year? Second? Third? Fourth, Fifth? Years Six through Ten?

note Note that you will be keeping two separate spreadsheets: what it costs to start your business, and what it costs to keep it running.

Although you will "crunch numbers" in the next chapter, as you prepare information for this section of the business plan, think about where you want to be in 5, 10, and 20 years. Knowing what life you want to be living in the future can help you make decisions about what services you offer and how much you work today.

Describing Your Assumptions and "What Ifs"

This section of your business plan performs two separate tasks:

1. It clarifies what assumptions you have made.

2. It provides you with objective measurements for closure and expansion.

In this section of the plan, you'll need to answer these questions:

- What assumptions have you made in order for your financial projections to work? What happens if those assumptions are incorrect?

- What assumptions have you made in your marketing and logistics? What happens if those assumptions are incorrect?

- At what point would it be impractical to run the business? At what point financially would you decide to throw in the towel—that is, how much money would you have lost (or risk losing), and for how long? If the business made money, would there be other factors that would make you consider closing or selling the business? (For example, your business is profitable, but will come under greatly increased regulation if you continue to operate it in to the next 3–5 years. Or your business is profitable, but requires you to be available weekends and evenings—something, perhaps, that you didn't realize at the time you started the business.)

- At what point would it be impractical to run the business from your home? For instance, at what point would you need to hire so much additional help that you could no longer operate from home legitimately? At what point would you have to purchase so much additional equipment that working out of your home would be impractical?

Defining Your Financial Assumptions and Contingency Plans

First within this section, you must answer the question, "What assumptions have you made in order for your financial projections to work? What happens if those assumptions are incorrect?"

Are you assuming that your spouse will continue to work at his job, where he can obtain sufficient health insurance? Then that assumption goes here. Along with that assumption, write a contingency plan. What if he changes jobs? How much extra would you need to pay for health insurance? (Granted, he might leave his job five years from now, but you should have some idea of the cost of any alternatives.)

What happens if your rent is raised higher than you anticipate? What if your homeowners association raises its rates beyond the expected $10/month?

Defining Marketing and Logistics Assumptions and Contingency Plans

Next, answer the question, "What assumptions have you made in your marketing and logistics? What happens if those assumptions are incorrect?"

If you find that you cannot use the space you set aside—say a lengthy construction project starts on that side of your home as soon as you set up an office—where else in your home would you place your business?

If you believe five of your current clients will come with you when you leave your employer, what happens when only three of them actually do?

What you need to do here is think of the obvious assumptions you are making and come up with a plan that addresses, "What if it isn't like that, after all," as outlined in these scenarios:

- You're assuming that you will work out of an area in your home. What happens if construction, noise, or natural disaster strike? What if you had to sell?

- You're assuming that you will have health insurance coverage for your family through your spouse or partner's employer. What if your spouse or partner were laid off?

- You're assuming that you can work and watch your children. What if you can't do that? What if you need to work and they need to be at violin lessons—at the same time?

List, one by one, all the assumptions you are making. This can be difficult—because the very nature of an assumption is that we just "assume" and don't think about other options or disruptions to the plan.

To be sure that you address all of your major assumptions, visualize a day in the future—your ideal business day. What do you do, during that day, step by step? These are your assumptions. They are right there—from assuming that the time you get up will be 7 a.m. to assuming that the phone will be quiet until your project is finished to assuming that you can get your work done before the kids return home from school at 3 p.m. Yes, this is a little like taking your dream and looking at it through nightmare-focused lenses, but that is how you unearth assumptions and consider alternate solutions in the event that those assumptions are incorrect.

Creating an Exit Plan

Next in this section, describe specifically at what point it would be financially impractical to run the business. At what point would you say, "I'm not making enough money?" Or, at what point would you be making enough money, but not enough to justify the hassle, sacrifice, or hard work? For many people, money and logistics will be tied together. In other words, perhaps at breaking even, you would not be willing to put up with as much sacrifice as you would if you were making six figures a year.

These are the lines in the sand that provide your best dreams and worst nightmares. How long are you willing to work (or how long can you work) and not make enough to meet basic expenses? What if you cannot reach your financial goals? Would your business still be worth running? What if you met your financial goals—but never got a weekend free?

Part of this question is answered in the next chapter, but in this section, you'll determine your financial limits. You might determine, for example, that you will have to close shop if you make less than $30,000 per year for two years. Also consider contingencies under which those limits might flex. For example, given the preceding scenario, could you continue to run your business if your children received scholarships paying part or all of their school expenses? Also in this section, consider at what point would it be financially or logistically impractical to run the business from your home.

To make this determination, ask yourself at what point you would consider moving to a separate location, outside your home. How many, and what type, of customers would justify a separate office, retail, or industrial space?

You might decide to move the business outside your home if you have more than 30 customers (for example, the maximum you think you could handle without hiring at least one employee). This type of expansion is discussed later in the book.

Summary

What you now have in front of you is the first draft of your business plan. As you work through this book, you will revise the plan, so it is always as accurate as it can possibly be.

Once your business is up and running, this plan will still need to be revised. Why? Well, as you run your business, the day-to-day operations will provide you with real, hard data. (Right now, you're making a lot of educated guesses.) The longer you operate your business, the more the data from the regular operation of your business will inform your business plan.

So, why make so many guesses when hard data is on its way? Simple. You need to know what you want to do, so you have some idea of the challenges you'll face in getting your business established. Estimating the cost—for both startup and operating expenses—is discussed in the next chapter.

Creating Your Business Plan, Part 2: The Money Pages

You know how you want to run your business, which room in your home will become your office, where your customers are, and how to reach them. But if you don't plan for financial realities—including changes—your business plan will fail.

Because budgeting is so important to the success of your business, this chapter is devoted to figuring out the financial aspects of starting and running your home-based business. From making sure that you have enough to start your business to knowing what funds you'll need to pay your bills, this section provides you with ways to reasonably predict how much money you will need and when you'll need it.

To do list

- ☐ Understand basic business income and expense categories
- ☐ Decide on paper or computerized bookkeeping
- ☐ Set up rows and columns of budget spreadsheet

Creating Your Budget Spreadsheet

You must know whether you are making money and whether you can pay your bills. This requires keeping track of hundreds of financial details—from the amount you spent on office supplies at the store yesterday to the cost of seeing your client in the city via public transportation to the amount of a client's check you just received. The information keeps coming, day after day, and you need to accurately track it to know how your business is doing financially. With so much important information—from income to your marketing expenses, from how much you spent in a month to how much you earned—you need to formulate a document for storing and tracking your budget in a way that allows you to view many pieces of information at once. To do this, you will set up a budget spreadsheet.

We will start with a spreadsheet that first gives you an overall idea of your startup financial picture. Then, much of that information will continue to be tracked and recorded on a paper or computer spreadsheet. I recommend that this be a computer spreadsheet using a program such as Excel or Lotus 1-2-3. However, you need to be comfortable with the program. See Chapter 6, "Getting Technology You Really Need (and Only What You Need)," which discusses technology options, if you're having trouble deciding which spreadsheet to use—or whether to use your computer or paper.

You'll need list

- ☐ Draft business plan from previous chapter
- ☐ Financial records, including pay stubs or W-2s, bills, and receipts
- ☐ Current household budget
- ☐ Tax returns (preferably for past five years)
- ☐ Spreadsheet (computerized or paper—whatever you work with)

Setting Up the Spreadsheet Columns

This initial spreadsheet will give you an immediate picture of what your business startup will cost and how much of that cost can be directly deducted from any income you earn this tax year.

Table 4.1 shows an example of this startup analysis.

Table 4.1   Startup Expense Analysis

Item Description	Startup Deductible	Ongoing Deductible	Startup Not Deductible	Ongoing Not Deductible
New Phone (for office)	$ 50.00			
Computer (for office)	$750.00			
Paper	$200.00	$20.00		
Office supplies—pens, pencils, plain envelopes, staples, and so on	$500.00	$75.00		
Repainting daughter's room			$150.00	
Maid service (monthly cost)		$25.00		$ 75.00
Laundry service				$200.00
Carpet cleaning	$ 25.00		$ 75.00	

Note that expenses concerning your business will fall in to one of four categories. Like Table 4.1, you will create a spreadsheet with four columns, one for each category:

1. **Startup deductible expenses.** These occur only once, when starting your business, and are deductible as a business expense. An example of a startup deductible expense would be a phone you purchase to use in your business. (You aren't likely to need to replace the phone for some time, so this would be categorized as a startup expense.)

2. **Ongoing deductible expenses.** These are ongoing, and they are also deductible as a business expense. An example of an ongoing deductible expense is copy/printer paper. Whenever possible, list in the spreadsheet the cost of this expense for one month.

3. **Startup expenses that are not deductible.** These are expenses you will incur as a result of beginning your home business, but they are not deductible as a business expense. For example, let's say that you switch your daughter's bedroom with the spare room so that you can use her current

room for your home office. You will repaint her new room to the color she desires. This will still cost you—but you cannot deduct that as a business expense.

4. **Ongoing expenses that are not deductible.** These are expenses you will incur as you operate your business, but are not a reasonable business expense. For example, let's say you decide to send laundry out rather than go to the laundromat. This gives you additional time to invest in your business because you are spending a few minutes to gather it and a few minutes to put it away rather than two hours or more at the laundromat. But this isn't a business expense per se, so you will not be able to deduct it as such. Whenever possible, list this as a monthly expense. This allows you to view a monthly picture of your expenses easily.

Check with your accountant or tax preparer to confirm that every expense you have in a "deductible" category is truly a deductible business expense. (Don't rely on the preceding examples—your circumstances might be different!) Or, download "Publication 334: Tax Guide For Small Businesses" and "Publication 4035: Is It Too Good To Be True? Home-Based Business Tax Avoidance Schemes" to help you determine whether an expense is truly considered a business expense. These publications, and much other helpful information, can be downloaded from the IRS website, www.irs.gov. Also, check with your accountant or tax preparer to determine if it makes sense to deduct some other expenses associated with your business, particularly a portion of your mortgage or property taxes attributable to your home business.

note Some expenses will have entries in both the Startup Deductible Expense and Ongoing Deductible Expense columns. For instance, you will initially purchase a number of office supplies so that you can operate the business. You will reorder supplies regularly, but not necessarily to the same extent as you did when you started. So, you would have an entry in each of the preceding two columns labeled "office supplies." In addition, many services you order for your home will apply to your home office, but you can usually only deduct the portion that would be applicable to the square footage of your office. So, in the example in Table 4.1, maid service is costing $100 per month, but because the home office takes up only 25% of the total home, 25% of the expense (or $25.00) is deductible.

caution **Watch Out**

Do not overlook categories 3 and 4! One way to underestimate your expenses is to assume you have nothing that fits in these two categories.

Setting Up the Spreadsheet Rows

Most home businesses operate as sole proprietorships. This means that you report your business income and expenses on Schedule C of Form 1040. To keep things simple, we will use the expense categories of Schedule C as major headings in the rows of the spreadsheet. (The first page of the Schedule C form appears in Appendix A, "References and Resources," of this book. There is a second page primarily for additional details regarding your vehicle and miscellaneous expenses. But for our purposes, we will focus on the first page only.)

> **tip**
> Your ongoing expenses can be for a month or a year. Recommendation: Use one month. This is more useful to you in planning. For expenses that come once per year (for example, membership fees), divide the cost by 12 and put 1/12 of the yearly cost in the monthly column.

You can download Schedule C from www.irs.gov or from your local IRS office. In either case, get both the form and instructions for using it; the instructions can help you determine which expenses should go in which categories.

Under each primary heading (from Schedule C), you will put the specific items that fit under that heading. For example, Line 17 is "Legal and Professional Expenses." Under this heading, you might have several specific entries, such as "Attorney Fees, Incorporation," "Attorney Fees, Standard Contract Preparation," and "Accountant Fee, Budget Review." (Note that all three of these line items are startup expenses.)

Later, in Chapter 5, "Setting Up Your Records and Preparing to Open for Business," you'll see an example of the expenses spreadsheet. A blank version of this template also appears in Appendix A.

You will then transfer some items to this Budget spreadsheet from your startup analysis. Why only some? This budget spreadsheet will focus on your *business* expenses only. Anything not considered a business expense will not be listed here.

Additional home (nonbusiness, nondeductible) startup and ongoing expenses should be added to your *home* budget. If you didn't have one before, it is now time to set that up!

Then, when you start your business, you will begin using a business spreadsheet just like this one; that spreadsheet, however, will be labeled "Actual" rather than "Budget," and will list the true expenses that you've paid for rather than the amounts you budgeted for those expenses.

So you might have to create four items:

- a Budget spreadsheet for your business
- an Actual spreadsheet, recording actual income and expenses, for your business

- a Budget spreadsheet for your personal household budget (if you have not yet set up a household budget)
- an Actual spreadsheet or similar records for your home (nonbusiness) if you have not yet set up something like this for personal household expenses

Don't overlook the household budget and actual expenses worksheets. They can be much, much simpler than your home business Budget and Actual spreadsheets, but you must know whether you can cover your personal household expenses. The only way to do this is to create a budget, track your expenses, and be sure that spending stays at a level you can afford.

Because it can be easy to overlook an item, create a draft of your business budget spreadsheet, and then check it twice. The first time, check your draft against the draft of your business plan (the one you created in Chapter 3, "Creating Your Business Plan, Part 1: What, Where, When, and How") to determine that your budget accounts for all the expenses and income resulting from the elements of that plan. Next, check your draft against Schedule C items. A sample spreadsheet is also provided to assist you in developing your own budget.

To do list

- ☐ List each expense you will incur in relation to your business.
- ☐ Decide whether the expense is startup only or ongoing.
- ☐ Determine whether the expense will be deductible as a business expense.
- ☐ Read any related IRS material for each particular expense.
- ☐ Make reasonable estimates of each expense, based on your own knowledge; make phone calls or perform other research if you are unsure of the amount.

Planning for Budget Items As Outlined in the Business Plan Form

In this section, we'll tick through each of the sections of your drafted Business Plan (refer to Chapter 3, Figure 3.2 for a clean version of the business plan outline). For each element of your plan that involves the income or expense of funds, follow the budget tips offered here to reflect those financial realities in your budget.

You'll need list

- [ ] Business budget spreadsheet and business actual spreadsheet
- [ ] Business plan
- [ ] An additional calculator

Introduction/Overview

There probably isn't much in item 1 that belongs in your budget.

The Basics

A. What is the business name? Is it a sole proprietorship, partnership, or corporation?

To account for expenses related to this element, be sure to include the following deductible startup expenses in your budget:

- Attorney fees for incorporation
- Attorney fees for trademark research and/or trademark application
- Fictitious Name Statement fees
- Business licenses

B. Where will the business be located? (Presumably, you have answered this, and the answer is in your home.) Is there a post office box?

To account for expenses related to this element, be sure to include

- Any special permit fees for business use of your home
- Cost of a post office box, if applicable

C. Will the business have a web presence? What is the domain name(s)?

Here, be sure that your budget accounts for these deductible expenses:

- Hiring a web designer and/or writer to create your website (usually an initial expense with regular or annual updates)
- Domain registration fees (can be purchased once every 10 years—you can also renew every year, but you're allowing someone else nine other chances to get your website name if you fail to renew on time)

- Website hosting fees (usually monthly, and separate from the development of the site itself)
- Expenses for regular web updates (for example, hiring a web developer or other person to regularly update your site if you are not doing it yourself)

D. Who is the proprietor(s)? What is it about the proprietor(s) that makes him/her/them the right person(s) to run this business?

Be sure to include this cost:

- The cost of renewing or maintaining any professional licenses; don't just put in the fee for renewal, but also the cost of continuing education classes if they are required to maintain the license.

E. What needs or wants of customers are being met?

These expenses are covered in the "Marketing" section, later in this chapter.

Business Overview

The budget-related items associated with this section of the business plan are discussed in each of the sections remaining. Because the business overview is more of a summary, it is merely providing a snapshot of what is discussed throughout the rest of the plan.

Marketing

This section of your Business Plan includes these elements that must be accounted for within your budget:

A. How does the business reach customers? What need or desire is being fulfilled?

B. What are the unique features this business offers that competitors do not?

C. How will the business interact with and retain customers?

To accommodate the expenses associated with these elements, be sure that your budget includes the following deductible expenses:

- The cost of letterhead and business cards. You will probably have initial design expenses with your first print order. Then, about once a year, plan on reordering both. You might eventually choose to have a complete redesign later, but this would be more discretionary and probably come during years 3–5 of your business.
- The cost of any mailings to new or existing customers (including development of the brochure or mailer by a writer and graphic artist, printing, and postage). Your initial mailing—letting the world know that your business

exists—will be quite large. Additional mailings your first year will probably be a bit more focused, smaller, perhaps even limited to one-on-one letters. (See Chapter 7, "Marketing for the Real World," for more information.)

- The cost of networking and joining chamber of commerce and other groups in order to gain clients. Be sure that you include not only dues, but also incidental fees, meeting fees, and so on. For instance, most BNI (Business Network International) chapter members pay an annual fee (to be a member) plus quarterly chapter fees (which cover the cost of room rental for their weekly meetings). Many chambers have monthly mixers, and if you assume that you'll attend at least 10 of these, you might be paying a $5 or $10 charge for entry and/or a drink.

- Display advertising; include the cost of developing the ad (for example, hiring a graphic designer), as well as the cost to insert the ad in the targeted newspaper or magazine. Your startup costs will include the design of the ad; running it repeatedly would be more of an ongoing cost.

- Cost of hiring a marketing strategist if you are unsure that you will conduct all of your marketing.

D. How is pricing structured in your line of work? What is the going rate for the service you provide?

It is unlikely this will be the source of *expenses*, unless you provide rebates under certain circumstances. We'll be talking about how to project income, and therefore pricing, later in this chapter.

note Most home businesses use the cash accounting method. This means that you record income as you receive it and record expenses as you pay them. If you want to use another method, check with your accountant or tax preparer. This budget is being formulated using the cash accounting method.

Logistics

Various elements of this section of your Business Plan must be accounted for within your budget.

A. Where is the business located? How much space is rented/allocated?

For this item, be sure to include

- The portion of your rent, mortgage, property taxes, and utilities that can be attributed to your home business. (Divide the square footage of your home business area by the total square footage of your home to obtain this percentage. For instance, 250 square feet used in a 1,000 square foot home means that the owner can deduct 25% of the mortgage payment, property taxes, and utilities.) This would be an ongoing expense.

- You might also want to budget for a percentage of maintenance on your home, such as carpet cleaning (if your home is carpeted throughout) and other recurring items. These would be ongoing expenses. Include a percentage of them in your business budget spreadsheet based on the percentage of the business use of your home. So for example, if 25% of your home is used for your home business, 25% of the carpet cleaning would be deductible. (Be sure and include the remaining 75% in your home budget.)

caution

You can't deduct home expenses that are completely unrelated to your business. Do not deduct a percentage of your home phone bill, for example. You also might have to repay some of what you deduct as a business expense for the use of your home (such as the portion of your mortgage payment you deduct). This applies to homeowners only (not renters). Talk to your accountant or see the IRS publications on the business use of your home, "Publication 523: Selling Your Home," for more information.

B. What equipment is purchased/needs to be purchased?

To account for these expenses, be sure that your budget includes these costs:

- Basic office equipment that you'll use, including computer, printer, scanner, fax, surge protector, and separate business phone. Most of these are startup expenses—you aren't likely to replace them for at least 3–5 years, and they should be deductible.

- Installation of high-speed, cable, or additional phone lines (for example, cost of line installation by an electrician or phone or cable company technician). Again, these are startup, deductible expenses.

- Paper, pens, pencils, and other office supplies as needed. (Refer to your favorite office supply store or catalog.) The initial office supply bill is likely to be a large one—kind of like your first grocery bill when you moved out of your parents' home. After that, however, you should have ongoing (but more modest) bills.

- Any special equipment specifically related to your particular business.

- Any mobile equipment to keep you in touch while you travel, such as laptops, mobile phones, wireless modems, and so on.

- Filing cabinets, bookcases, and other furniture for the office. This is usually a startup expense. Decent office furniture really doesn't wear out for some time, so unless something unusual occurs or you outgrow the furniture, it should last quite awhile. (You might get sick of it and decide to buy new, but that would be assuming you have the income to do so—it's discretionary.)

This item usually will not be the source of any additional costs:

C. What arrangements have been/need to be made with other businesses in order to provide the product(s) and/or service(s) offered by the business?

If you must occasionally make deposits on clients' behalf, you might want to allocate a separate fund for this purpose.

Financials and Assumptions, Expansion, and Exits

You are accounting for these two sections of your Business Plan by working through this chapter to draft a business budget.

Accounting for Expenses As Listed in Schedule C

Now, refer to Schedule C to make sure that your budget accounts for all expenses and income that will be listed on that document.

You'll need list

- ❏ Business and home budget spreadsheets
- ❏ Business plan
- ❏ Calculator, if desired

Listing Gross Receipts, Returns, and Costs of Goods Sold

Though you might have little or no entries for some of these categories, as appropriate, make sure that these lines are complete:

- **Line 1. Gross receipts.** Meaning all the income generated. We'll cover this more when we discuss pricing.

- **Line 2. Returns and allowances.** These are actual product returns. So, if you are selling widgets, and you estimate six customers will email you requesting a refund (and returning the widgets), the price of the returned items goes here. Line 3 is merely a result of lines 1 and 2.

- **Line 4. Cost of goods sold.** These are the actual cost of products you sell. Include the cost to make or purchase any products you sell in your budget—both as a startup and as an ongoing expense.

Costs of Advertising and Car/Truck Expenses

To account for line 8, Advertising, include any and all types of advertising expense in your budget. Don't forget these expenses:

- Newsletters
- Booths at conferences
- Ads in school or community posters, such as high school sports schedules

Line 9 lists Car and Truck Expenses. To budget car and truck expenses correctly, be sure to read the IRS' publication "Publication 463: Travel, Entertainment, Gift, and Car Expenses." Note that you will need to provide quite a bit of information on the back of Schedule C, too.

> **tip** If you are using a car or truck for both personal and business trips, you will need to carefully document how many miles you traveled for your business. Keep a mileage log that shows the date, start time, end time, destination, and beginning and ending odometer readings. Be sure that each trip is clearly labeled—for example, were you driving kids to soccer practice or seeing a client? Be sure that you can easily tell whether a particular trip is business-related or not.

Accounting for Commissions, Fees, Contract Labor, and Depreciation

To account for expenses associated with Line 10, Commissions and fees, be sure to include these expenses in your budget:

- Bank fees incurred when you open a separate business bank account
- Referral commissions paid to those who provide you with business leads that turn in to actual business
- Any commissions you will pay to other independent contractors to work as your sales representatives

For line 11, Contract labor, be sure that your budget includes costs associated with any labor you might hire to help you complete your work or run your business, including bookkeepers, contract clerical staff, and project subcontractors.

Expenses associated with costs listed on lines 12, Depletion, and 13, Depreciation, usually aren't applicable for most home businesses. Check IRS guidelines or with your accountant for more information.

Budgeting for Insurance Costs

Line 14 of Schedule C lists the costs of Employee benefit programs. You probably won't have employees, so again, this is not likely to apply.

To account for costs listed on line 15, Insurance (other than health), be sure that your budget includes costs for any of these types of insurance that you'll use for the running of your business:

- Professional liability insurance (or errors and omissions insurance); this insurance covers any mistakes you make in your work and provides legal assistance if you are sued as a result of a mistake you make in your business. If you have a good track record in your profession and are in a low-risk business, this can be as low as hundreds of dollars per year. If you are in a high-risk business, or if you have had legal action or professional complaints in the past, you will pay a much higher fee.

- Disability insurance. Don't overlook this! You know that health insurance is important. And if you pass away, you have life insurance. This covers that in-between possibility—that you are alive, but not able to run your business for some period of time.

- Unemployment insurance, if you choose to purchase it (some states allow sole proprietors to purchase this; it is rarely worth the premiums, however)

- Life insurance; be sure that you cover yourself (so that your family has enough to live on if you pass away), as well as your spouse or partner (particularly if you depend on his/her nonmonetary services, such as child care and housekeeping)

- Renters or homeowners' insurance should also be considered, although this type of insurance would be entered on "Form 8829, Business Use of Your Home" for tax purposes. Be sure that any liability insurance covering your home would also cover someone visiting your home for business reasons.

Planning for Costs of Interest and Legal and Professional Services

Line 16 lists business-related costs of interest paid throughout the year. To cover these expenses, make sure that your budget includes

- Mortgage interest (but see the earlier caveats about deducting mortgage and other expenses)

- Other interest, including interest on business credit cards and business lines of credit

To account for expenses associated with line 17, Legal and Professional Services, your budget should include

- Attorneys' fees

- Accountants' fees

- Coaching or consulting fees to help you establish your business

DISABILITY INSURANCE IS IMPORTANT!

In some cases, disability insurance is actually *more* important than life insurance. Although in life insurance, your personal living expenses are no longer a consideration (because you are dead when it is collected), disability insurance helps you cover expenses while you are alive, yet unable to contribute. It's replacing your income, while caring for you at the same time.

Social Security offers disability coverage, but this should not be relied on—guidelines are fairly strict; you might have too many assets to qualify, and you might not qualify for the coverage even if you cannot run your business.

See www.ssa.gov/notices/supplemental-security-income/ for more information, including a screening tool that allows you to put in possible scenarios based on your own personal circumstances.

Even if you qualify, Social Security disability assistance is almost never enough to cover your regular living expenses, additional home care you might need, and the expenses of your business.

Some states offer disability coverage that is open to self-employed individuals as well. (California is one of those states.) Check with the state where you live, and see if this is offered. Again, restrictions will apply, so you might not be able to purchase it right away. (There might be a minimum number of years you must be in business.)

If you don't qualify for a state-run program, or if premiums would be too high, purchase private disability insurance. Again, be sure that it would cover all four types of expenses: a) your medical care, b) keeping your business running, c) additional services you would need (such as a home health aide), and d) living expenses for you and the rest of your family.

Premiums will vary, depending on your age, your occupation, and possibly your medical history. See Appendix A for insurance resources if you need to find an insurance agent who carries this type of insurance.

Budgeting for Office Expenses

Line 18 lists the costs of office expense. Here are just some of the items you must budget for when planning business expenses:

- Supplies, both the initial purchase and ongoing
- Toner for your fax and printer
- Computer technical support
- Training on new software

- Office furniture
- Purchase of software and hardware

You'll also want to include postage, phone bills, Internet bills, paper, letterhead and business cards, and just about everything else that keeps your office running smoothly.

For many home businesses, this is the largest category of expenses. Because it can be such a significant part of your budget, it is worth reviewing twice.

Accounting for Pension and Retirement Expenses

Line 19, Pension and Profit Sharing Plans, lists some important costs. Because you do not have employees, you would not enter anything on this line when filling out Schedule C. As a home business owner, however, you are responsible for your own retirement savings, so be sure to budget for

- Regular contributions to your individual retirement account (IRA)
- Regular contributions to your savings account

Contributions to your IRA are deductible—not on Schedule C, but on the very front of Form 1040 (the primary form used to file your income tax return with the IRS).

If you've been able to squeak by with 1040-EZ or 1040-A, well, those days are over! Don't be afraid, and don't listen to all the daunting "big, bad, lost-in-the-woods 1040" stories you hear. Yes, the form 1040 is long; yes, it can be tedious. But if you stay on top of your expense and income tracking and work with a bookkeeper and/or accountant, it will be much easier than you think!

Accounting for Rent/Lease, Repair, Maintenance Expenses, and Other Necessary Supplies

Line 20 lists costs related to your rent or lease. To account for these expenses, be sure that your budget includes these items:

- Leasing costs of any vehicles or equipment you will need.
- Cost of leasing some office equipment, such as copiers. Leasing may be a preferable option, at least initially because you might not be certain that you will really need the equipment. It is a way to "try it out." On the other hand, technology often advances so rapidly that leasing can be seen as preferable, particularly when having the latest technology is important to the functioning of your business.

Line 21 lists costs of repairs and maintenance. Include here the cost of repairing or maintaining equipment. Home maintenance also needs to be considered, but would go on Form 8829 for tax reporting purposes.

Line 22 records the costs of supplies. These are things you need to run your business that are used regularly (such as office supplies), but particular to your own business. Examples of the latter group include reference books for writers, standard disclosure forms for real estate agents, gloves and shovels for landscapers, and so on.

Budgeting Taxes and Licenses and Travel Expenses

Line 23, taxes and licenses, is used to record all the expenses you pay for business licensing and special taxes. (If in doubt, read the directions for completing Schedule C.)

On line 24, you'll record costs associated with travel, meals, and entertainment. These expenses are relatively self-explanatory, but note that although travel is fully deductible, meals and entertainment are only partially deductible. Be sure to budget for the nondeductible amount as well. But this category can be confusing: Your car, when used for business, has its own line item. Rental cars, if leased while traveling, would be covered here. Your cell phone is probably used all the time and should go under "Utilities"—the next line item.

Listing Utilities, Wages, and Other Expenses

Line 25, Utilities, records expenses associated with phone, fax, and Internet services dedicated solely to your business. Electricity and gas will be covered under Form 8829, as only a portion of those bills apply to your business.

Line 26 records wages you pay throughout the year. Again, because you have no employees, you probably will not use this line.

Use Line 27, Other, to record deductible expenses for anything that doesn't fit in one of the preceding categories—for instance, use of local public transportation. There is a business use of your car on Line 9. That's for local travel. There's also Line 24 for Travel—meaning going outside your local area and getting around. But local public transit doesn't fit, really, in either category. So you can include it here and explain what it is on the back.

You really shouldn't have too many things in "Other." Think about your expenses carefully, and in almost all other cases, you'll realize that there's a category that fits. Don't assume that you can just load up on anything and put it here come tax time, either. There's room on the back for an explanation as to what these "Other" examples really are—and the IRS will want to know, in detail.

Planning for Estimated Tax Payments and Other Expenses Not Included in the Form

What isn't included on this form? There are several expenses you will still need to budget for, including estimated tax payments.

As someone running his/her own business, you will need to pay what you think you will owe for the tax year, generally divided in to four equal payments. Be sure to budget for federal, state, and local taxes. For federal taxes, you will pay 15.3% Social Security/Medicare tax on everything earned over $400. In addition, you will pay income tax based on what you owe—this percentage changes and is available at www.irs.gov/businesses/small/. As for state and local taxes—these will depend on what state you live in, which city/county you live in, and whether your state or city even has an income tax. Cities in California do not have an income tax. Some states, such as Nevada, have no state income tax.

As a general rule of thumb, however, taxes will take roughly 30–40% of your income after business expenses are deducted. In other words, if you take in $150,000, and have $100,000 after expenses are deducted, taxes will consume about $30,000 to $40,000 of that income.

Also, you might need to plan for an additional increase in your electricity and water usage, to accommodate the utilities you'll use in your home office. However, a percentage of your utilities will be deducted on Form 8829, covering Business Use of your Home. You need to be sure, however, that if your electric bill is currently $50, you aren't budgeting for a $50 electric bill (when everyone is gone most of the day), but perhaps a $75 or $100 bill (when you are now home all day, running office or other equipment, using lighting and heating, and so on).

Reviewing a Sample Business Budget Form

In this section, we take a look at a sample budget spreadsheet. Sam is a graphic artist with no dependents. He rents his apartment, and will be working from home there. Note that Sam only includes in his spreadsheet the category headings he really needs.

Table 4.1   A Sample Business Budget (Sam the Graphic Artist)

Line Item	Deductible		Not Deductible	
	Startup	Ongoing (Monthly)	Startup	Ongoing (Monthly)
Advertising				
Newspaper ad	75.00	6.25		
Special section article (writing)	150.00	12.50		
Special section article (insertion)	300.00	25.00		
Car and Truck Expenses				
Car mileage and maintenance		50.00		
Insurance (other than health)				
Renters'	200.00	17.00		
Liability	300.00	25.00		
Health* (Deductible on the front of Form 1040, but not as business expense)			250.00	250.00
Car (portion deductible for business)		150.00		150.00
Legal and Professional Services				
Accountant fees—budget review and estimated tax (Check and see if all is deductible as business expense)	250.00	25.00		
Attorney fees, preparation of standard client agreement	500.00			
Office Expense				
New computer	750.00			
Carpeting (check with accountant)				
Supplies	500.00	75.00		
Software	3,000.00	25.00		

Table 4.1   Continued

Line Item	Deductible		Not Deductible	
	Startup	Ongoing (Monthly)	Startup	Ongoing (Monthly)
Supplies				
Digital camera	2,000.00			
Special lighting (for creating photos when needed)	2,000.00			
Taxes and Licenses				
Business license	120.00	10.00		
Utilities				
Additional phone line (Installation plus monthly service)	200.00	50.00		
Business Use of Home (25% of home used for business)				
Rent		250.00		750.00
Electric/Gas		25.00		75.00
Taxes				
Federal Income				500.00
Federal Social Security (1/2 deducted on front of Form 1040)		255.00		255.00
State				50.00
Local				5.00
Savings and Retirement				
Savings				50.00
Retirement				50.00
Client			500.00	
Advance Fund (may advance funds to printers)				

We'll work more with the Schedule-C based spreadsheet—including forecasting beyond your startup phase—in Chapter 8, "Avoiding Expensive Mistakes."

To do list

- ❏ Determine accurate pricing for your services, and by extension, likely potential income
- ❏ Plan on cutting expenses and following necessary frugality measures while your business is in startup.
- ❏ Determine how much you will need in savings to cover both startup expenses and less income the first two to four years.
- ❏ Review this information and compare it to your budget from the previous section.

Planning Your Incoming Funds: Where Will the Money Come From?

Now that you have determined how much is likely to go out, you need to figure out how much you can reasonably expect to come in to meet your expenses.

Although you'll depend on the marketplace to supply some of your income, you have some ability to control your cash flow. Your pricing structure, for example, will play a role in determining how much income you make. You also can plan for having a savings and/or investment account from which you can draw necessary funds or tap in to in case of an emergency. How you use those incoming funds matters, too; by cutting back on expenses and saving wherever possible, you can stretch the dollars you earn further.

To plan for all these factors, you need to realistically assess your current situation and plan for the future. You might need to go back and forth several times, adjusting income and expense projections until you have a budget that meets your needs.

You'll need list

- ❏ Business budget spreadsheet
- ❏ Startup analysis spreadsheet
- ❏ Calculator (if desired)
- ❏ Business plan

Developing a Pricing Structure

Part of your budget will require developing a pricing structure for your business. How do you know what to charge? You don't want to charge too little; not only might you fail to make ends meet, but also you can damage your credibility in the marketplace and limit future earnings potential. Yet, your prices must be competitive; overcharging can damage your credibility, as well, and you don't want to charge so much that your clients go elsewhere.

The following sections discuss techniques you can use to develop a pricing structure for your home business. Because pricing is so important, you are going to calculate your pricing according to three different variables. Then, you will compare and reconcile the three results.

Method One: Calculate the Going Rate

First, find out the going rate for your particular service. You can do this in several ways:

1. Call and ask your competitors what they are charging for their services.

2. Ask around. Have any of your friends, relatives, or acquaintances used this service lately? What did it cost them?

3. Visit websites, and learn all you can about the going rate in your particular field. Many professional organizations conduct surveys of their members on a regular basis and make these survey results available online.

When you have the average going rate in your field, you need to use that rate to calculate a projected yearly income. Use one of these methods:

- If your industry charges by the hour, multiply the going rate by 2,000 hours (50 weeks × 40 hours a week = 2,000 hours).

- If your industry charges by the day, multiply the daily rate by 250 (the number of average work days in one calendar year).

Remember that some of your time will be spent handling administrative tasks, marketing, and other duties that aren't always directly billable to your clients. If you absolutely must work no more than a 40 hour week, reduce the hours in your calculations accordingly. Most home business owners can expect to work at least 55 to 60 hours per week initially, with at least 15 to 20 hours of nonbillable work. As you grow your business, your nonbillable hours might stay the same or decrease, as you find more efficient ways of operating and gain clients. (The preceding standards already assume that you will still want two weeks' vacation per year.)

Here is an example:

The going rate for graphic designers in the San Francisco Bay Area is approximately $75 per hour. Sam, who is planning his own home business, only wants to work 40 hours per week and assumes that he can get nonbillable work done in 10 hours per week.

$75 per hour × 30 billable hours per week × 50 work weeks per year

75 × 30 × 50 = $112,500

If Sam charges the going rate, he has the potential to earn $112,500 before expenses (including taxes and benefits).

Method Two: Convert Your Salary to a Self-Employment Income

Another way to calculate your pricing is to use your current income and multiply it by two. Then, divide by 2,000 hours (or however many hours you want to work) to come up with an hourly rate. This gives you a rough idea of the amount of money you need to match your current salary and its capability to meet your current expenses (assuming that you aren't spending more than you make).

Why multiply your salary by two? Most companies not only pay your salary, but also offer benefits, including health insurance, life insurance, liability insurance, vacation days, sick days, and employee discounts. Doubling your salary is a good rule of thumb to quickly gauge the cost of those benefits.

Here is an example:

Sam is living in San Francisco, and currently earning $40,000 per year.

Twice Sam's salary is $80,000 per year. He only wants to work 30 hours per week, which comes out to 1,500 hours per year (30 × 50 = 1,500).

$80,0000 ÷ 1,500 hours per year = $53.33 per hour

Method Three: Pricing Based on Current Expenses

Finally, you need to look at your current monthly living expenses. (Refer to your home budget from earlier in the chapter.) You want to be sure that your pricing will allow you to meet your living expenses and allow you to pay taxes, insurance, and other expenses you are now taking on as you move into self-employment. You will also need to have money for investing back in to your business as well.

Taking all of these expenses into account, calculate your average monthly expenses, multiply by 12, and then divide by 2,080 (hours in a typical work year) to approximate an hourly rate.

You will need about the same amount of money as you are currently bringing home, plus an additional amount to cover taxes, business expenses, insurance costs, and retirement contributions.

Reconciling the Results of the Three Methods

Your next step will be to reconcile these three approaches to determine how much income you'll require and how you must price your products or services in order to acquire that income.

In Sam's case, he knows that he can charge up to $75.00 per hour, which—if he works about 130 hours per month (30 billable hours per week x 4.3 weeks per month)—seems to be about what he will need to cover his expenses. Plus, he will have some periods when he just cannot find enough clients to work 30 billable hours in a week (or 130 billable hours in a month), so the going hourly rate gives him some financial cushion.

If Sam manages to work a full 130 billable hours per month, he will receive $9,750 per month, or $117,000 per year. When about $35,000 (roughly 1/3) is subtracted for tax payments, this leaves Sam with $82,000 per year. Sam will still have to pay insurance, retirement, and business expenses, but considering that he's been living on only $40,000 per year, he should be able to afford these additional expenses comfortably. This would be a best case scenario.

If Sam works only 100 hours in a month, he will receive $7,500 per month, or $90,000 per year. Less about 1/3 for taxes, this will leave Sam with about $60,000— $20,000 more to cover insurance, retirement, and business expenses. This is a middle of the road scenario. It should be Sam's goal to reach this no later than his first year in business. Even at this rate, however, Sam will have to carefully monitor his expenses. There really isn't much breathing room.

If Sam works only 50 hours in a month, he will receive $3,750 per month, meaning that Sam brings in only $45,000 per year. (Bear in mind that he was bringing in $40,000 per year as an employee—and had many items, such as Social Security and health insurance, fully or partially paid by his employer.) Sam can't stay at this level for very long—it only provides him with an additional $5,000 per year for business expenses, insurance, and retirement—that's a little more than $400 per month for all these expenses! At this stage, he will have to draw money from his savings. Although it's okay to be in this mode as long as his savings last, he will need to see a steady increase in his billable hours if he's going to stay afloat.

These are the best, average, and worst-case scenarios for Sam. To determine whether your own pricing will work, take the hourly rate suggested by the three methods used (falling back to the going rate) and look at what your income would be if you work 130 hours per month, 100 hours per month, and 50 hours per month. If you cannot make enough money at 100 hours per month to get by, you will have problems making a profit. You either need to rethink the service you offer (it might not be profitable), raise your rates, or reposition your services so that you are doing less for the prices charged.

Trimming Back Expenses

The less money you spend, the less money you must make, and the more money you can save.

Money in the bank gives you options. You can use the money to support yourself while you start your business, you can save the money for a month in the future when your income is small, or you can use the money to expand your business by buying better equipment or additional services.

Money frittered away on 500,000 cable channels and junk food limits that power. Excessive unnecessary spending increases the chance that you will not have enough money to get through dry times, or that you cannot expand your business as you would like. It increases the chance that, when you are feeling burnt out from overwork, you cannot take a vacation because you do not have the savings to do so.

However you trim expenses, do not pull money out of your retirement savings. Retirement funds should be treated as someone else's money—because they are. Retirement funds are the money of the "future you," not the "current you." Once you are self-employed, it will be up to you to add money to this account. An employer will not be automatically deducting this money from your paycheck.

Planning Necessary Savings

Chances are, you will not make the maximum amount of money your first day in business. In fact, you might not make any money at all. You might have to wait a week, a month, or even a year to see your first business income.

Ideally, you should have money in the bank to help pay your bills during your first year in business. Your savings will also provide you with money for your startup expenses.

If you are going in to a new or unusually risky field or one that is not terribly familiar to you, you should have the equivalent of one year's worth of living expenses in the bank. If you are going into a lower-risk field, are more comfortable taking on risk, or have extensive experience in the business, you might be able to make do with only four to six months' of living expenses to reasonably run your business, not including one-time expenses.

CUTTING HIDDEN EXPENSES

Sometimes unnecessary expenses are well hidden. Have you thought of

1. Tracking your expenses for a week to see if you have regular patterns of unnecessary spending?

2. Renewing your library card to reduce the expense of books (other than this one, of course)?

3. Cutting back to one car (if part of a couple) or relying solely on public transportation?

4. Eating fewer meals out?

5. Buying fewer clothes that require dry cleaning?

6. Making, not buying, gifts? Or, setting out to buy a gift with the amount in mind, not the item?

7. Reusing paper rather than buying writing tablets?

8. Conserving as much energy as you possibly can by turning off the television more often, and looking for other energy hogs in your home?

9. Buying the food you really need rather than a lot of extra snack foods (such as soft drinks)?

Considering Contributing Factors

Before you decide on how much money you truly need in your savings, however, you also need to consider other factors that will impact how much money you are likely to need. Those factors include

- **The cyclical nature of your business**—Plan for any time of year that is likely to result in reduced business, as well as those that will be your busiest. Tax specialists and some areas of law are quite busy during December, whereas many other businesses slow down to a crawl. Yet, many attorneys find the summer months to be much slower than the rest of the year. You will need to think about what month you have in mind for your business opening and how that will be affected by the cyclical nature of your particular trade or service.

- **Lead times**—Don't forget to think about lead times. Gift baskets for the holiday season need to be advertised by October or November. And in most industries, clients can pay an invoice as long as 30 days after its receipt, too. This means that gift baskets you plan to sell for Christmas, for example, will require marketing in October, order taking in November, and delivery and

invoicing in December. Even more importantly, payment for those baskets might
not reach you until January. That is a lead
time of four months!

- **Your personal situation**—Do you have
  a spouse or partner who earns enough to
  meet all expenses? Can you take a part-
  time job (one that will pay all or most of
  your bills) if money is tight? Can you obtain

work through a temporary agency to supplement your business income?
These factors might allow you to have less money in the bank.

- **Your particular line of business**—How large of an investment do you
  need to make to begin work? If you are going to write, your investment might
  consist of dedicating a computer solely to
  work-related activity. For a basic, home
  office business, $3,000 to $5,000 in startup
  expenses is not unusual. If you have special equipment to get, such as special
  printing machines, a dedicated terminal,
  tools, lab equipment, or a web server,
  your startup expenses will be considerably
  higher.

> **note** Don't forget to take in to account billing cycles for clients who are slow to pay. This situation can cause serious cash flow problems for business owners. For more information on dealing with this issue, see Chapter 8.

> **caution** *Watch Out* If you are single, you might actually need to be more conservative than someone who has a working spouse or partner, as you do not have a safety net in the form of someone else's income.

Estimating Savings

Your savings should equal the amount of your total startup costs *plus* a gradually
reduced amount of funds needed to subsidize your business. As you increase your
clients and cash flow, you should need to dip in to your savings less often in order to
meet living expenses.

But how do you know how much you will need to meet your bills?

Let's say your maximum earnings, as calculated previously, is

$75.00 per hour × 35 hours = $2,625 per week × 4.3 weeks per month = $11,287.50

Now, $11,287.50 per month would be the absolute maximum you can make at your
current billing rate. You certainly won't make that amount your first week—perhaps
not even your first year.

A good rule of thumb is to assume that you will earn 20% of your potential during
year 1, 40% of your income in year 2, 60% in year 3, 80% in year 4, and 100% in
year 5.

This means that

Year 1, you need 11,287.50 × .80 (or $9,030.00) × 12 months in savings.

Year 2, you need 11,287.50 × .60 (or $6,772.50) × 12 months in savings.

Year 3, you need 11,287.50 × .40 (or $4,515.00) × 12 months in savings.

Year 4, you need 11,287.50 × .20 (or $2,257.50) × 12 months in savings.

You might need less in savings—or decide not to worry about savings—if your spouse or partner makes enough to cover living expenses. *But* you should still have at least three months' worth of your *business* expenses set aside in savings (unless your spouse or partner is able to cover those, too).

BEING PREPARED TO GET BY ON LESS

Here are some ways to economize:

1. **Prioritize your needs.** For instance, you might not need a website or letterhead right away. Get business cards printed, and get the rest prepared after money starts coming in.

2. **Look for free help.** No attorney? See if your area's Legal Aid organization will provide assistance to you regarding the legal issues surrounding your business. Likewise, don't overlook the Small Business Administration (SBA) or the Service Corps of Retired Executives (SCORE) and the Small Business Development Center (SBDC).

3. **Look for student help.** Designers too expensive? Contact your local art school, and ask for referrals to students who can do your work. They will probably charge much less than a designer who has been in business for several years.

4. **Learn all you can and do it yourself.** Do you automatically need an accountant your first year in business? Perhaps not. But this means that you must be the one to visit the IRS website, read through the mountains of tax regulations, ask questions, and work through the tax forms.

5. **Barter for services by helping other new business owners.** If your business will be in accounting, offer tax help in exchange for help from a designer or other service provider.

6. **Get help from small-business development programs.** Visit your county and city offices, as well as your local Chamber of Commerce. Do they provide any assistance with business setup?

To do list

- [ ] Consider other sources of funding
- [ ] Weigh the risks involved in alternate funding sources
- [ ] Adjust budgetary figures as needed

Pursuing Other Sources of Funding

After reviewing your budget, you might be wondering where you can get a loan.

That will be difficult. Right now, you are an unproven entity. You have no track record as a business owner. Your business plan is entirely untested, as is your ability to retain clients, do good work independently, and juggle the many responsibilities of home business ownership. Plus, as a home business, part of your expenses are going toward your home, not your business. (In other words, you really cannot pay just 25% of your rent or mortgage; that is, the part that is considered a business expense.)

That doesn't mean funding sources don't exist—but you need to be aware that funding your business outside of your own savings (and perhaps your partner's or spouse's income) is highly unlikely. Having said that, this section of the book discusses some of the best options for outside funding.

You will have a better chance of receiving funding from any outside source, however, if you

1. Have your budget and business plan fully prepared for review.
2. Can show exactly how much of a loan you are requesting, and specifically where the money will go.
3. Have operated a business before, with a good track record.
4. Have a good credit score (showing you can manage money).
5. Have a proven track record in your business and can document this.

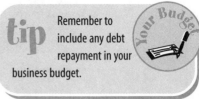

tip
Remember to include any debt repayment in your business budget.

You'll need list

- [ ] Business budget
- [ ] Business plan
- [ ] Startup analysis

REVAMPING YOUR PRESENTATION FOR THE BANK

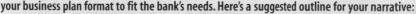

We've focused your budget and business plan on the information you will need to start your home business.

But a bank considering your loan will not want to see the same level of detail for each of the areas of your plan. So, before you head off to your meeting with your banker, revise your business plan format to fit the bank's needs. Here's a suggested outline for your narrative:

- Executive Summary—Similar to your own overview.
- Market Analysis—Include your market research. Why your services? Why now? Why here?
- Company Description—Description of your business. What services does it offer?
- Organization and Management—How is the business organized? Who are you (management)? Why are you suitable for the role of business owner?
- Marketing and Sales Strategies—How do you plan to capture clients? What do you have to offer that's truly unique?
- Service or Product Line—Description of these in detail.
- Financials—Spreadsheet—extend your projections for the next 3–5 years.
- Appendix (supporting documents)

Small Business Administration and Local Government Agencies

The Small Business Administration is the government agency charged with supporting smaller businesses—from offering advice on starting a business to financing. Its programs range from seminars to encourage small businesses to bid on government contracts, to special loans, to providing resources that businesses can use throughout their life cycle.

Visit your local SBA (Small Business Administration) office, or find it on the Web at www.sba.gov. State, county, and local development offices might also offer some additional assistance.

Banks

Start with the bank where you have your accounts. The employees know you best and are most likely to view your loan request favorably. The first question from other banks will be, "Why didn't your home bank give you a loan?"

Home Equity Loans

If you own a home, you can obtain a home equity loan and use the proceeds to finance your home business. This is usually tax deductible, so it might be a very cost-effective way to finance your home business.

A Caution About Credit Cards

Credit cards should not be considered a source of funding. Having one or two cards for emergencies and using a separate business credit card for expenses are fine.

But credit cards are not sources of operating capital. Interest is high and will continue to pile up, leaving you deeper in debt and in need of even more funding. In some instances, companies might be able to have you charged with fraud if you ran up credit card debt with no other means to repay the money.

Relatives and Friends

Like business partnerships, borrowing money from relatives and friends can be a dicey proposition. Do you really know what the friend or relative expects from you in return?

Any arrangement needs to be formalized in a written agreement. (Discuss it first, draft the agreement, and then have an attorney review it.)

Summary

Dealing with home business financing can seem like a never ending, dizzying array of duties to perform and details to track. But, as you learned in this chapter, these details are very important. Assessing how much money you realistically can expect to make in your business and comparing that to your projected expenses tells you whether you can pay your bills, whether your business is growing, and even whether your business is worth continuing.

Just remember that your budget is never "complete." You are always gaining new information. As you read through the rest of this book, your budget will probably change significantly—you'll remember an expense you didn't consider, or increase the budgeted amount for a particular item based on additional information.

Some areas of your business will need more attention when budgeting—including your technology needs. In Chapter 6, we'll discuss what technology you need, in detail, and help you fill in any questions you have about what you need and what it is likely to cost.

5

Setting Up Your Records and Preparing to Open for Business

You can avoid many legal problems associated with your business simply by keeping accurate records. This chapter helps you set up your business records the right way, so you can accurately—and legally—track your business activities from your first day in business and avoid many problems down the road. You will be giving notice, setting up your physical space, and creating a solid record-keeping system. It is exciting, but it has to be done correctly.

This chapter is relatively short, but take your time. Double-check everything, and make sure that you are ready to begin your home business.

You'll need list

- ❏ Self-employment journal
- ❏ Business plan (from Chapter 3)
- ❏ Business budget (from Chapter 4)
- ❏ Calculator or spreadsheet
- ❏ Your technology needs, furniture, and other items for your physical home office

To do list

- ☐ Set up customer records
- ☐ Set up business management records
- ☐ Set up expense and income records
- ☐ Learn to record expenses properly
- ☐ Create an invoice and income tracking record

Setting Up Basic Records

As you set up your office, there will be several basic sets of records you will need. Some of these will be for tax purposes, whereas others will provide you with the information you need to run your business efficiently and make intelligent business decisions.

The following sections outline only the basic record-keeping items you will need. Depending on your chosen field, you might want or need to keep additional records. Check with a professional organization, your accountant, or your attorney if you are unsure about what other records to keep.

You'll need list

- ☐ Computer with spreadsheet and/or database programs installed (or spreadsheet paper and notebook, if working manually)
- ☐ Calendar
- ☐ Contact manager or rolodex (however you will keep track of customers)

Important Electronic Records

In most instances, your contact management records, calendar, and business expense and income records will be maintained electronically—usually on your computer. These records are the heart and soul of your business. Years from the time each entry is first recorded, they will continue to provide important information to you about how to make basic business decisions, where and how to grow, and what markets to target. Five years from now, you might see a pattern that shows February is a slow month—always. That is good to know because you can make plans to accommodate that trend. You might notice which clients have provided a lot of steady income, which have been one-hit wonders, and which have been sporadic yet highly profitable. You might also notice that, in five years, your revenue (income before expenses) has tripled. That's a great way of telling others how well your business is doing.

In fact, these records provide important information to third parties as well. If you should ever choose to sell your business, these vital records document the value of your venture. Should you ever be audited, the IRS could seek financial records from you—and go back as far as you have owned your business, if they feel it is justified. On a more positive note, should you decide to seek a loan, it is absolutely necessary to provide the financial history of the business. And, should you choose to sell your business, you will need to maintain the records that provide so much value.

In most instances, we talk about these records as if they are all kept separately in separate software files. Can you combine some of these records in prepackaged software? Sure. Just be sure that any piece of software works well for you and provides you with all the information you need and want to run your business. Don't try to fit your needs in to the software—rather, the software should allow you to customize it to fit your needs. Use software on a 30-day trial basis if you are uncertain whether it is the right tool for you. If you need resources to help you find the software you need, see Chapter 6, "Getting Technology You Really Need (and Only What You Need)," or, for more resources, Appendix A.

Setting Up Business, Calendaring, and Contact Management Records

First, you'll want to keep an electronic copy of your **business plan**. (You learned about this plan in Chapter 3, "Creating Your Business Plan, Part 1: What, Where, When, and How.") Remember, as your business grows and changes, you will be updating this regularly. Review this weekly at first, as your business starts, then monthly. After the first one to two months, reviewing your business plan every three to six months is a good idea.

You'll also want to maintain an electronic **calendar**. There are many excellent calendaring programs, and they are usually combined with a contact database. (Lotus makes Lotus Organizer, which might come with your IBM PC. ACT! is also a popular calendar/contact management software.)

The calendar has several purposes. Primarily, double booking people is a big no-no (but you already knew that). Equally important, however, is that your calendar will help you budget your time. If you see that you already have several "To-Do's" on a given day, you should not schedule a lengthy meeting. Get in the habit of putting anything that needs to be done on your calendar. Don't forget to block out time for personal commitments, such as special family outings, doctor's appointments, and school functions.

You should also build and maintain a **contact database**, holding your clients' names, addresses, phone numbers, email addresses, and so on. Contact databases have several purposes as well. Primarily, the most important phone numbers and addresses are right where you need them—at your fingertips. Second, you will be able to send out mass mailings directed toward a particular group—that is, prospects who never became clients; clients from this year who should receive a holiday gift; clients who also gave referrals; all contacts who are attorneys (for a mailing aimed directly at attorneys); and so on. Programs with preset fields include ACT! and Entourage. For more freedom and flexibility, try database programs, such as FileMaker Pro or Access.

You can incorporate a **phone log** in to your contact manager, or, if you prefer, create a spreadsheet. Your phone log should be updated every time you pick up the phone to make or receive a call, as well as every time you receive a voicemail message and should look something like the example shown in Figure 5.1.

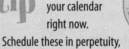

tip   Put two items on your calendar right now.
Schedule these in perpetuity, once a week:

a) Back up your computer files, which should take 15–60 minutes

b) Review your business plan, which should take 15–60 minutes.

note   Also, as part of your contact management database, you should track how much money you have collected to date from each client. (You'll learn more about other aspects of tracking income in the next section of this chapter.) Your client database should tell you how much business you have done with each client, when that business has taken place, what invoices pertain to that account, and so on.

Note that you will record the date and time of each call, its length in minutes, who you spoke to, the company, the phone number, and the message or (if you actually spoke to a live person) what you talked about. (You might not want to repeat all these details if your contact manager is up-to-date, but be sure that the person's name and company name is covered regardless.) The numbers next to "minutes" and "hours" are the actual amount of time spent on the phone, to date. Gathering this information will help you gauge how much phone time is required for various projects. The column heading "VMS" is a place for you to indicate the nature of the phone exchange—was the call incoming or outgoing? Were you talking to someone or leaving a message on her voicemail?

FIGURE 5.1

A simple phone log helps you keep track of commitments and who contacted you when.

[Current year] Phone Log						
		VMS	Length			
Date	Time	Minutes:	5642.50	Person	Co./#	Message
		Hours:	94.04			

A SIMPLE CUSTOMER DATABASE

These fields can be used in a database program (such as FileMaker) or even at the top of a spreadsheet program (such as Excel), in the form of a sortable list. If you use a contact manager, from Act! to Entourage, you might want to import some of these fields from that program.

Last Name:

First Name:

Company:

Title (if needed):

Address:

City: State: Zip:

Work Phone:

Cell Phone:

Home Phone:

Email Address (work or primary):

Email Address (home or secondary):

Customer Status: (Is this an active, current customer? Prospect only? Referral source only?)

Last invoice: Amount: (When did you last bill the customer? For how much? You might want to import this information from your bookkeeping software or spreadsheet for expenses.)

Notes: (What is special about this client that you should know? Are there certain times she prefers you call or not call? Does she have an assistant whose name you should always remember? Jot down the personal information that keeps you on a good footing with her.)

This example doesn't list every possible field, but should get you started when it comes to designing your own customer database document for keeping track of customer information. As you use your database, you might think of other fields appropriate to your business. If you're a writer, for example, you might want to note the rights sold to each customer; if you're a lawyer, you might want to keep track of the matters handled; and so forth.

This log serves several purposes. Primarily, you will have an automatic memory aid as to when you spoke to someone, what you promised or said, and what you have discussed with whom. Should you be involved in any dispute, this log will also help you document facts related to that dispute.

You also should have an electronic inventory of all of your writing, designs, marketing plans, ideas, or any other creative property. If copyright issues are involved, this **work database** will also serve as the information source regarding what you have licensed to whom and when. This database will vary, based on the kind of work you do.

Table 5.1 provides a basic structure for keeping track of intellectual property work.

Table 5.1   Intellectual Property Structure

Title	What is the name of the work created? If this is a working title, make it as descriptive as possible; additional notations or fields, such as the number of pages, date created, and so on, might need to be added if you cannot identify the work by title alone.
ID Number	A unique identifier to distinguish this record from other, similar works.
Status	Is this work placed with an initial client? Can the work be resold, or is the work solely for this client? Is the work merely an idea, or query, at this point? Options might include • Idea • Active Query • Placed with Initial Client • Completed Initial Client; Reuse (Syndication) • Completed Initial Client; Proprietary
Entity Type	Who did you sell or license the work to initially? This is good marketing information, so you can recognize patterns in sales of your work (knowing, for instance, that a certain type of work is bought initially by corporations, and later by smaller businesses). Options might include • Non-profit • Small Business • Individual • Medium/Large Corporation
Type of work	What type of work was it? Photo? Written work? Graphics? Invention? Other? If you deal only with photos, was it black and white? Color? Digital? Print? Be as specific as you can when creating categories for type of work. Again, this is valuable marketing information.
Subject	What topic or subject does the work in question cover? Subjects will vary, depending on the type of work you do.

Table 5.1   Continued

Date Sold, Rights Sold, Entity Sold To, Amount Sold For	These four fields will "repeat"—so when you license a work again and again, you can see who it was licensed to, and when; the "rights sold" also indicates whether you can continue licensing the work, and to what extent.
Total sold this item	This totals the "amount sold for" field in the prior row. At a glance, you can tell how hard this particular piece of intellectual property is working for you.
Archived?	In many instances, you will want to "retire" a work or cease licensing it. Once archived, the physical paper file should be stored in a different area than your current, working files.
Notes	Any special circumstances surrounding the sale or licensing of the work.

Setting Up Business Expense and Income Records

If you'll be taking on all the tasks associated with owning and running a home business, you will need to keep systems as streamlined as possible. A little bit of effort now in organizing your expense and income records will save you days and days of frustration later. In addition to saving you tons of extra work and frustration at tax time, keeping your income and expenses relatively up-to-date will give you an always-current picture of how much money you have brought in and how much money is going out.

Before you begin, review the budgeting categories discussed Chapter 4, "Creating Your Business Plan, Part 2: The Money Pages," so that you are familiar with the type of expenses you will need to track.

The easiest way to set up income and expenses is to base the categories within your records on those in Schedule C of your federal tax return. To obtain the most current Schedule C, go to www.irs.gov and download the most recent form. Print it, and read through the directions. (This is the same form we used in Chapter 4 as a template for the home business budget, so it might already look familiar to you.)

> **tip**
> Schedule C will be a major part of your tax return every year, and most banks and certifying organizations will want to see copies of it from prior tax years.

Recording Expenses

Figure 5.2 shows the heading of a typical spreadsheet for a home business. It provides a column for the date, as well as a description of the income or expense. Note that the line numbers from each category are included in the headings. After you input the date and description, you enter the amount of each expense or income in the appropriate column. The 0.00s just below each column description are where the column totals should go. Not every business will use every category. You might want to start, however, by listing every category on Schedule C and eliminating those that you do not use regularly after the first two years.

FIGURE 5.2

Using Schedule C as your guide, create headings across a spreadsheet that will provide you with clear categories for each type of expense.

		1-Gross Income	8-Advertising	11-Comm/F 001	15-Insurance (non-health)	16b-Internet (Other)	17-Legal/Pro n	18-Office	20b-Rent (other)	21 Repair nt	22-Supplies	23-	24a-Travel	24b-Mea	24b 50% of Meal/Ent	25-Utilities	27-Other (local ent)	30-Home total	30-Home (%, or total)	0.00	Total expenses
Date	Description	0.00	0.00	0.00	0.00	0.00	0.00	0.00	0.00	0.00	0.00	0.00	0.00	0.00	0.00	0.00	0.00	0.00		0.00	Net Income

Note, too, that special columns are set up to handle entertainment expenses and home-based expenses. Most entertainment expenses are only 50% deductible, so although you will want to track the total amount spent, only 50% should be deducted from your income.

The percentage of home expenses will depend on how much of your home you actually use as your home office. Let's say that you have a 1,000 square foot home, and of that, 250 square feet is used as your home office. Therefore, you use 25% of your home for a home office. That means 25% of your utilities and rent/mortgage will be deductible as a business expense.

If you plan to sell your home shortly, discuss the home expense deduction with your accountant or tax preparer. When the home is sold, you might have to repay some of this amount.

At the end of the categories, you should have two numbers off to the side. One is labeled "Total Expenses," and it will add up all the expense columns—simply create a formula that adds up all the expense column totals, not including the working-number columns for entertainment and household expenses. This supplies you with the total amount you have spent to date this year. The other number is labeled, "Net Income This Year." This is the result of taking the total of all "Income" columns and subtracting the "Total Expenses" number. This number is the amount you have actually earned after deducting business expenses.

Much of this spreadsheet is tax related; however, don't forget to also keep track of other, tax-related information, including home mortgage interest, charitable deductions, and IRA contributions.

Tracking Invoices and Income

For most service-based work, you will need to send an invoice to your clients. You should number your invoices in sequential order, although what number you start with is up to you. Record each invoice number, as well as the date, description, marketing code, and amount of money invoiced. The description should briefly state who the invoice was sent to and what project or work it covers. (More detailed information will be on the invoice itself, as well as in email communications and contracts with the client.) Figure 5.3 shows a sample spreadsheet used to track invoices; a sample invoice tracking document is also included in Appendix A.

FIGURE 5.3

A sample list of invoices.

Invoice #	Date	Description	Marketing Code	Amount

The sample invoice tracking document shown in the figure records the following information:

- **Invoice #**—This is the number of your invoice. Like check numbers, these should be sequential (for example, 1001, 1002, 1003). Start with any number you choose. However, it is not a good idea to start with "0001," as that makes some clients nervous.

- **Date**—This is the date on the invoice itself. (See the sample invoice form in Appendix A.)

- **Description**—This should list the client's name and the project name. You should be able to tell, at a glance, what you did and who you did it for.

- **Marketing code**—This is the code that will let you know how you obtained this client, so you can better target your marketing, and know what works and what doesn't.

- **Amount**—This is the total amount of the invoice.

You can use your invoice-tracking document to help track the source for each project you invoice. That way, you know what marketing methods have been the most successful in your business. Adding a "marketing code" to your invoice tracking document is one way to record this information. Because it is your business, you will develop your own codes. Some suggestions are as follows:

P for postcard mailings

G for groups you belong to

W for former co-workers or those from your former company

R for referrals from current or former clients

M for magazine ads

You might also want to make these codes more specific; for example, "P" for referrals from your PTA contacts, "1QP" for the first quarter postcard mailing, and so on. As I said, the system is really up to you. The goal is to keep track of what kinds of advertising and publicity work best for you so that after your first year, you can clearly see exactly where to put your marketing dollars and why.

If you sell products, you probably won't send an invoice for each book, basket, or piece of jewelry sold. However, you should set up a separate sales record spreadsheet that keeps track of these amounts, as well as any sales tax you collect. An example of a sales record is shown in Figure 5.4.

FIGURE 5.4
Sample spreadsheet for sales tax purposes.

Date	Event/Internet	Quantity	Title	Amt. Before Tax	Tax Charged	Total Collected

Here is the information recorded in the sales record shown in this example:

- **Date**—This is the date the sale occurred.
- **Point of Sale**—This records the place or event at which the sale occurred. It's important to keep track of where you sell items, so you can track which events are most successful for you. Compare the dates of Internet sales to the dates of any changes you make to your website, so you know which changes have attracted more customers.
- **Quantity**—This records how many items you sold.
- **Product**—This records the product or service sold.
- **Amount before tax**—This records the base price of your item, multiplied by the quantity sold.
- **Tax charged**—Check your state's tax tables for the total taxable amount, and record that charge here.
- **Total collected**—This records the total amount collected from customers, which should be the total of the amounts recorded in the preceding two columns.

note If you haven't done so yet, obtain your sales tax license from the appropriate state agency. This allows you to purchase some raw materials without being charged any sales tax and authorizes you to collect sales tax on products you sell.

Must-Have Hard-Copy Records

Electronic documents are easy to store and take up much less space. But as of this writing, there are still some things that should be kept on paper. Technically, you can scan every scrap of paper you might keep and store it electronically. However, you might prefer, instead, to keep the paper version for awhile, and only go the scanning route if you are certain the document is likely to be kept for archival purposes only.

Also, some legal documents can come into a gray area. If you signed a contract with a client, keep the paper copy. It's much easier to prove the contract was actually signed. Here is a list of the paper records commonly maintained by most businesses:

1. Client contracts. These are the contracts you and your clients sign when you agree to perform services. If the agreements are email/letter exchanges only, be sure to print those out and keep them in the same place as your other contracts. Get any verbal agreements confirmed in writing, even if it is only an email or letter reiterating your conversation.

2. Working papers of current and past projects. These are the notes, research, drafts, and other items from each project. If you have a database of your work, these files should have the inventory number of the appropriate work.

3. All business-related receipts (even if only part of the expense is business-related). Credit card slips should be saved, even though you will also have a monthly statement. Expenses in which only part of it is a business expense (for example, your electric bill) should also be saved.

4. Informational files. These are files about groups you belong to, issues affecting your service or subject matter, and copies of all marketing materials.

5. Copies of tax returns, beginning with the year you start your business. (You should probably keep your returns from prior years, too, although for non-business reasons. Check with your accountant or with the IRS website, www.irs.gov.) The same goes for state and local taxes.

6. Previous versions of your business plan. As your business plan changes and grows, you will want to keep past copies. Print your business plan and file a hard copy once every six months, or just before and after making broad changes to it.

How Long Should I Keep These Records?

The length of time for which you must maintain your business records varies by type:

- **Client contact information.** As long as a client is active, all contact information should be readily available. Records for clients who are not active, but with whom you are on good terms, should be kept, too—these contacts are excellent sources for mailings, and provide additional value should you choose to sell your business down the road.

DON'T FALL FOR COMMON TAX MYTHS

Say the word "taxes," and most adults have strong reactions—the vast majority negative.

As a home business owner, you need to move away from the negativity (at least a bit). Try to view taxes as an expense, just like any other listed in your budget. You will have regular, quarterly payments (as well as an additional payment in April if you still owe more tax). You will be able to keep track of your tax expense and (to some extent) minimize the cost. Most of all, avoid these common errors in thinking:

* Spending money is always good for the business because it lowers my taxes. No, spending money should be justified. If you need a piece of equipment, buy it. If a piece of equipment is unnecessary, don't purchase it just so you can avoid paying taxes. The math just doesn't add up. For example, let's say that you see a $10,000 piece of equipment you don't really need, but think you "should" buy to reduce your taxes. If you make $50,000, an additional $10,000 means that you now make $40,000. Without the purchase, you pay $16,500 in taxes (assuming roughly 1/3 of your income is tax). Using the same rate at $40,000, you pay $13,200. In other words, you just paid $10,000 to save $3,300.

* I'll never get audited, so I don't have to worry about records. Guess again. All types of businesses get audited, from one-person, home businesses to large corporations. Keep current, accurate records—always.

* I'll just keep a separate set of books (or pay folks under the table) to avoid complications. Guess again. You could be looking at fraud charges if you are caught, along with a host of other legal and financial problems. Do it right, aboveboard, the first time—always. The IRS is well aware of the temptations available to cash-based small business owners, and has increasingly targeted its audit efforts at these very problems. On a more pragmatic level, you simply will not have time, as a business owner, to keep track of the many lies and cover-ups. Honesty is not only good for you, it's also much more efficient.

- **Working files** should be kept for at least several years—long enough to be sure that the service or product provided has been paid for and its value not called in to question. What are working files? They are the notes, drafts, papers, and other items you accumulate as you work on a project. They are not the finished project itself, but the preliminary drafts, discussions, and note that lead to the final version.

If there are legal, ethical, or other considerations in your profession, you might need to keep your working files longer. (For instance, attorneys, accountants, and insurance agents might be required, either by laws or the ethical canons of their profession, to maintain records for a set period of time. If you are in these businesses, you should know those regulations quite well.) Personal preference comes in to play, too. I know some writers who still have working notes from stories published 20 years ago—and I know other writers who toss all papers as soon as a story is published and they are paid. Keeping working files for at least three to five years, however, is not a bad idea.

- **Financial records** should be kept as long as you own your business. Because it is relatively easy to maintain a lot of records on your computer, you can keep the basic information there while archiving physical paper files to a storage facility after several years. If the electronic files get too cumbersome, move them off your computer and onto a CD-ROM or DVD. It seems odd to keep years and years of financial records handy, but as you run your business, you might want to have these files readily accessible. Even if you move the records to some type of electronic storage each year, keep the records handy. The information stored in them is valuable to you, as you watch for year-to-year trends, and compare each year with prior years.

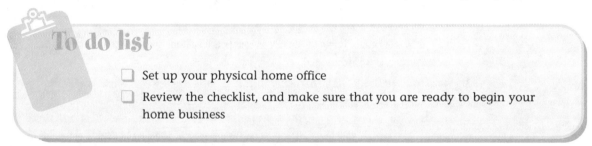

To do list

- ☐ Set up your physical home office
- ☐ Review the checklist, and make sure that you are ready to begin your home business

Setting Up Your Office Space

You have your record-keeping functions in order; now you're ready to set up your office space. But before you connect all that shiny, new equipment from the last chapter, make sure that these items are in order:

- Is your electrical system up to the task? Are the outlets where they need to be? Are the phone jacks near the actual phone base? Is the wiring "iffy"? Then have it inspected and upgraded before proceeding.

- Is your office space dry and free from water leaks? Leaks can damage costly equipment, so address the problem right now.

GIVING NOTICE

What is your current employer's policy regarding unused vacation and sick leave? If you can, you will want to use up any leave you have earned, especially if you aren't reimbursed for unused leave. You might want to get in one last checkup on your employer's dime before you go.

As a safeguard, you should also have any personal items ready to go and boxed up. Your work computer should be cleared of any personal files, including resumes and personal emails. Your voicemail should be completely cleaned out. Do all of this prior to giving notice, even if your company does not escort people out the door right away. Your boss' reactions might be hard to predict, and you need to be prepared.

If your employer supplied you with a computer for home use, be sure that this computer has been cleared of any personal files and emails. Be sure that it is in "ready to return" condition. If you are able to do so, bring the home computer with you on the day you give notice. If you do not want money taken out of your final paychecks for things such as charitable deductions, be sure to ask payroll to stop those deductions about one month before you give notice. (You do not have to explain that you are leaving the company. Just say that you are reviewing your personal budget and making some changes.)

Check your state's laws regarding employment, notice, and final paychecks. Must you give 14 days notice? Is this specified in your employment contract? Here are some reasons why giving 14 days notice might be a bad idea:

1. This avoids the potential problem of misbehavior and harassment by your immediate boss. If such behavior seems likely, you might want to avoid the last two weeks of misery.

2. It allows you to focus fully and completely on your new life rather than having to pretend to be interested in your old life for another two weeks.

3. While two weeks' notice might be custom, there is no guarantee that your employer will honor this custom. Many employers will say that they expect two weeks notice, but will immediately cut off anyone as soon as they give notice. If you are fairly certain you will be escorted out of the building as soon as you turn in your resignation, many of the advantages of giving 14 days advance notice disappear.

But giving 14 days notice is not always a bad thing. In fact, it could start your business off on an excellent footing. Here are some reasons why giving 14 days notice might be a good idea:

1. If you give two weeks notice, and your employer allows you to continue working for those 14 days, you might have an opportunity to market your new services to people within the company. (Just remember to stay within the parameters of your employment contract.) In fact, your current employer might become one of your first clients.

GIVING NOTICE (continued)

2. It gives you two weeks to practice your marketing pitch—think of all of your co-workers and colleagues in other departments who will give you a lot of practice as they keep asking you, "Oh, where are you going to work when you leave?"

3. It will make it easier to use your boss as a reference.

In short, if your employer will let you continue working the last 14 days, giving notice is a great way to make your transition and let everyone know about your new business.

Some bosses will become visibly upset when you turn in your resignation. They might even beg you to stay at the company, and make a counteroffer to get you to stay. If you receive a counteroffer, I recommend that you refuse it. In many cases, your boss over time, will come to view you as expensive and disloyal, rather than as someone who stayed on at the request of the company. Meanwhile, the problems you had before you gave your resignation will still be there. And you must consider that if your employer really valued you, he would have made you a satisfied employee before you gave notice. At the time you give notice, you are closing the door on your employment with that company. (That is why it is so important to be well prepared when you do so.)

- Give your home office that extra coat of paint if needed. Buy a new rug, hang your favorite painting, and make it comfortable. You will be spending a lot of time here. Make it comfortable!

- Your home office might have been the family junk room before you took it over—end that pattern! Furniture, wall hangings, or knickknacks that just don't fit in other parts of the home are not allowed in your office.

Get your physical home office as ready as you possibly can. You will want to start operating out of this office right now (if you haven't been already).

Summary

At this point, your office is set up, your phone log is waiting to be filled, and you have probably given notice. Now is the time, if you have any doubts or questions, to go back and reread any section in the book, to rerun your budget figures, or to revisit an issue about which you solved yet are still feeling uncertain.

If you are ready to go, you are probably wondering what you are going to do now. After all, you have no clients—just a sparkling business plan and a new home office.

Be sure that you set the alarm clock for your regular waking time. Even if the phone never rings tomorrow, you will need to put in a full day at your home office.

caution

Watch Out!

Before you move forward, take a moment and double-check your steps. Have you

1. Reviewed your personal situation, making certain that there are no "show stoppers" (events that could prevent or hamper your ability to start your own business)? Review Chapter 3, as needed.

2. Checked your budget figures and made sure that you are fully capitalized? (In other words, do you really have enough money to do what you want to do?) This is so important—businesses that are underfunded have a difficult time catching up—and many never do. Review Chapter 4 as needed.

3. Resolved any conflicts with family or household members, zoning laws, or your employment contract? Review Chapter 3 as needed.

4. Obtained health insurance? Review Chapters 3 and 4 as needed.

5. Made sure that you have enough money in the bank to forego a regular salary until your home business starts providing an income? Review Chapter 4 as needed.

Getting Technology You Really Need (and Only What You Need)

6

In this chapter:

* Reviewing technology you already have

* Deciding what additional technology to purchase

Technology is key to a home business. Unlike traditional businesses, there is no phalanx of employees standing by, and customers don't regularly walk through the door. A home business lives and dies by email, phone/voicemail, the Internet, faxes, and postal and delivery services. If your phone or computer isn't working, you don't exist.

Mistakes in this area can be extremely costly. Knowing when to cut corners, and how, will make the difference between an office that works for you and an office that works you. That is why we'll trust you to buy your own pens, paper, and file folders—but a whole chapter is devoted to what technology you need and how to buy it. In this chapter, you learn how to assess the technology needs of your business and determine what technologies you own, what you need, and how your budget is prepared to meet those needs. You learn how to use antivirus and firewall software to protect your business computer and the documents and records it holds. Finally, you learn how to get your business website up and running.

You'll need list

- ☐ Self-employment journal
- ☐ Business plan (from Chapter 3)
- ☐ Business budget (from Chapter 4)
- ☐ Calculator or spreadsheet

To do list

- ☐ Assess technology needed for your business
- ☐ Take an inventory of current technology and review budget and business plan in view of technology needs and gaps (if any)
- ☐ Purchase necessary equipment and software
- ☐ Protect your electronic assets with antivirus and firewall software

Meeting the Technology Needs of Your Business

Before you know what you need to purchase, let's look at what you truly need (and what you already have).

Bear in mind, however, that this chapter can only speak in generalities. As such, we're focusing here on the most commonly needed technology. Your own business might need more, or less, depending on the specific business you operate, your client base, and other factors. So think of this as more of a guide than an absolute "must."

If you need more specific help, turn to Appendix A, "References and Resources." This lists a wide variety of technical consultation assistance available for small and home businesses.

What Do You Really Need?

This is a basic list of what your home business needs:

- **Computer(s)**—You should have a pretty good idea whether your customers and colleagues will expect you to have a personal computer (PC) or a Macintosh—or other computer technologies (such as a mainframe computer or Linux workstation). For instance, most graphics-related professions will be expected to work on a Macintosh platform. You also might need a laptop in addition to (or instead of) a desktop computer. Consider your need for mobile computing when making this decision.

- **Software**—More than any other category, software purchases are largely dictated by your customer base and your own working preferences. Most business owners will need a word processing program and a spreadsheet program (for your business budget and keeping track of income and expenses). Most home businesses will benefit from purchasing an "office suite," such as Microsoft Office or Lotus SmartSuite. These office suites bundle a word processor, spreadsheet, presentation software, and sometimes other useful programs into one package, providing a lower price and additional enhancements than if you purchased each program individually. Some businesses will also want a separate database program for keeping track of customers and other important information, whereas other businesses will make use of the spreadsheet programs for this purpose.

- **Printer(s)**—Whether this is color or black and white will largely depend on your specific business and the expectations of your clients. Laser printers, both color and black and white, dropped in price significantly over the last decade. Because of their superior print quality, and this price reduction, they became the standard. Unless your business requires voluminous internal reports or has other special needs, avoid dot matrix, inkjet, or other types of printers. Look at the printer's ppm (pages per minute) rate, too, particularly if you print lengthy reports.

- **Fax machine or fax software**—If the majority of faxes you send and receive are documents created in a word processing or spreadsheet program, you can use fax software rather than a fax machine. Fax software lets you fax these types of documents directly to and from your PC, bypassing the need for a fax machine. This method is particularly useful for faxing documents whose information you will be manipulating. Because you can view the faxes on your PC without printing them, fax software eliminates the need for fax-machine toner and prevents spending money (in the form of toner) on "junk" faxes, an all too common problem. If you're uncomfortable with fax software, however, and need faxes primarily for reference or communication only (rather than to manipulate their content), you might want to stick with a regular fax machine.

- **Phone and phone line**—Don't try to use your home number as your business line. Install a second phone line for your business (and a third, if you will be using a dial-up connection and/or an actual fax machine). In fact, if you use a dial-up Internet connection, consider making the third phone line a combination fax/Internet line. Voicemail should be purchased for your office line, too—this can often be done for a monthly fee on your phone bill, and your customers will expect that they can leave a message if you do not answer the phone.

- Technology that allows you to save files for **long-term storage**—Most computers come with read/write CD-ROM burners. You might also want to consider tape backups, too. Zip drives and CDs can deteriorate over time, so you'll also need to plan on resaving crucial data every few years.

- **Internet access and website**—The Internet is quickly taking the place of the phone book, and potential clients will look you up to see your website (as well as what the world is saying about you).

- **Copier**—If you are right across the street from a copy shop, you might be able to put this off initially. Scanners and fax machines might allow you to make some copies, and might be okay for office copies, but most businesses require (even if only occasionally) high-quality, presentation-style copies that are clean and professional looking.

caution

If you plan to use your scanner or fax machine to produce copies, don't assume that the quality will be acceptable. Test the machine to determine that the quality of the copies meets your needs.

- **Mobile technology**—Personal digital assistants (PDAs) have become indispensable, particularly for those frequently away from the office who also have to make a lot of appointments. Likewise, you might want to invest in a laptop with a wireless modem, as well as a cell phone. (PDAs can do much of what a laptop and cell or wireless modem can do, but they tend to be quite small and might not be well suited to the amount of work you must do remotely.) If you travel more than you'll be based at home, reverse the process: Get a laptop with a docking station for your home office, making the laptop your main computer (with a spare very handy, of course). But don't forego the land line: Cell phones can drop or cut out, particularly during lengthier calls, and customers will view a cell-only phone listing with suspicion.

- **Other small items**—You might want or need a calculator or adding machine separate from your computer.

Take Inventory

With the preceding list in your hand, look around your home. Do you have any of the equipment already listed? Could it be put to use in your home office?

If you already have the equipment, you'll be saving a significant amount of money by delaying the purchase of new technology. (After all, starting your business is expensive enough—if you can delay some purchases by using what you have, do it!)

Be completely hard-nosed and realistic when viewing the equipment you have. Unrealistic expectations can be expensive. Is a particular piece of equipment completely suitable for the long-term, or merely "OK" to get you through your first year? Adjust your inventory, and your budget, accordingly. (Computers might not be worth the "merely OK" status, however, since you might have to reinstall all of your software and data files on a new computer relatively soon.) So if your computer is five years old, can't handle scanners and printers with USB (universal serial bus) cables, which are the new standard in peripheral connectivity, and you have difficulty finding software that will run, it might be time to buy a new computer. If your computer is three years old, be sure to realistically budget for a new computer in either year 1 or year 2; by year 3, the new computer should be in place. Consider why you originally bought your technology, too—a three-year–old computer might get you through the first year. However, a three-year–old computer that was bottom-of-the-line three years ago and was purchased strictly so "the kids could fool around on a computer," might have been inappropriate for your business even at the time of its original purchase.

At the same time, be sure that your needs are driven by what you will actually have to use, not by advertising pressure. Remember that 30 years ago, no business "needed" a computer, cell phone, high-speed Internet connection, or fax machine. Then again, advertising expenditures were much smaller, too. Your business today might truly need most of these items, but be sure that you're responding to actual requirements, not market hype. (See the tips later in this chapter for how to avoid over-reliance on marketing pressure, and be sure to use Appendix A to find reliable help if you need it.)

Be sure to revisit your budget (see "Planning for Budget Items As Outlined in the Business Plan Form," in Chapter 4, "Creating Your Own Business Plan, Part 2: The Money Pages") and include any additional purchases you need to make. Be sure that your list of available technology equipment is listed in your budget. You might, for example, list "Computer (have) $0" to show that you have the computer you need and haven't overlooked this expense.

Don't assume that you can deduct expenses for equipment you already have. Check with your tax preparer or the IRS (www.irs.gov) if you have any questions. You should know, prior to purchase, what is and is not a business expense for tax purposes.

You'll need list

- ❏ Copy of equipment budget
- ❏ Technology needs assessment

Purchasing Technology for Your Business

Chances are, you will need to purchase at least some of the technology you need for your home business. Heed the following caveats:

- Avoid the common mistake of looking at hardware first and purchasing software as an afterthought. You could have the best computer in the world, but if it won't run software required in your business, it isn't worth very much to you.

- Choose an operating system that matches the needs and practices of your business and your clients. If you decide to have a single computer, you probably will need to choose a single basic operating system from which to work. The first choices typically are between the Windows and Macintosh operating systems. The Macintosh's ease of use, combined with enhanced security and reliability, make it worth considering for most home businesses. Still, many businesses use Windows-based PCs, and in many industries your client base will rely on this type of operating system, as well. Do the research, and compare the latest versions of both operating systems to determine which looks right for your business and which you can anticipate will be the most common within your client base. You should be able to find literature on both systems at their respective websites (www.apple.com and www.microsoft.com).

> **note** What about Linux? Indeed, many users have Linux computers. As with Macintosh and Microsoft, you need to really find out what software is available to run on a Linux station, how readily support is available, and how Linux compares in crucial areas such as security and ease of use. Added to this might be concerns about Linux's future: Do you know who will own or dominate the operating system five years from now? Whoever that is will dictate what the future holds for Linux users.

Consider issues such as compatibility with other systems, ease of use, security, and time/money spent on maintenance. But most importantly, consider your client base and the type of operating system most likely to be used by the people you'll be working for and with. You need to be sure that you can share files with them and communicate with them in a hassle-free way.

- Acquire full-featured versions of important programs, rather than dumbed-down 'home' versions. Carefully review pre-loaded software that comes with a computer you are considering purchasing. Almost every computer has software already installed, and beyond the operating system, a lot of it is useless to you and your business. If you must acquire basic software packages, look for a commonly used office suite, such as Microsoft Office or Lotus SmartSuite. Such packages typically contain a word processing program, spreadsheet program, calendar/email program, presentation program, and database program, along with other programs useful for small businesses. Home versions tend to reduce special tools for presentations, such as advanced formatting, tables, and other business report-style features, and emphasize the "fun" stuff of making cards and announcements more easily.

If you are comfortable with learning new software (or already work with databases), purchase a basic database program, such as FileMaker Pro, and develop your customer contact list, invoicing, and other databases yourself. By purchasing one database program, you save a lot of potential headaches stemming from compatibility among customer contact, invoicing, and other record-keeping programs. Plus, you get to set things up in a way that works for you rather than relying on a format someone else thinks is a good idea. Flexibility and cost savings are rolled into one! If you don't know much about database software, see Appendix A for resources.

- When buying a computer, buy as much as you can afford. If a computer with twice the storage space is slightly more, and you can budget for it, buy it. While the industry only expects the average computer to last two or three years, you can make your computer last much longer, particularly if you buy smart. At the same time, remember that the technology you purchase is for your business. Extras such as fancy speakers, game peripherals, and advanced video capabilities shouldn't be the focus of your purchases unless your business actually requires these items.

caution

Avoid computers where you must "buy in" to a service. You should be able to purchase your computer all by itself. Avoid any "deal" that requires you to purchase services, or make other commitments, as part of your purchase. All of these caveats lead to the same problem: The seller is really going to make money when selling you the services, almost always at a higher-than-normal price. Some of the services you might not even need. And again, buying in to a bundled package means that you are limiting your support options—and again, making technical support more expensive because your choices are greatly limited.

Likewise, technology consultants who also sell equipment have a conflict of interest. Purchase your equipment separately from your services. A technology consultant might make recommendations on what to purchase, but she should not be selling equipment to you directly.

- Think carefully about purchasing custom-built computers. Some out-of-the-box computers meet software requirements for some specialized applications such as engineering, CAD, and graphics. Unless you are building the computer yourself (and are in this line of work), the labor costs involved in purchasing a custom-built computer are usually unjustifiable and a needless drain on your budget. Plus, custom computers limit your support options to the person or company who built the machine—making technical support in general more expensive. If you want specific features on a computer, order it directly from a reputable, name-brand computer manufacturer. Many large computer manufacturers will provide you with a computer built to your specifications, and often for much less money than other options. Plus, your support options are not as limited.

- When purchasing fax machines, copiers, and printers, consider the cost of replacement cartridges, too. How many pages are expected from one toner cartridge, and what is the cost on a per-page basis? This gives you some idea of the long-term cost.

> **tip** A CD-RW drive can be a real benefit to your business. If you'll be exchanging a lot of graphics files or other large electronic files with your customers or other vendors, a read/writable CD drive will let you exchange those files via CD rather than over the Internet or through a sluggish dial-up connection. The drive will also be useful for creating and storing archives and backup files.

Choosing the Right Antivirus and Firewall Software

Security is a huge issue now that you have your own business. An infected computer will not only be a nuisance, but it could also cause you to lose relevant client files and tax information. The ramifications might include missing client deadlines (and even losing clients). Don't overlook these purchases, and take your computer security seriously.

Your two most important security measures will be acquiring, installing, and learning to use good antivirus and firewall software. *Antivirus* software protects your system against computer viruses, which are programs created to cause problems with regular computer operation. When you try to load and read a virus-infected file, the antivirus software detects and alerts you to the virus. Such programs are updated regularly to provide protection against newly developed viruses. This means that you can't install and forget the antivirus software; you need to visit the website of the software's manufacturer to find and download updates. *Firewall* software provides a layer of protection between your computer and the Internet, minimizing the ability of someone to snoop on (and steal information from) your computer.

MY WAY

Personally speaking: When the subject turns to technology, people ask what computer I use. I can proudly say that my IBM personal computers have lasted for six years so far, with nary an incident. Slightly more expensive when I purchased them, they have saved me a lot of money on computer support. In addition, the IBM PCs came with Lotus SmartSuite software included in the price—making the total purchase a real bargain. For about the past year, I've also been working on an Apple eMac. Similar to my IBM, the eMac is powerful and problem free, and the eMac's features make working in a mixed PC/Mac environment no problem at all. I also like Macintosh's additional security features.

When purchasing security software, consider the following important points:

- No antivirus or firewall software will replace common sense. Most of us have heard the adage of not opening unfamiliar email attachments—and if you haven't, you need to invest in a class on computer security before you open your business. Foolish decisions by end users are the biggest culprit of virus infections.

- Antivirus software usually has to be updated regularly. Though some periodic updates are offered as free downloads from the manufacturer's website, periodically you'll need to update the entire software version, so you'll need to budget for this expense. Ironically, the updates cover viruses only after a virus has spread. So you will remain vulnerable while the initial attack is launched. Such updates are helpful, however, if you must receive files from a large number of people because your chances of receiving an infected file (even after the initial infection) are much higher.

- You can help protect your business records from viruses by using one computer for the Internet only and another computer (off the Internet always) for your financial and work records. Likewise, don't host your own website—pay for a company to host your site on its servers, reducing further the need for firewall protection.

> **tip** Try out any antivirus or firewall software on a 30-day trial, so you can see how it will work with your particular computer and the software you regularly use. Don't rush out and buy it—do your homework. You'll find resources for free downloads (including McAfee and Norton) in Appendix A.

- Spyware programs are a much bigger concern for most Internet users. "Spyware" refers to any program secretly installed on your computer, often "piggybacking" on legitimate programs, which seeks to use your Internet account or other personal information for the attacker's gain. There are a lot of free anti-spyware programs. Get one, and install it on any computer linked to the Internet.

There is no absolutely foolproof method of protecting your computer. By carefully considering how you connect to the Internet, which computer connects, and how you act when online, you can greatly reduce your chances of victimization.

caution

Your Budget

In fact, you should never rush out and by the "latest" hardware, software, or gadget for your business. Anything that is brand new is also expensive. Prices go down after a product or piece of software or hardware has been on the market for awhile. Most software releases have small problems that are not discovered until people buy the software and start using it regularly. Don't be the unpaid guinea pig of software manufacturers—never purchase "version 1.0" of any software program if you can avoid it.

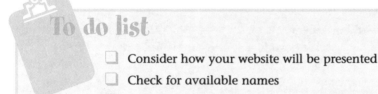

To do list

- ☐ Consider how your website will be presented
- ☐ Check for available names
- ☐ Get and review quotes for website creation

Designing and Maintaining a Business Website

Although much of the technology you purchase is sitting right in your office, two key pieces of office technology might be relatively invisible to you: your website and Internet access. In this section, you learn about the basic types of websites used by most small businesses, and you review some important pieces of information for consideration as you choose and design the site that's right for you.

Choosing the Type of Website for Your Business

Don't assume that you don't need a website. Increasingly, people are looking to the Internet in the same way that, 20 years ago, they looked at the phone book. That being said, not every business needs a high-end site. Most websites fall into these categories:

- **The "brochureware" site.** This website is really little more than an online brochure, hence its name. If you are uncertain how extensive your website needs to be, this is a great place to start. Also, because many programs exist that allow users to create their own, you might be able to put up a website on your own with little cost (just be sure that it really does attract people, rather than driving them away). Although some web designers and developers will use the "brochureware" name pejoratively, it is usually still better to have such a site than no website at all.

- **The brochure plus site.** This site provides basic information about your business, but also adds some relevant features as well. For instance, your brochure-plus site might offer e-commerce (the ability to purchase items directly from your website) or a feedback form (an electronic form on your website that will send the comments from the user directly to you).

- **Dynamic website.** This site might or might not have e-commerce or a feedback form, but is well beyond "brochureware" because it is capable of being updated regularly. It allows you to update the "latest news" every week or every day, or provides updated information about available products or reservations to the general public. For instance, let's say that you want to keep the public (and prospective clients) informed about the schedule for your speaking engagements, which changes all the time. Your dynamic website would allow you to go into the site and update the text of one or more pages, so your clients and prospects can always get the latest information on when and where you will be speaking. It's a great way to keep your website from going "stale."

Deciding on a Site Design

You'll probably need to consult with a professional website designer about the design and creation of your business's website. But before you talk to web designers or marketers, do your homework. What sites do you visit often (and which of those are run by businesses similar in organization or operation to your own business)? Why? What do you like about them? What would you change? What makes a site readable (or unreadable)? Look, too, at legal notices covering copyright and privacy issues. Will you want (or need) a separate page to cover these items?

tip Remember to include any marketing professionals (such as marketing strategists or public relations professionals) in the construction of your website. Like other materials you create, the website needs to mesh with the rest of your business advertising materials (which are usually referred to as collateral).

PREPARE TO BE SEARCHED

Don't forget to ask your web professional about designing a site so that it works efficiently with search engines. Search engines, such as Google, are the 411 operators of the Internet. Many of your potential customers will use a search engine to find resources (such as your business) by searching on a specific word or phrase. Search engines operate by looking at "keywords" from a website. Your web designer should be able to maximize your site by ensuring that all the most important keywords or phrases appear in your site content. That way, searches will return your site's web address, and prospective customers can readily find you when they are searching for your particular business. (Note that being first on the search engine list is rare—most of those slots are actually paid for.)

Then, talk to three web designers, and ask all of them to prepare proposals and quotes for you. A good designer/developer will be able to suggest applications for your website that will attract potential clients. When you're considering a website design, don't just find out what looks good online, but find out how easily a website's text could be updated (by you) on a regular basis. Keeping a site fresh is vital. Remember that the most basic website is fine for beginning, but sites age quickly—and an old-looking website might make clients think that you are no longer in business.

When choosing a name for your site, match your business name as closely as possible. Visit a site, such as www.Register.com, which provides you with available names and allows you to purchase the website name that is right for you. (Again, any marketing professionals you are hiring might be helpful with this, too.) You will also need to decide whether your email address should come from a third party (for example, AOL or EarthLink), or whether it should be based on your website domain name (for example, *owner@businessname.com*). Make this determination by evaluating how you work, whether you have an email address that already establishes your business, and your marketing goals.

note You might want to wait until you have read Chapter 7, "Marketing for the Real World," before you finalize your website.

Summary

Technology is a special part of your purchases that requires particular attention. It is your lifeline to potential clients and the rest of the outside world. Without it, customers might think that you are no longer in business—or worse, that you no longer care about them.

Don't rush into your technology purchases. Take your time. While it might feel good to make every purchase in one Internet session, you might come to regret it later. Don't over look the advice of friends, relatives, and co-workers, either. Just about everybody uses a computer, and the input of people you know can be invaluable when trying to decide on a particular model or brand name.

Part II

Putting Your Plan to Work

Marketing for the Real World

Say the word "marketing" to any group of people, and you'll see reactions akin to eating a sour lemon. People tend to think of marketing as some sleazy, hard sell gimmick or game that lures the unsuspecting into purchasing something they neither want nor need.

But that isn't necessarily marketing (and it certainly isn't good marketing). Marketing is simply letting everyone know about you and your business in order to attract clients. And because you will be doing the marketing, and representing your home business, your marketing will have your personal imprint.

Here's the most important thing to know: Next to the actual service you offer, marketing is the most important thing to do. If you don't market, you won't have to worry about bookkeeping (well, not much, because not much money will be coming in). You won't have to worry about expanding, organizing your office, or filing. Without marketing, your home business is nothing more than a well-kept secret.

You'll need list

- ☐ Business plan
- ☐ Calendar
- ☐ Rolodex, address book, or contact manager (however you keep track of people you know and their contact information)

Understanding Real Marketing

We're going to start at the end for this section. Here's the maxim you need to remember:

You should be marketing full time or as close to full time as possible. Whenever you are not working on a project for a client, you should be marketing. Whenever you have nothing scheduled on your calendar, you should be marketing. When you have a quiet afternoon, you should be marketing.

Marketing should take up a full work week until you get your first client. For the first one to three years of your business, you might spend 50% or more of your time marketing. After three years, that might drop to 35%. No matter how busy you are, you should still spend at least 20% of your time marketing.

If that sounds like a lot, let's consider the marketing cycle. Using the preceding definition, ("letting everyone know about you and your business in order to attract clients"), let's run through the typical marketing cycle.

The Marketing Cycle: A Typical Story

John is a friend of your favorite aunt. He heard about your business, and is considering hiring you. It is late January. You and John talk on the phone. You both like what you hear—he's your ideal client, and to him, you are his ideal service provider. So, you arrange to meet in early February.

There you are in February, snow swirling outside your favorite coffee shop, discussing possible projects and getting to know John a bit better. After an hour or so, the two of you come to the next step. John would like to see what you discussed in a formal quote, with a contract.

You race home from the meeting and prepare the quote and contract. John receives it, thanks you, and says he'll review it—but he's going on vacation, so it will probably be early March. He calls you on March 3 and says all is going well. However, he'd like to expand the use of your services. Would it be possible to rework the quote and present it to his business partners as well?

The two of you agree on a date when you will go to his company and make a presentation. It is now late March. Although you are nervous, the presentation goes extremely well. Everyone checks their calendars at the end of the meeting. Tentatively, you could start on the project in early April. You'll receive the signed contract, and a deposit, in the mail shortly.

Have you noticed that more than two months went by from initial contact to signed contract? Depending on the size of the project, the time could be more or less. The client, too, might be very busy, and simply not as attentive as John was in the previous example. From the time you make first contact until you close, the business could be months, if not a year or more.

This is why marketing every day, day in and day out, is important. You need to work on your marketing today in order to have business coming in next month, next season, and next year.

Plus, John might not have turned into a client. Something might have gone wrong, or you or John might have realized that there wasn't a good fit. That can happen, and it might happen after you have prepared a quote, made a presentation, and performed other marketing work. Figure 7.1 shows the process graphically.

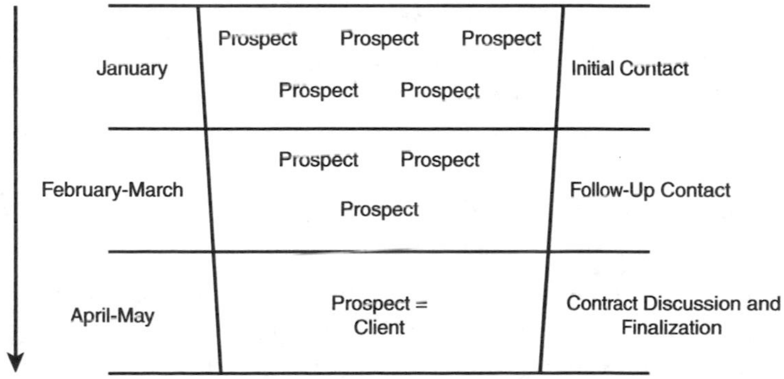

FIGURE 7.1

The marketing funnel shows three basic stages of obtaining clients and a typical reduction in prospects over time.

January	Prospect Prospect Prospect Prospect Prospect	Initial Contact
February-March	Prospect Prospect Prospect	Follow-Up Contact
April-May	Prospect = Client	Contract Discussion and Finalization

Note that, as time goes by, the number of prospects turning into customers decreases.

Slow Frying Fish: Understanding that Marketing Takes Time

Yes, marketing is a special kind of slow frying fish. You have to grab the fish out of the pond today and throw it into the pan, so you will have fish to eat next month, next season, and next year.

Sometimes the toughest part of this process is that, when you are sitting in your office with a quiet phone and clean paper and a blank computer screen, it's tough to get going. After all, what's one day spent playing solitaire (or Tomb Raider or Pro Skater 4)? Plenty. This could be the day you were destined to catch a very large fish.

That's why you need to flesh out the Marketing section of your business plan. You're going to come up with a list of things you can do, and put them both in your business plan *and* on your calendar. You're only allowed to move them off your calendar if client work or a bona fide emergency crops up (with bona fide emergencies generally involving police, fire, or hospital personnel). This is something you need to do. And you need to keep doing it for as long as you own your business.

To do list

- ❑ Draft or revise your marketing plan.
- ❑ Make a list of everyone you know.
- ❑ Write your introductory business letter and send it to your list.

Marketing You and Your Business

One of the more interesting questions I get is the question, "How do you market yourself?" or "How do you market your business?" Perhaps the question itself isn't as interesting as the implications that go along with it. The person asking the question is awaiting my answer, expecting it to be succinct. He is hoping to find the one silver bullet that will kill the need for any constant marketing efforts, the one-step, easy routine to riches.

Usually, he is disappointed. I tell him to think of a dozen ways to market himself, and I have probably tried them (and gotten clients from most). No, Virginia, there is no microwave dinner style solution to marketing.

But this is a good thing. Most of the time, you don't have to pursue a lot of options that just don't fit your business or your personality. (There's one big exception here; most marketing requires getting in front of people sooner or later. But just about everything else is negotiable.)

In the later section, "Marketing on a Budget," I've prepared a table that lists some of my favorite low-cost marketing solutions—the ones I typically mention when I respond to the "How do you market your business" question. But first, let's look at some basic, tried and true marketing ideas that every business can benefit from.

You'll need list

- ☐ Address book/Rolodex listing of business contacts, associates, friends
- ☐ Computer and word processing software
- ☐ Business plan
- ☐ Calendar

Announcing Your Business

So, here's one basic marketing exercise to get you started.

Go through your Rolodex (or contact manager or address book). Write a letter announcing your business to almost everyone you know—anyone who might conceivably use your business or recommend it to someone who might use it. Put the letter on your new letterhead.

Why send a letter to *almost* everyone you know? Everyone who knows you, and might refer people to you in a positive manner, should be aware of the opportunity to do so. One of the most overlooked chances to get new clients is failing to mention the business—or failing to directly ask for referrals.

Why write a letter? A letter provides the recipient with a visual reminder, written information about your business, and (because you will tuck business cards inside this), cards to hand out to referrals they meet. Well crafted, this letter should provide the recipient with key words and (if room) suggestions of people to look for (for example, "Do you know anyone who…").

Choosing the Right Recipients

Because I said "almost" everyone you know, there are, obviously, a few exceptions. You might not want to send the letter to

- People who know you but don't like you. Stick to people who respect and admire you.
- People who simply are not in a position to refer your business to others, such as those who are seriously ill or in prison (unless those groups are part of a key target audience for your business).
- What about people you know who are students or unemployed? These are judgment calls. Generally, students are not good referral sources unless they are in graduate studies or working as interns. Unemployed people are likely to be so stressed over their job search that they won't think to refer you to

someone—and it might even be awkward. ("Well, because I blew that interview and you won't hire me, how about using a friend of mine? He just started his business.")

 - In general, the closer a person might be to your potential clients, the more likely you should send him a letter. So, a retiree who stays in touch with the corporate office is worth the letter. But a retiree who is out on the water jet-skiing, having eschewed contact with former colleagues, should probably be skipped.

Although your list can be winnowed, don't overlook people simply because of how you know them. Yes, you know Betty because you both have kids in the "Mommy and Me" class you both attend. But Betty isn't restricted to that role even though she might be a full-time mother. She still knows people, stays in touch with them, and could be extremely helpful if she knows the details of your business.

Writing Your Letter

Your letter should include four short paragraphs:

 - A brief opening paragraph announcing that you are now in business. Specify what kind of business you are in, and whether you will be limited by geographic boundaries.

 - In the second paragraph, let them know what you hope to provide that your competitors do not. Keep this brief—no more than three sentences.

 - In the third paragraph, ask for their help in soliciting business. Ask them to let you know if they are interested in your services and to refer you to anyone who might be interested in your services. Give them one or more examples of people who might use your services.

 - Close the letter. Thank them for their attention/support. Let them know that you appreciate the warm relationship you have with them. Let them know how to reach you at your business (sometimes as simple as "I can be reached at the phone number below if you have any questions.")

 - Don't do a simple "mail merge." Personalize the letter, so the recipient knows you took the time to think of him directly. That means addressing him as you normally would (for example, as "Sam," not "Mr. Jones" if that is how you address him) and perhaps including a sentence or two unique to his letter. ("If you have questions, I'd be happy to answer them when we work out Monday morning.")

- Be sure to sign each letter in blue ink (which is friendlier, and makes sure that the reader knows you really did sign it, as opposed to having your scanner and printer do it for you).

Here's an example of an introductory letter used to announce the opening of a writing business:

January 12, 2005

Ms. Jane Smith
123 Profit Lane
Friendly, CA 94702

Dear Jane,

I just want to let you know that I have opened my own writing business. Focusing solely on nonfiction, I am offering to write articles, reports, press releases, and other business and marketing documents. As part of my business, I am also offering writing instruction so that clients have the option of learning to write better themselves.

You probably know a lot of other writers, but my business stands out in several important ways. First, I offer writing instruction as well as writing services—I'm not insistent on doing the writing myself because I know many small business owners would rather do their own work. In addition, my background includes a broad base of journalism, technical writing, and marketing. This is rare, as most writers specialize to an extreme. With my varied background and business focus, anyone you refer to me will get the professional writing services they want—not overly specialized experience they don't need. My clips and references confirm this. (See my website at www.*[your site here]*.com, where I've included testimonials from several happy clients.)

Several of my business cards are enclosed, along with a full list of the writing services I offer. If you know of someone who has a writing deadline looming, and can't quite get to it, please mention my name and offer one of my cards. I would be more than happy to meet with them and see if I can help.

Most importantly, however, I want to thank you for all of your inspiration. My conversations with you after Job Club really helped me to focus on what I want to do, and what I do well. With this business, I have both.

If you would like more information, please don't hesitate to contact me at the phone number below.

Sincerely,

[your name and business name here]

To do list

- ☐ Approach local media regarding articles and interviews.
- ☐ Set up a time and date to perform regular marketing activities. Pick out which ones you will do ahead of time, so you are prepared.
- ☐ Obtain quotes from service providers (as needed) such as printers, marketers, and mail houses.
- ☐ Research networking and speaking opportunities.

Tried and True Marketing Techniques

The following sections describe some traditional and low-cost marketing techniques available to home businesses. You probably won't want to use all of them, but almost any business can benefit from some variation of these types of marketing.

Display Advertising

This is advertising that is displayed, usually in a newspaper, magazine, phone book, and so on. (Website ads are discussed in the next section.) If you are a retail organization, display advertising needs to be part of your marketing plan. If you are not a retail business, however, display advertising might just be an expensive exercise in frustration and expense. So, before you hire a graphic artist and start calling for ad kits,

- Do your homework, and do it well. Display advertising really needs to be researched thoroughly if you are going to do it at all. Which venue? Your local newspaper or the national magazine? (There's a huge difference in price, believe me.) Can you handle the response if the ad works as projected? Will you get inappropriate calls? What is your break-even point? How many clients or how much business will you need in order to make more than the cost of the ad? Can you handle that much work?

- Understand why you want the ad. Display ads might be a prudent move for other reasons than a direct line to potential customers. If it is important that you or your company be well-established (for example, a building contractor), it might be a good idea to invest in display ads. The impression that your company can spend the money for a large display ad, repeatedly, can make a customer choose to do business with you because he knows that you didn't just arrive in the community yesterday. Also, many of these ads appear in nonprofit venues, such as theater programs and school sports calendars. So, you might be placing the advertisement more as a way to show community support. It's a great way to build what's known as "goodwill," but you might not see a direct return in dollars and cents in the near future.

- For a service business, display ads might backfire. Let's say that you need a good mechanic. Which would you rather use: Your friend's recommendation or someone from an ad? That's right; you're going to go with your friend's recommendation if at all possible. So if you're the mechanic, and you've placed a display ad, who is going to call? People who can't reach their friends in time, are new to the community, or don't like their friends' answers. In other words, clients who are more likely to be both desperate and a bit picky (or downright difficult). It's a great way to reach people new to the community (or perhaps new to having the need you're addressing, such as folks who just purchased a used car). But you will also have to screen prospective clients more closely, and the percentage of callers who just aren't a good fit will be higher. (You can mitigate this by choosing your venue carefully—perhaps a display ad in the Welcome Wagon package targets the newcomers you want, while avoiding less desirable customers.)

> **tip**
>
> For most service businesses, money on display ads is better spent in other areas. If you decide that a display ad is a good option for your business, however, do be sure and pinpoint your audience as closely as you can. Remember that, with a business line, you will probably receive a listing in the phone book free of charge. (If the phone company doesn't mention it, be sure to ask and be sure that you know how you're listed, double-checking the spelling.)

Website

If you're a service business, your website acts as a sort of virtual brochure. It will be rare that someone contacts you strictly after seeing your website with no other contact. Websites are vital, but they work best in conjunction with other forms of marketing.

Although updating your website might be considered part of your marketing work, don't fixate on your website to the exclusion of meeting real people and connecting.

Cold Calling

I've never tried this, and quite frankly, never want to. Before the "do not call" list went into effect, my responses to telemarketers ranged from professional but abrupt to downright nasty (for which I've done penance). Because most of us feel the same way, why would you want to market your business in such an annoying way? Can you imagine someone barging into your home any time they feel like it? This is what cold callers are doing—barging in, and unilaterally attempting to change the recipient's calendar and priorities. Because it's also time-consuming, draining, and rarely the image you want anyway, you will probably want to avoid it in most instances.

How do you get the attention of that ideal client who is a business? If you can't find a personal connection, send a marketing package (cover letter and brochure minimum—press clippings if you have them) to the key decision maker. Make a follow-up call one week later, asking if he received the package, and does he have any questions. But even here, be prepared for a low return—many decision makers have gatekeepers, and/or routinely discard unsolicited mail.

Avoid any "pseudo-cold-calling" strategies. In other words, don't call strangers and say that you're conducting a survey, providing information only, or any other strategy used to weasel out of saying that you're cold calling.

With the Do Not Call registry in place, calling consumers (for example, private individuals) can be a costly mistake. Businesses are not covered by this registry, however, and some exceptions for calling consumers include calls from charities and calls from political organizations.

If you'd still like to make cold calls, particularly to private households, be sure to check out the Federal Trade Commission's Do Not Call website, www.ftc.gov/donotcall/. Contact a lawyer if you are uncertain whether the specific calling you are doing is prohibited.

Press Release

This is an announcement to all relevant media outlets (radio, television, magazines, newspapers), letting them know that you have news. A lot of these are recycled, particularly if they're little more than, "Yay! I started my business." Send one out if you really have something newsworthy to announce—but be sure that it is truly newsworthy. What type of story is the media outlet expected to write or air? Why is the beginning of your business newsworthy? Unless you are doing something no one else has thought of, or you are holding a big event, it probably isn't. And, after you come up with a newsworthy press release, your work isn't done. Plan to spend time calling to follow up on each release sent to each contact. The combination of an extremely newsworthy idea and persistence will work. Anything else will fail. (See Appendix A, "References and Resources," for press release particulars.) Keep this type of marketing in mind. It isn't likely to be a good fit when you start your business, but you can certainly build your business to a point when you're ready to do this—perhaps one to three years down the road.

Marketing on a Budget

I hear you scoffing. "Radio and TV ads? What, when I win the lottery?" It sounds like the marketing plan for some large, multinational business. And here you are—small, new, feeling poor (or actually poor, or both).

> **note** Though you're unlikely to pursue radio and television advertising when your home business is young, you might want to consider it down the road. Because they usually hit a broad audience, the cost (both for the time to air as well as the production of the ad) of these ads is only slightly less overwhelming than the response. Depending on your business, this might be a good move after three to five years, but not the best source of marketing when your business is just getting started. Contact a public relations specialist with experience in broadcast media (TV and radio) to help you.

There are many ways to market your business without spending five or six figures—or even four. Because the touchstone of good marketing is getting out, meeting people, and telling them about your business, many effective marketing techniques take time, but not much of a direct outlay of cash. You will still spend money, but we're talking tens or hundreds of dollars, not thousands.

So it's now up to you to get out and meet people—or prepare to do so. Remember that list of ways to market my business I'm asked about? Here are the ones that work for me. (Most don't cost very much.) Choose one, and do it tomorrow. No clients yet? Phone still quiet? Choose another one, and do it the next day. Still no response? Keep going.

No "To Do" or "You'll Need" lists for this section because you'll find all those details included in Table 7.1. Enjoy!

Table 7.1   Options For Marketing Your Business

Activity Description	Cost and Materials	Comments
Postcards	Postage; purchase of cards from office supply store (to run on your computer) or from graphic artist/printer	Send to people who have at least heard your name. (This is a good way to follow up with the "maybe" people.) Avoid buying marketing lists—there's no connection to you, and the cards go right into the garbage. If you aren't graphically inclined, hire someone to design the card for you.
Voicemail	You've probably already included this cost in your budget.	Set a quiet time in your office, and write out what you want to say in your outgoing message. You don't have much time, but you need to include enough information to intrigue a prospective client. If you offer multiple services, be sure and mention them all—it makes cross-selling much easier.
Networking groups	See Appendix A for networking resources.	Your Chamber of Commerce. Networking groups such as Business Network International (BNI). They're everywhere, and they work. Get out there, and get to know people. Go for the long term. Don't try to attend every one-off mixer. Stick with meeting the same crowd, week after week, month after month, to ensure best results.
Former co-workers	See Chapters 1, 2, and 3.	As long as your employment contract allows you to contact them, send a letter (as in the introductory exercise in the prior section) to every contact who might help you get a contract.
Join a professional organization	Fee for joining, possibly additional time for continuing education.	If you want a good building contractor, you go to their professional organization to find one. People will do the same for your profession.
Send a pointed query	All you need is some time to write a well-crafted letter or email, and the contact information of the person you need to reach.	If you see an opportunity you'd like to have, go for it. But do your homework, and tailor your query to the decision maker for that project or company. Best chance: It's a company or project that isn't advertising for assistance. Worst chance: It's posted on every email list and job board.

Table 7.1   Continued

Activity Description	Cost and Materials	Comments
Join an email list	Find out what email lists your potential customers belong to; can you join them?	The idea here is to "hang out" with prospective customers, so they know you. Do the one-on-one marketing off the list, after someone has expressed a need for or interest in what you do.
Contact current clients	The cost is simply letterhead or email.	Tell your current clients, "I'd love to have more clients who are as wonderful to work for as you." Then ask them to refer you.
Keep your eyes and ears open while doing your work	Just being there and knowing how to respond is key.	Let's say you are visiting client A for a meeting. You break for lunch, and meet B, client A's colleague. B expresses an interest in what you do—in fact, he needs someone himself. Be ready for such an unanticipated opportunity.
Volunteer	Choose a cause you care about, and pitch in.	This is a low-key way to market. You shouldn't be handing out your business cards with every food basket or vitamin. But by volunteering, you will meet like-minded people you didn't know before, expanding your social circle and increasing the chances for a personal referral. Worried about conflict between paid and volunteer work? Do something that isn't exactly the same thing you do for a living. It keeps the volunteer/paid distinction cleaner and allows you to stretch a little. Regardless of what you do, be very specific about your duties and time commitment, so you avoid "scope creep."
Write an article	Not much needed in the way of materials; just a computer and word processing program. Then, just sit down and do it!	The easiest way to write this article is to give your readers 10 tips related to what you do. (See "The Ten Marketing Truths" Sidebar as an example.) Don't tell them everything you know, but give your readers information they didn't have before they read your article. Be sure and put your name, business name, and contact information at the bottom. Don't worry about national publications, either—start by asking your community paper or chamber newsletter whether they're interested in the article as written. Don't be put off if they decide to interview you instead—save the article for another venue and enjoy the publicity!

Table 7.1   Continued

Activity Description	Cost and Materials	Comments
Speak	Find out who meets on a regular basis, and why, in your community. Talk to them and share yourself and your business.	This is similar to the written article, but instead of writing those 10 tidbits, you'll be incorporating them into a talk. Start with local groups, and offer to talk free in exchangefor mention in their program and distribution of your marketing materials. Squeamish about public speaking? Join Toastmasters, BNI, or any other group where you can practice your public speaking skills. Limit your free speaking offer, however, to 10–30 minutes. In most instances, if they ask for an hour or more of your time, they should be paying you!

TEN MARKETING TRUTHS

1. **Be honest and remain true to your business.** Don't be coerced into writing or saying something that doesn't fit you or your business. Keep your marketing message true to who you are and what you can do. Sometimes, when money is tight or things just seem exciting, you might be tempted to agree to something out of your field. Don't do it. Stick to your plan. (To be prepared, have referrals ready for people who can perform services that mesh with yours.)

2. **If you haven't left your office, you probably aren't marketing.** There might be exceptions to this rule, but they're rare. Get out of your chair and meet some people face to face. This is the best way to connect with them, and they're more likely to respond to you in person than through email or the phone. If face-to-face isn't practical, be sure that you connect well over the phone.

3. **Getting along with others really counts.** A lot of decisions are based on whether people like you. Yes, it is sometimes just that simple. Are you nice? Do they feel they have common ground with you? In particularly competitive fields, this factor can weigh just as heavily as technical skills and experience.

4. **If you have a personal connection, your skills are enhanced by that connection.** Your technical ability might be off the charts, but if no one knows about it, no one can recommend you. The personal connection is the difference.

TEN MARKETING TRUTHS (continued)

5. **It's okay to admit that you just started your business.** They'll know that soon enough, anyway. Chances are, you have been doing what you are doing for someone else, so be sure and mention that. Your prospective client will walk away feeling good because a) they have a skilled service provider, and b) they are helping a small business owner launch their business while getting something they want or need.

6. **Money does not equal results.** You might spend hundreds of thousands of dollars, but if it isn't directed to the people you are most likely to attract as your clients, it's wasted. On the other hand, successful campaigns have been waged with forty bucks in postage and some postcards printed on a laser printer.

7. **Always carry your business cards and be ready to discuss what you do.** Marketing opportunities are not always planned. You might be at a barbecue or Christmas party, chatting with someone you don't know, and suddenly, he blurts out that he needs the services of someone such as yourself. Be prepared. You should always have your business card with you. Of course, there are times when you don't want to launch into a full-scale marketing discussion (a holiday party really isn't the best time, after all), but you can still provide him with your card and tell him you'll follow up the next business day.

8. **Periodically assess the effectiveness of your marketing methods.** After the first three to six months, you'll have plenty of marketing opportunities to analyze. Don't overlook this important step. What worked? What didn't? Do you know why a particular attempt didn't work? Could it be modified, so you could try again? Are your efforts reaching your intended audience—or are you receiving phone calls from prospects who are less than ideal? Adjust what you do based on the feedback you receive.

9. **Don't be afraid to bring up the tough subjects.** At some point, the "dog and pony show" or "getting to know you" phase has to end—or pause long enough to discuss the details. Before your prospective customer becomes an actual customer, be sure that he is willing to pay your fee, have the deposit ready, and understand that part of the project depends on his own responsiveness (for example, to review a draft and get back to you promptly). Good clients will expect these subjects; bad clients will show their true colors. Which leads to item 10.

10. **There are two decision makers in every business agreement.** Your prospective client is deciding whether to hire you. But you, too, need to make a decision. Is this someone you want as a client? Is it worthwhile to continue to pursue him through your marketing efforts? Later in the book, we'll talk about clients you don't want (and how to recognize them). For now, however, you need to simply be aware that you, too, are making a decision, whether you want this person as a client.

How Much Marketing Is Enough?

The suggestions in this chapter can make marketing sound like a never-ending process. Although it will continue for as long as you own your business, there are several circumstances indicating you might need to take a break:

- When you are tired of talking to strangers (or people, period), give yourself a break. That's enough for the day. If you still need to do some marketing activity, focus on researching prospective clients or some other activity that doesn't involve meeting the public. (Just don't make "research" the only marketing task you perform.)

- When you need all of your time to perform work for clients, go ahead and take a brief marketing pause. (By brief, I mean one to two weeks.) If you are always taking "breaks" from marketing, you might need to look at your schedule and figure out a way to make the marketing process a more natural fit. For instance, you might make Friday night a postcard-labeling-and-stamping party, with pizza afterward. When you receive responses from the postcards, schedule the meetings when you would be taking a break from working anyway—perhaps at lunch or over mid-morning or mid-afternoon coffee.

- Longer projects might require your full-time attention. That's okay—but compare your marketing cycle to the project's time frame and schedule marketing appropriately. For instance, let's say that you are working on an intensive project lasting six months. Your marketing cycle (from initial marketing activity to signed contract) generally lasts two months. This means that during month four of your large project (at the latest), you need to gear up and begin marketing again. Why? You don't want to come off a large project with nothing to do and no money coming in—you want to have other work to do as soon as the large project ends.

At some point, your marketing will downshift. When you have steady work coming in, month after month, you are probably at a point when you don't need to do special marketing "pushes," such as postcards or ads. Here's one example: Let's say that it is early April. You look at your spreadsheet and see you have work lined up for this month (April), as well as May and early June. In a week or two, work for the rest of June is pretty much lined up. At this point (and assuming your monthly total of all business is sufficient to meet your needs), you can probably avoid huge mailings (for example, mailing postcards and flyers), speaking strictly for marketing reasons, and other marketing activities that seem to take up too much of your time. At this point, you want to shift to "maintenance marketing"—one or two regular activities you do each week that will continue to generate fresh leads, yet take a minimum of time and money. (By the time you get to this stage, you will know precisely which activities those should be, based on what has worked and not worked in your business.)

Here's an example: Several years ago, I "downshifted" to a maintenance marketing schedule. While I might send out a postcard mailing every one to two years, on special occasions, I'm not sending two to four mailings a year, as I used to do when my business was new. Nor do I write as many articles or perform as many speaking engagements solely for the publicity. But every week, I attend BNI (Business Network International), and network with other small business owners for about two hours. This is now my primary marketing activity. If I see a company that would make a particularly good client, I might write the key decision maker a letter introducing myself. For the most part, however, the bulk of the marketing is being done during those two hours per week. (I also meet with BNI colleagues over lunch or coffee, and this might add another hour per week.) That's not a lot of time, really—particularly when compared with the early years of my business, when marketing was a 20–30 hour per week commitment. The loss of a client, a project falling through, or other setback might bump up my marketing to 5–10 hours per week, but only for a brief period of time.

Using Professionals to Help You Market Your Business

Although you can do many of the low-budget marketing activities on your own, it also makes sense to hire someone else to help you in many instances.

The most likely people you will want to speak to are a marketing strategist and/or a public relations specialist:

- A **marketing strategist** looks at your overall marketing plan and recommends ways to improve it. She might suggest how to improve your current marketing efforts (such as making your current web presence more effective) or suggest a venue you aren't currently using (such as appearing at a special event). She might also suggest ways to bring more focus to your marketing approach and minimize a scattered, trial-and-error strategy. When considering a marketing strategist, look for someone with broad marketing experience and a knack for maintaining focus and organization.

- A **public relations specialist** works with you to get you noticed by the media. This means suggesting story ideas involving you and your business to television, radio, and newspapers (also called "pitching" a story). When hiring a public relations specialist (or publicist), look for someone with key media ties. He might have actually worked for one or more media outlets. He can also usually help you craft a press release, and if hired, might insist on doing the writing himself (with your input) to achieve the desired result.

For both of these professions, they should be able to provide you with a set price for a one or two hour consultation. This allows you to invest a relatively small amount of money while also making sure that each is the right person to undertake more expensive projects. After the consultation, consider what was suggested and whether you'd like to extend your marketing efforts with the professional or simply act on the advice provided.

Also, both of these professions tend to specialize, so ask what industries their clients generally come from—for example, publishing, high-tech, small retail businesses, or some other specialty. Be sure that they have the industry background you desire, while providing sufficient assurances that work on your particular project is not merely a cookie-cutter repeat of what they have done for your competitors. During or after the initial consultation, each one should be able to tell you what is unique (and marketable) about your business so that the boilerplate approach is avoided or minimized.

Other marketing professionals commonly used include

- **Image Consultant/Voice Coach**. This person might help you appear more professional when you meet people or focus solely on a particular venue—for example, how you look on television or sound on radio. The idea is to get the world to notice you, and not bypass you because of the way you look or sound. Most will offer a set fee for classes, making budgeting easy to do, with the option of more one-on-one consultations if desired. Your publicist should know of someone to refer—or ask friends who appeared on television or radio who they used.

- **Marketing Coach**. This is someone who acts as a coach with a focus on helping you market your business. This person might offer many of the services provided by a marketing strategist or publicist, but generally do so with an emphasis on providing you with tools, help, and insight to do the work on your own, as opposed to doing it for you. As such, they should be both certified coaches and have a strong background in marketing. Visit the website of the International Coach Federation (www.coachfederation.org) to find a certified coach specializing in this in your local area. Other coaches specialize in helpful, marketing-related activities, such as public speaking.

Finding Professionals to Hone Written Marketing Materials

Here is a list of the most commonly used professions to help you market your business via written documents—and what to look for:

- **Graphic designer**—This is someone who takes care of how your marketing materials look. He will take the text, logo, and other information you give him, and lay it out in a way that is visually pleasing. You might believe you can do these tasks yourself, but think carefully about this decision. Layout and design is both an art and science, requiring a professional sense of what catches the eye, how much whitespace is needed, and whether the page is balanced to laying out the materials in a way that fits web or print specifications. Some designers will do web materials as well as printed matter, although most who do will limit their activity to technically simple sites (for example, with no e-commerce or linking databases).

> **tip**
>
> When choosing a graphic designer, you should ask for work examples similar to the work you have in mind, as well as a written estimate of cost and turnaround time. Ideally, this person will have a close relationship with a printer, or will have worked with many local printers, so that the two aren't pointing fingers at each other should something go wrong during the design/printing handover. If you are going to use a printer the designer has not worked with, ask what programs they will use to design your work—and be sure that the printer can use these file formats without charging you additional money.

- **Printer**—Yes, this is the person or business who prints your materials from postcards to flyers to brochures to business cards. When selecting a printer, ask for samples of her work and a written estimate of cost and turnaround time. Look for the little details that can make your life easier, too, such as free local delivery and an explanation of why it is best to print a particular document in a certain way. Don't be afraid to ask about price breaks, either. Most printers can offer substantial per-piece discounts when more of a particular item is printed. So if you're thinking about printing brochures, for example, ask for an estimate to print both 500 and 1,000 brochures. The price difference might be minimal. Some printers specialize in environmentally friendly inks and paper, but their prices might be substantially higher than traditional printers.

- **Writer**—These individuals can craft the language you use in your flyers, brochures, and other printed or web materials. They might also help you write speeches or come up with written handouts to give to audiences when you speak. As with the printer and graphic designer, the writer should be able to provide you with a written cost/time estimate and relevant examples.

Delivery of the text should be relatively easy, too—be sure that the writer has the software you need, or can easily email text to you in a useable format.

Using Pros to Craft Your Web Presence

And what about your web page? There are several basic functions you will need to cover when you have a web presence, and it is very rare to find one person who has all of these skills. However, you should be able to find

- Webmasters, who have the technical know-how to create and maintain the site you want. Some might only create the site, leaving you to go elsewhere for maintenance.
- Web designers, who are more concerned with how the site looks (from a graphic design perspective).
- Web marketers, who can help you drive traffic to your website, and get it noticed.
- Web hosts, of course, merely keep your site on display on the Internet.

Because of the many specialties needed, you might have a webmaster who consults with your marketing person and graphic designer (to keep your website focused on your message and to give it the same look and feel as your printed materials, respectively). Covering all the duties involved is more important than what a person might call himself.

Summary

Marketing isn't sleazy, yucky, expensive, or phony—unless you make it that way. (And of course, you won't.) How you market your business will largely depend on the type of business you run and your own personality. But don't be fooled into thinking that you are marketing because you've responded to Internet ads all day—getting out in front of other people is vital.

In fact, marketing isn't really a separate activity at all, but an integral part of how you operate your business. In Chapter 8, "Avoiding Expensive Mistakes," we'll talk about the "how" of running and operating your business to avoid some common problems. Most of those problems are best avoided through targeted marketing, and the "how" becomes easier if you address these issues during the marketing phase of your work.

Avoiding Expensive Mistakes

8

inancial forecasting is simply the process of projecting how much money you expect your business to bring in, when you expect those funds to arrive, and—in turn—how much money you expect to spend over a given period. In the process, you are making sure that you have enough money to run your business and meet your basic household needs.

This is important. And don't let the word "financial" confound you. The process is really very simple—and vital.

In fact, this whole chapter is dedicated to the proverbial ounce of prevention. Forecast today, keep money flowing tomorrow. Set up some ground rules today, keep clients happy tomorrow. Think about potential problems today, and—yes, that's right—avoid certain disaster tomorrow. It's a pattern that sets you up to succeed. And we'll do it in a way that is quick and painless—honest!

* Develop a business forecast (and learn why you need one)
* Plan and prepare to avoid common problems
* Learn how to manage four essential functions that will make or break your business.

You'll need list

- ☐ Business plan
- ☐ Calendar
- ☐ Spreadsheet, calculator, and/or budgeting software—whatever you will use to keep track of financial information and invoice clients

Making Financial Forecasting Work for Your Home Business

Don't let the phrase "financial forecasting" fool you. You aren't as large as Wal-Mart or IBM, so we aren't going to go to the lengths companies that size might need when they perform financial forecasting.

Look at the two words again—financial, as in having to do with money, and forecasting, as in predicting what will happen in the future (or what is most likely to happen). That is all we are doing—working through a set of assumptions and goals so that you have some idea how much money will come in and roughly when it will arrive. When you were employed, this was relatively easy. You knew what day you got paid—perhaps even the hour that your paycheck hit your bank account and was ready for withdrawal. Based on that, you paid certain bills, or withheld others. You made purchases (or not). You gave your kids permission to spend money (or not).

We'll do the same, only the income is less predictable.

No matter how meticulous you are, two annual events could easily knock you for a loop your first year or two in business—and you might never see them coming!

Warm weather and longer daylight hours in the summer make it easier to have fun. The problem is, unless your business involves selling ice cream (or swimming pool supplies), you might see a large drop in business. With many people on vacation and away from the office, proposals move more slowly, invoices are approved a little later, and your next project's start date is stalled until after Labor Day (when the kids are back in school and everyone returns).

Time flies quickly again in the fall, and, before you know it, it is Thanksgiving Day. Every one of your clients is busy spending time with loved ones and celebrating one or more holidays to pay too much attention to work. And when they don't pay attention to work, your clients don't sign contracts, don't sign checks, and don't approve invoices—specifically, *your* contracts, *your* checks, and *your* invoices.

Your particular business might not follow this precise schedule. But every business has slow periods and peak periods during the course of the year. By recognizing and planning for slower times of the year, you will be ready for them. Instead of frittering away extra cash during your busier times, you will have a clear picture of the amount of money you need to save to sail through the entire year smoothly. Forecasting will also allow you to see a slow period coming—at any time, whether predictable or not—and do something about it while you still can. By regularly adjusting and reviewing your forecasts, you'll be able to see a slow period arise months ahead of time—when you can still do something about it, rather than having it surprise you at the last minute.

In addition to knowing how much money will be coming in, you need to know how much you can spend. Do you have your eye on a new color printer? You might want to plan to buy it a month or two after your "peak" month when all those invoices are paid and you have some extra cash in your pocket. Or, perhaps you want to put off that purchase even further because you need to save up for an impending slow period. Then there are taxes—remember those? They're due four times a year in equal installments. Even if you aren't making a lot of money, you'll need to be sure you can make estimated payments that cover your Social Security (15.3% of anything you make over $400). That can add up quickly—$3,000 on just $20,000 of profit.

Forecasting also provides you with the information to make business decisions. In addition to helping you plan when to purchase items for your business, you'll be able to tell whether it's a good idea to take a discounted project. (You learn more about setting pricing policies and avoiding problems with clients in this area in the "Pricing" section later in this chapter.) If your slow period is December, and you have nothing forecasted for the month, why not take a lower paying project? (But be sure and read the sidebar, "Don't Devalue Your Business" before you offer that discount.)

To do list

- [ ] Set up your financial forecasting for the next calendar year
- [ ] Schedule regular financial forecasting
- [ ] Adjust business plan and future budget as necessary

DON'T DEVALUE YOUR BUSINESS

Though taking discount work occasionally might be a good business decision, you need to do so carefully and only with real forethought. You don't want to risk devaluing your business or the services you perform, and you don't want a reputation as a 'bargain' business.

Think back to your employment days. The first day you were without a job, did you take whatever job was offered—even if you were a highly paid technical consultant and the fast food restaurant had a "Help Wanted" sign in the window? Of course not. Yet self-employment brings out a bit of panic in all of us. That's understandable. Income that came in on regular, predictable, installments will now come in wildly unpredictable, irregular amounts. Forecasting helps alleviate some of that up and down swing, but in our hearts, we know that we have to get out there and get some work from clients, or we won't eat.

And that motivation is usually a good thing. You need to value your clients—to treat them well and with respect. But you also need to value yourself and the services you provide. *Devaluing either one* means business failure.

So when is a discount justified? If the discount offered is

* To tide you over a specific slow period (such as the summer or the holiday season), and not done as a way to generate more business in general.

* Offered to clients for a limited time only. Be clear that the offer expires on December 27, for example, and that the work must be **started** (for example, contract signed or deposit made) by that date. The clients need to understand that this is a temporary condition—a slow season—and not a reflection of your regular business.

Generally, you will want to move away from this time-related discount as your business grows. Even by limiting the time and scope of the discount, there is still some danger that other clients will hear of the discount, and—rightly or wrongly—try to get the same rate.

Alternatively, a discount is justified if a client will use a significant amount of your services. How is "significant" defined? If you can forego some of your marketing activities because of the contract, you can share some of the cost savings with the client. For instance, let's say that SuperClient A provides you with a contract for $50,000 worth of business over the course of three months. You realize that you will probably save around $5,000 in marketing costs—you'll have to market more toward the end of the project, but you'll be cutting back on your marketing quite a bit for the first two and a half months. You might also be able to cut overhead, such as sending fewer invoices, because you are dealing predominantly with one client. You can choose to give your client the entire $5,000 as a discount (meaning a 10% discount), or give him part of the savings (say, only $2,500, which is a 5% discount).

DON'T DEVALUE YOUR BUSINESS (continued)

You might want to increase this amount further if some of the work overlaps. Let's say that your standard charge for a logo is $1,000. But a client orders both a logo and letterhead, and built in to your letterhead design price is the cost of designing the logo. So naturally, you might want to discount the cost of the logo from the client's total invoice.

In either case, however, you have to be sure that the client sticks with his original order. Some clients might ask for the discount up front, only to cancel or scale back an order after you've already given them a break due to volume. Your best bet is to offer a *rebate*—that is, a discount back to the client *only after all of the work is done, invoiced, and paid*.

Last, offering a discount is a good customer service gesture if you have made a mistake. Discounting an invoice or offering free work is a good way to maintain goodwill with a client when you have made an error. (See what else you should do for an angry client in Chapter 12.)

Learn more about the problems associated with giving clients a discount rate in the section "Pricing" later in this chapter.

Creating a Simple Forecasting System

Forecasting can be as simple or complex as you need it to be. This is a basic forecasting system you can adjust to fit your business and your own preferences.

We'll cover forecasting income first and then expenses. Not only will it be easier than you think, but you've already done the first part of the work. (Remember that business budget created back in Chapter 4, "Creating Your Business Plan, Part 2: The Money Pages"? That was really a forecast.)

You'll need list

- ❑ Business Plan
- ❑ Spreadsheet and other records used to record and track your business budget
- ❑ Calculator, spreadsheet, or other method of calculation

Forecasting Income

Somewhere—in your spreadsheet, within your customer database, or in your budgeting program—you should keep a record of past, present, and future invoices: Past invoices provide you with a good historical record; present invoices, of course, tell you who owes you money; and future invoices are your major forecasting tool.

On a spreadsheet, your forecast might look something like Table 8.1. In this example, you see a financial forecast for a freelance graphic artist named John. In his spreadsheet, John has numbered each invoice (in the column headed "Number") and dated it (see the column headed "Date") and marked it in bold after it was sent. The "Customer/Description" column lists the specific client and which project or time frame the invoice covers. The "MC" in the second to last column means Marketing Code. John's shorthand indicates how he obtained the client: "A" for article; "BNI" for BNI, his networking group; "P" for postcard marketing mailing; "Q" for a direct query (meaning that John approached the client directly); "R" for referral from an existing client (not BNI); and "V" for clients obtained via his volunteer work with the school's literacy program. The "Amount" column lists the total amount of the invoice.

Finally, John puts a "?" in front of future invoices for which a contract still hasn't been signed. This indicates that there's some uncertainty as to the client's commitment, so the money shouldn't be counted on 100%.

Set up your spreadsheet similar to John's. If you tend to think of the total in the "Amount" column as money that is guaranteed to come in, avoid entering any amount for entries with a question mark (?)—in other words, the $15,000 John has listed for 6/25/05 would not appear.

As business comes in, is verified, or falls through, John's spreadsheet changes. As the spreadsheet changes, so, too, does the long-term outlook for John's business—with the most immediate invoices having the best chance of turning into actual closed business.

Table 8.1   Forecasting for John, Graphic Artist, May 30, 2005

Number	Date	Customer/Description	MC	Amount
1005	05/01/05	Smith Company; flyer	R	$ 500.00
1006	05/05/05	Jones Co.; website graphics	P	$ 1,000.00
1007	05/15/05	Building A Better Tomorrow; fundraising brochure	BNI	$ 5,000.00
1008	05/25/05	Gottit & Howe; annual report	Q	$10,000.00

Table 8.1   Continued

Number	Date	Customer/Description	MC	Amount
1009	05/30/05	Anna Martin; graphic design lessons, May 2005	A	$ 125.00
	05/31/05	Parkhurst School System; graphic design classes	V	$ 250.00
		Total May 2005:		**$16,875.00**
	06/01/05	Smith Company; website	R	$ 1,000.00
	06/07/05	Jones Co.; flyer	P	$ 200.00
	06/15/05	Building A Better Tomorrow; fundraising website	BNI	$ 5,000.00
	06/25/05	? Gottit & Howe; brochure and website	Q	$15,000.00
	06/29/05	Anna Martin; graphic design lessons, June 2005	A	$ 125.00
	06/30/05	Parkhurst School System; graphic design classes	V	$ 125.00
		Total June 2005:		**$21,450.00**
	07/31/05	? Anna Martin; graphic design classes	A	$ 75.00
	08/31/05	? Anna Martin: graphic design classes	A	$ 125.00
	09/30/05	? Anna Martin: graphic design classes	A	$ 125.00

Even though John just started his business a short time ago, we can already tell a few things about his business. First of all, let's hope that he's saving some money from May and June because July is looking like a very lean month!

A closer look reveals some of the reasons for fluctuation. It appears that John is wrapping up a lot of big, corporate projects in May and June. He anticipates keeping his steady private client, Anna Martin, through the summer, although she is going on vacation for part of July. Anna also goes back and forth about how long she'll continue the lessons, so John has question marks in front of those invoices after June 2005. Likewise, Parkhurst schools haven't said whether they will ask John to return, so after school lets out in June, he isn't sure whether he'll receive additional business.

note Even without the title, you can tell it is May 30 or early on May 31 because John has not invoiced the client for 5/31/05 yet.

KEEPING TRACK OF POTENTIAL CONTRACTS AND CLIENTS

So why would John include the Gottit & Howe amounts at all? As a reminder—he still has a potential client outstanding. (We can tell it's outstanding because of the "?" in front of it.) For those with a question mark, John needs to follow up with the client periodically and see whether a decision has been made (or if the client needs more information from him). This should be marked on his calendar.

Note, too, that John has several other possible contracts in the works. But he's reasonably confident about Gottit & Howe—he's at least 80% certain that the contract will come through. The firm loves him, and he's done a lot of other work for it before. The firm is a regular client.

His other prospects aren't on the spreadsheet yet. That's because they're newer, and John isn't as certain that they will actually turn in to work.

Where are these prospects John isn't certain of? On a white board, or in a tickler file on his desk. Be sure that you, too, have set up a system to keep track of potential clients. Don't let them fall through the cracks!

Even the month of June isn't as lush as it might seem—well, not that we can say for certain yet. Gottit & Howe has not yet signed the contract for the brochure and website work, so John knows that his June invoices might be more than $20,000 or as little as $5,000.

The financial forecast you saw in Table 8.1 allows John to make some decisions:

- **Financial decisions**—John has been approached by his local art college to do some heavily discounted work. He's agreed, provided that the project lasts *only* during the month of July, and has limited his involvement to 20 hours per week. (More on how John should handle this situation is coming later in this chapter.) This will keep some money coming in, reducing the feeling of panic and keeping John in touch with potential clients. This also prevents him from appearing too desperate or pushy to Gottit & Howe. After all, even if they don't sign this contract, there might be others—and he wants to keep them as a client for the long term.

- **Marketing decisions**—John sees that BNI and referrals from customers are paying off very well. He has made his money back (and then some) from the postcards, and the article has brought in more individual business. Over the next several months, John is going to rework his article and place it in publications where more businesses will see it. He's also going to make sure that he maintains his involvement in BNI, so the referrals keep coming in. In addition, he's going to write his current satisfied customers a letter asking for referrals. Their referrals have panned out nicely, but he'd like to have some more. He's going to hold off sending more postcards until he comes into contact with more people who would be good candidates for the mailing list.

As John continues with his business, he will have more information available to him—as you will. For instance, you will be

- **Mapping and recognizing business cycles**—If John has been in business not one year, but two or three, and every July there is a big "dip," he'll know to prepare for it. He might decide to write a graphic arts book with a deadline for late July. He might save enough money to take off the entire month and enjoy the time with his family. It's up to him—but he has the knowledge that July has been ridiculously slow in the past, and therefore he can make good decisions based on the additional information.

- **Financial planning for the entire year**—What about December? John's spreadsheet actually covers an entire calendar year with 2006 on a separate page. He isn't as worried about December (at least not yet), but come September, he's going to be looking at October, November, and December very closely.

- **Avoiding overbooking**—This forecasting will also help John from becoming overcommitted. If someone calls with a large project due in July (or later), John can easily take on the work. If it's due in June, however, he knows that he'll have to pass or hire some temporary help. (More on that dilemma in Tool 5, "Keeping Up When You Have Too Much Work.")

- **Planning for financial necessities**—Above all, this forecasting will help John avoid financial disaster. If he doesn't have enough work and doesn't have enough in savings, he's going to have to make other arrangements to pay his bills. (More on that situation in Tool 4, "Surviving Lean Times: No Work, No Money.") By looking ahead and assessing his situation, he has time to think through his options and take needed action. (Of course, he'll also have to look at his expense projections, which we cover later in this chapter.)

- **Planning discretionary spending**—John also has time to change his spending, his business plan, and other important parts of his business. He might forego some additional purchases, for example, until he knows that business will pick up in the fall.

Forecasting Expenses

Remember the business budget you created while reading Chapter 4? That was a pretty good forecast of your expenses.

So continuing to forecast those expenses will be fairly simple. Starting with the budget you created, you will add expenses as you incur them, begin reviewing actual versus projected expenses, and adjust your future spending or your future budget accordingly. Let's take these steps one at a time:

1. **Add expenses as you incur them.** In Chapter 4, you stepped through the process of creating a budget spreadsheet that included columns used to track expenses. You need to use this spreadsheet religiously. Several times a week (at a minimum) you will need to input your expenses. You might want to combine this task with your income forecast review and bill-paying tasks so that you handle all of your financial matters at one time. Also, the more frequently you have small expenses with no receipt (for example, for bridge tolls), the more frequently you should enter expenses, if possible. Little expenses—those that cost less than $8, such as bridge tolls and public transit fares—can be forgotten too readily—and they can add up!!

You should have a receipt for every expense. Travel and entertainment expenses should be easily tied to your business via your business calendar. In other words, anyone looking at your calendar should be able to match the meeting/travel dates and times with reasonable expenses on your spreadsheet.

2. **Review actual versus projected expenses.** One month after you start your business, compare what you have actually spent the first month with what you budgeted for your first month. (For the first month only, include startup expenses.) Are you on track? Are you spending more than you planned?

3. **Adjust your future spending or income as needed.** Being over your budget means you either a) underestimated the true cost of one or more parts of your business operation, or b) you are spending more than you really should.

What do you do if you underestimated an expense? Let's say that Chamber of Commerce dues were $250 when you did your initial research, but by the time you joined, the chamber increased its dues to $300. Where is that $50 going to come from? You will either have to cut $50 in expenses from some other category, earn at least $50 in additional income, or take $50 from your savings. Savings is the least desirable of the three options because you are taking away from your financial cushion—and sooner or later, if you keep repeating this, you will have no financial cushion left!

If you tried to budget accurately, however, your overall budget should be on target. You might be a bit low here and a bit high there, but the total should be very close to your target.

As with income, reviewing your expenses and scrutinizing them closely is important. Unlike income, however, you need to watch expenses very closely from the day you decide to start your home business—because you will probably begin spending money sooner than you earn it.

Scheduling Regular Reviews and Making Changes

As you set up your business, during your first year, review your forecast spreadsheets at least once a week. When business becomes more substantial—that is, when you have enough work to keep you busy at least 2–3 hours per day—make a habit of reviewing your forecast spreadsheet at least 2–3 times per week.

Schedule time for your forecast review on your calendar! Give yourself at least 30 minutes initially. As you become more comfortable with the process, and with your own business, the time is likely to decrease to fewer than 15 minutes.

Why so frequently? Things change. In our society, they change rapidly. When your home business is fully operational, you will need to capture the changes as they occur, so frequent spot checks are important. For instance, in one week, you might have three new clients come on board, two clients expand or decrease the amount of work they order from you (and hence, increase or decrease your income), one project that is shifted to another month, and one client who incurred additional charges that weren't originally anticipated. Can you imagine how often your income would fluctuate?

Then, in the same week, a dues increase might arrive in the mail, as could the bill you forgot about when you drafted your budget—as well as the rebate on another bill, reducing that amount. Suddenly, your expenses have shifted, too. Or, during a meeting with a potential client, he suggests lunch (and you anticipated coffee), or dinner (and you anticipated lunch). No one thing is likely to cause you to panic, but a series of events can cause a significant change in your planned expenses in a very short time.

By keeping your spreadsheet updated, and also briefly reviewing your long-term business income picture, you will have an accurate understanding of how much work and how much money is coming in today, tomorrow, next week, and next month.

> **tip**
>
> As you update and review your projected income and expenses, make sure that there is enough money in your bank account to meet expenses for the next several weeks. (You might even pay bills at the same time.) Because invoices are listed in front of you, this is also a good time to contact any clients whose payments are overdue.

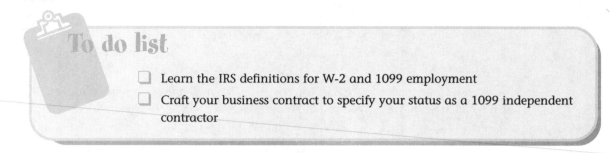

To do list

- ☐ Learn the IRS definitions for W-2 and 1099 employment
- ☐ Craft your business contract to specify your status as a 1099 independent contractor

Avoiding Risky Business

You take a lot of risks as a home business owner. Generally, having a client hire you isn't considered one of them. But two common mistakes in taking on clients can result in reduced payment, the potential for being involved in legal action, and even business failure. Avoid making these mistakes:

- Misunderstanding the difference between working as an independent contractor and an employee. Gratefully, the IRS provides us with a lot of information to help eliminate such confusion.
- Agreeing to work for bad-risk clients who are unlikely to pay. Avoiding this mistake requires using your discretion and qualifying clients.

In the sections that follow, we'll go over the general rules for both situations, so you don't end up doing risky business.

You'll need list

- ☐ Computer with Internet access or contact information for nearest IRS office
- ☐ A copy of your business contract form

Avoiding the 1099/W-2 Tax Trap

If, as most home business owners, you are a sole proprietor, refuse any work that is not on a 1099/independent contractor basis. Not only will this keep the IRS happy, but your business' long-term success will also benefit.

If you are a sole proprietor, the IRS is very concerned with whether you are an independent contractor. A W-2 contractor (technically) doesn't exist, although this term is used to describe someone who is a W-2 (that is, a regular employee) of a temp agency, contracted out to a client site. An independent contractor (or, 1099 contractor), is someone who is an independent, one-person business.

Understanding 1099 Versus W-2 Employment Status

You might be looking at the preceding paragraph and thinking, "Boy, that's quite a fine line." In fact, there are huge differences between the two statuses. As a W-2 employee, your agency is your employer, even if you work at the client's site. Most agencies offer very little in the way of benefits, so you will have to figure medical, vacation, down time between assignments, and other factors in to your hourly rate. You will probably work exclusively (or almost exclusively) at your client's site. Some clients treat their contractors just like employees and try to include them in company picnics and other activities. Although you can deduct job-hunting expenses if you itemize your federal income tax, you won't be able to deduct the cost of commuting to the client site, and it is questionable whether you can justify any home office deductions. You might be hired for a specific set of skills, but will probably be invited to staff meetings, and you might wind up with duties you weren't planning on, such as reordering office supplies. (The client is free to treat your presence as "staff augmentation"; in other words, the client temporarily needs more people and sees you as having similar responsibilities as an employee.)

As a "1099 contractor," you are self-employed. According to the IRS determination, among other things, an independent contractor buys her own supplies, has her own office, has more than one client, and is not provided with specific work hours by her client. As an independent contractor, you will probably do your own marketing or enter in to a relationship with an ad agency or public relations firm to do your marketing for you. You will pay for all of your medical insurance, retirement, and other benefits (but these are often deductible). You will pay all of your own taxes, including Social Security tax. Depending on the nature of your business, you might have an hourly rate, a project rate, or per diem rate. Also depending on your line of business, you might need to register your business with your city or state and obtain licensing.

Protecting Your Independent Contractor Status

Your status as an independent contractor is important because if you are someone's employee and not an independent contractor, the employing organization can be held responsible for your taxes, employee benefits, and related items. Nevertheless, you will run into potential clients who want you to be an independent contractor, but will want to also treat you as an employee. They do not want to pay your taxes, benefits, or anything other than a project fee, yet they will try to insist that you come to their office and perform work for them onsite during specific work hours.

IRS TAX TOPIC 762–INDEPENDENT CONTRACTOR VERSUS EMPLOYEE

The IRS sees these two ways of contracting as vastly different, and has guidelines to determine whether you are an employee (W-2) or independent contractor (1099). These guidelines can be found at the IRS website, as Tax Topic 762, which I've reproduced here:

> To determine whether a worker is an independent contractor or an employee under common law, you must examine the relationship between the worker and the business. All evidence of control and independence in this relationship should be considered. The facts that provide this evidence fall in to three categories—Behavioral Control, Financial Control, and the Type of Relationship itself.
>
> **Behavioral Control** covers facts that show whether the business has a right to direct and control how the work is done through instructions, training, or other means.
>
> **Financial Control** covers facts that show whether the business has a right to control the financial and business aspects of the worker's job. This includes
>
> * The extent to which the worker has unreimbursed business expenses
> * The extent of the worker's investment in the facilities used in performing services
> * The extent to which the worker makes his or her services available to the relevant market
> * How the business pays the worker
> * The extent to which the worker can realize a profit or incur a loss
>
> **Type of Relationship** includes
>
> * Written contracts describing the relationship the parties intended to create
> * The extent to which the worker is available to perform services for other, similar businesses
> * Whether the business provides the worker with employee–type benefits, such as insurance, a pension plan, vacation pay, or sick pay
> * The permanency of the relationship
> * The extent to which services performed by the worker are a key aspect of the regular business of the company

For more information, refer to Publication 15-A (PDF), Employer's Supplemental Tax Guide. If you want the IRS to determine whether a specific individual is an independent contractor or an employee, file Form SS-8 (PDF), Determination of Worker Status for Purposes of Federal Employment Taxes and Income Tax Withholding.

—From the IRS Website, http://www.irs.gov/taxtopics/tc762.html

Does this mean that you should never go to a client's location? Of course not. What it means, however, is that you need to understand when it *is* problematic. Attending a meeting at a client's location, regarding a project or potential project, in and of itself, is not a problem. A client asking you to attend a staff meeting, or asking you to arrive at 8 a.m. and leave at 5 p.m., every day, signals a potential problem.

Note, too, that Tax Topic 762 (see sidebar) considers the whole picture, looking at whether you are expected to have set hours to whether you have a desk and chair at the client's site, and even whether your contract is time limited or open-ended.

Working as a W-2 employee also has numerous disadvantages for you as a home business owner. After all, how much marketing can you reasonably do if you are sitting in another company's cubicle from 8 a.m. to 5 p.m., Monday through Friday? You need to have more than one client, and it's tough to do that if you are sitting in another client's workplace, using its phone and email.

To make the situation even worse, such an arrangement tends to be a slippery slope. After all, if you are in a cubicle during regular hours and show up every day, most of your colleagues will assume that you are an employee and treat you accordingly. This means that they will include you in office parties, ask you to order office supplies for the company, attend staff meetings, and do all the other things you thought you had left behind. So instead of being a business owner, you are now an employee again—but this time without benefits.

So how do you avoid the W-2 trap? Follow these guidelines:

1. Review the IRS guidelines mentioned previously, and be familiar with them. If you still have questions, read the additional recommended material or consult your accountant or attorney.

2. Whenever a client or prospect edges you toward specific no-nos, such as requesting that you spend more than a few days of set work hours at their place of employment, educate them about the IRS constraints. Make it clear, too, that you cannot provide the same services as an employee. You have other clients to think about, and your office is based at your home, not at their address.

3. Be sure that your contract has clear language indicating that you are an independent contractor and won't be expected to remain on site for set hours or perform other tasks that would make you an employee.

4. In addition, your contract should be very clear as to the scope of your duties, and, most likely, these duties are tied to a very specific project (and set amount of time). If the prospective client tries to add language that sounds vague, such as a job description, explain why that isn't acceptable.

Amazingly, many prospective clients will not know about this distinction. By educating them in a positive tone, you help them avoid unnecessary problems and keep the door open for actual work in the future.

Avoiding Bad-Risk Clients

As a small business owner, clients who don't pay can make a significant dent in your profits—not to mention your ability to pay the bills on time. Although doing business involves some risk, there are several warning signs that most bad clients will exhibit long before you begin working for them. Consider carefully whether you want to accept work from a client if

- **The client asks you for money to be considered for projects.** You should never have to pay a client to obtain work.

- **The client balks at basic concepts in your standard contract.** Every contract is negotiable, and it is usual for a client to request changes to a contract. However, if the client complains about a number of basic tenets of the contract that protect you (such as when you receive a deposit, your standard rate, or the scope of the agreement), the client might be signaling that she expects something for nothing.

- **The client offers a standard or corporate contract that is nonnegotiable.** Every contract should be negotiable. A bad contract from a large company is still a bad contract—so if the client will not negotiate, and the contract is problematic, consider walking away.

- **The client indicates that the project is not a sure thing, but expects you to begin working.** Why work on a project when you have no contract, no deposit, and no guarantee that the client even wants the work?

- **The prospective client is not the decision maker for the company (if the company is smaller) or for the department (if the company is larger).** You should be meeting with the person who has the authority to sign a contract, a check, or both. You might have to meet with someone else for the first meeting, but the second meeting onward should include whoever makes the final decision.

- **A prospective client calls you (out of the blue) and asks for a rush job.** This is fine, provided that the client is willing to pay a deposit for most or all of the job. After all, you don't know her, and you're being asked to possibly reschedule other clients (and maybe your personal life as well) just for her.

- **A prospective client acts in a way that is unacceptable to you—and the behavior appears to be a pattern.** Having a client hire you is a bit like a marriage. Whatever you saw that you didn't like about her is not going to change; it's just going to bug you more. Was the prospective client rude? Did she arrive late? Did she insult you (repeatedly and deliberately)? Did she waste your time, asking you to wait, perhaps, while chatting on her cell phone with a friend? Don't count on rude clients to become less rude over time. You will either have to accept that this behavior is part of working with the client—for instance, submitting a bid that takes in to account hours wasted while he chats away with his friend—or walk away from the project altogether. (See the following sidebar, "What if the Client Is Difficult—But I Need the Money?")

> **tip**
>
> There's a difference between convincing a client you're the right contractor for the job and tolerating a client's hostile attitude that doesn't go away. Such a client might say something like, "My brother is a [writer/graphic artist/whatever you are] and could do this for less," or "I was going to go find a student in [whatever profession you are in]," or "I could probably do this myself. Why should I hire you?" There are plenty of people who really need you to do what you do. If this prospect has someone else who he thinks is better, cheaper, or faster, then you shouldn't be wasting your time discussing a contract. You will certainly have to do some convincing during a meeting with a prospective client, but if the hostile attitude continues, don't push it. You don't want this person as a client.

- **The prospective client is reluctant to provide a deposit.** As a service provider, you have very little tangible items to withhold if she doesn't pay. If you're a printer, you can hang on to her print job. If you're a grocer, of course, people should pay before they leave the store. But if you're a writer, lawyer, accountant, consultant, coach, engineer, or other profession that provides a service and invoices in arrears, the initial deposit is your safety net. By being reluctant to provide you with one, the prospect is saying that either she doesn't know you well enough yet or she doesn't really plan to pay. You can provide her with reassurances if it's the former. If it's the latter, nothing you say will make a difference.

- **Other service providers have worked on the project and have left.** Self-employed individuals usually do not leave mid-project unless there is a very good reason.(After all, why walk away from the work and the money?) Be sure that you know why a prior service provider is no longer available. Even if the prior service provider is at fault, the project could be problematic—accept the job with contingencies that allow you to charge extra to chase down or re-create missing files, straighten out problematic records, or fix other mistakes.

WHAT IF THE CLIENT IS DIFFICULT– BUT I NEED THE MONEY?

There it is in front of you—the contract that you hoped would feed your ego, your bank account, and your reputation.

But you've started the contract, and now you're having second thoughts. Your main contact on this project is rude—taking personal calls while you wait, arriving late for every meeting, and making others wait (and wait and wait) while he finally delivers the data you need to do what you've been hired to do. Or maybe you knew it would be like this from the start—but you need the money or the credibility, and you simply cannot walk away from the offer.

How do you handle *that*?

1. Relax. Be grateful that you are working with this person only on a particular project, and you're not a co-worker, supervisor, or underling. It's one project, not a lifetime. There will be an end to your interaction.

2. Be sure that you build up positive relations with other contacts, if possible. So one person on a project is a pain—what about other contacts with the same company or organization? Chances are, everyone knows this one person is a problem child. If you get along well with everyone else, people will know that you aren't the problem. (In fact, most of his co-workers are probably well aware he's a problem child—and that might be why you were hired in the first place—no one else wanted to deal with him.)

3. When you know the behavior pattern, do your best to work with it. (That's part of what you're being paid to do.) For example, if he's habitually late to meetings, tell him an earlier time, or plan to have the meeting take longer (while you wait for his arrival).

4. If your contract allows for additional hourly charges for the wasted time, consider billing them. Should the client ask, however, you need to be ready with specific dates, times, and other details.

5. Understanding his motivation helps. Is he surly with everyone? Or was he upset that the contract was awarded to you (and not his friend)? If he's surly with everyone, his churlish comments are his way of saying "hello." If you think he's going to carry a grudge, realize that you can only do your best—and don't let the sour grapes bug you.

6. If the behavior is truly nasty, do something positive to offset it. Hopefully, you'll never be in a position in which you must suffer rude comments or boorish behavior. But it might happen. If so, be sure and give yourself plenty of time to unwind. Putting some distance between you—working via email or phone, perhaps—might also make it easier to take.

7. You might still want to do business with this client—but next time, take the behavior in to account. This means adjusting your estimates, or stipulating certain additional charges or ground rules, in the beginning, anticipating the difficult behavior you encountered last time.

8. A successful home business is the best revenge. When you reach a point at which you can get rid of some clients—these go first. (See Tool 5, "Keeping Up When You Have Too Much Work," for more information.)

Some clients might turn out to be very good to you and your business, even if they exhibit one or two characteristics on the preceding list. If you are unsure, get to know them better and gather more information before you make a decision. You might ask for complete payment up front on your first project with them, rather than just a deposit, so you minimize the risk to your bottom line.

Here are some other ways to protect yourself from taking on bad-risk clients:

- Check the client's reputation within your professional organization. Ask people within your industry, whom you trust, whether they have worked for the company. Word spreads very quickly about clients that do not pay or make unreasonable demands.

- Check the client's record (if any) on Dun & Bradstreet (www.dnb.com), with the Better Business Bureau, and in the general media and Internet—in other words, Google 'em. If a company is having financial difficulty, it might not be a good client—and you should know about its precarious situation before you take on a project with it.

- Many smaller clients won't show up in many of these databases, so the amount of independent information you can obtain about them is limited. Ask around. Who has done business with this company among your most trusted business contacts?

- As you meet with a prospective client, listen for clues. Did she mention that her credit cards are maxed, or that bill collectors are calling? Does she seem to have a lot of experiences with service providers who "ripped her off"? (Most everyone gets cheated at some point, but someone with story after story about poor service and bad service providers might be the cause of their own problems. Don't hesitate to ask questions about what went wrong.) Listen to her carefully. After your meeting, review her comments. Did anything she said or did (or didn't say or do) strike you as being odd?

Four Areas That Will Make or Break Your Success

If you have a significant disagreement with a client, walk away from a client, or have a client fire you, one of these areas will probably be the cause:

- **Pricing**—You and your client will disagree over whether additional charges were incurred or whether certain hours were required to finish the project.

- **Scope**—You and your client will disagree over whether the set price you quoted covered a specific part of the work or whether it should result in an additional charge.

- **Payment**—Not just the amount of what you are to be paid, but how soon you are to be paid, and why.

- **Communication**—A disagreement over what was said, not said, or should have been said will ensue, with exclamations from either you or your client, such as, "Why didn't you **tell** me? I could have fixed that!" or "I wished I'd known that at the time!" or "Why wasn't I notified?" or "That really would have made a difference—if I'd known!"

Avoiding problem clients is the best way to enhance your reputation. Establishing sound policies in these four areas will go a long way toward eliminating problem clients. That leaves you time for good clients, who you can serve with pride.

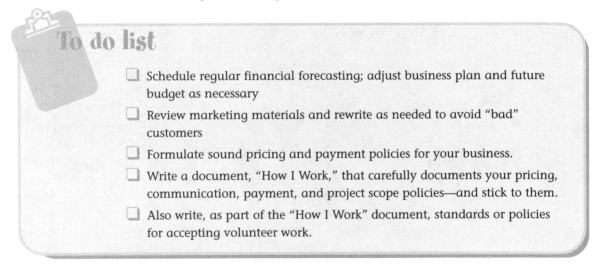

To do list

- ☐ Schedule regular financial forecasting; adjust business plan and future budget as necessary
- ☐ Review marketing materials and rewrite as needed to avoid "bad" customers
- ☐ Formulate sound pricing and payment policies for your business.
- ☐ Write a document, "How I Work," that carefully documents your pricing, communication, payment, and project scope policies—and stick to them.
- ☐ Also write, as part of the "How I Work" document, standards or policies for accepting volunteer work.

Maintaining a Pricing Structure

Did you research your rate thoroughly? Good. After you have set your rates, stick to them for everyone, discounting your rate only under conditions that benefit you and your business (see sidebar earlier in this chapter). By sticking to your rate under most conditions, you avoid numerous problems. The following subsections discuss various situations in which you might consider adjusting your rates, and some advice and examples to help illustrate the caution with which you should approach this decision.

Maintaining the No-Discount Rule

Client A comes to you with a possible project. You're eager to do the work and provide your hourly rate (or standard quote). Client A gasps. She's a small business owner, like yourself, she reminds you plaintively, as she explains why your rate is so out of her budgetary reach. And you know that she's a nice person. Isn't there any way you can reduce your rate for this project, she asks sweetly? You know the rent is due soon, and your invoices are looking a little weak. This might be a good project to take at a cut rate, you think.

Don't do it.

You are discounting your work for reasons that have nothing to do with you and your business priorities—you haven't made a mistake, you're not in the middle of a slow season, and there's no volume purchase or other associated benefit of taking a discount project. Client A now knows she doesn't have to pay your going rate —not now, and maybe not ever.

But the real problem lies in the other half of the agreement. You discounted your rate, but client A will still expect full service from you. This gets easily manipulated so that any apparent infraction, any whim not catered to, will make it seem as if you aren't holding up your end of the bargain. You said you'd cut your price, not your service, you are reminded (explicitly or implicitly).

The best response here is to hold your ground. Hold to your standard quote or hourly rate. If the person asking represents a charity, give your work away free if you are comfortable doing so. But avoid the messy middle ground of "discounted" work. (See the sidebar earlier in this chapter that talks about the rare exceptions when discounting your work is okay.)

Volunteering Your Services

How you price your services directly affects the perceived value of those very services. Volunteering is great, but offering those same services in a volunteer setting can lead to a weird devaluing of your services. You are less likely to run in to this if the work given is provided to an audience you would never have as a client in their current status. For instance, providing free writing sessions to homeless families would not cause a problem. Providing free writing sessions to the local chamber might. Also, problems are less likely to occur if the work is limited in scope. One free writing class at a local fair can be a great marketing tool. Free writing classes to every member who joins a particular group, on an ongoing basis, will cause your work to be devalued to the entire membership.

Part of this equation is the culture of the organization requesting your help, too. Although you are doing the work free (or in exchange for good karma, community kudos, or whatever), you should look closely at the organization just as if it were a paying customer and judge it against the standards discussed in this chapter.

TWO VOLUNTEER EXPERIENCES

A number of years ago, I volunteered for two separate organizations—each of which I was a member of at the time I volunteered. The experiences I had with these organizations illustrate the range of experiences you might have when volunteering the services of your home business.

Organization 1 asked me to gather stories for a newsletter. I was given a list of contacts, called or emailed people as needed, and drafted the copy. People responded in time, unless they were on vacation or other circumstances prevented them. I then gave the copy to the volunteer editor. (This was definitely a low-budget organization.) The newsletter was photocopied and mailed (or emailed) to members. Fees to join the organization were nominal. I volunteered for organization 1 for several years.

Organization 2 also asked me to gather stories for a newsletter. But the request was last minute. I accepted anyway. (Perhaps that was my first mistake!) As I dove into creating copy for the first issue, I was told that I also needed to do the layout and purchase software specifically for this purpose. This was told to me in a meeting with another volunteer, who took call after call on her cell phone, all of them personal, all of them social, and all of them highly optional. (The meeting ended when, in the middle of the third "chatfest," I stood up and walked away.) Oh, and I had to figure out who to bug for stories and contact them. (And they were always late, if they responded at all.) The organization felt whoever did this should really serve on the board, too, and contacted me hours before the board meeting for that month, wondering if I could attend. (I said no, not at the last minute.) As time went on, it became readily apparent that the (rather high) dues were paying for many services comparable to my writing and editing, including the work of printing and mailing the newsletter. Yet my time was expected to be voluntary. The printer (who was being paid) quit days before an issue was to be taken to him for printing. It fell to me to find another printer and negotiate the placement of an ad in exchange for the printing. I quit after that issue was out.

Even though an organization is nonprofit or recruits a lot of volunteers, problems can arise just as they would in a situation with a paying client. So choose your commitments wisely. Nonprofit organizations don't have the resources that businesses usually do, so things won't be perfect, but they will still set a pattern of treatment for their volunteers that has little to do with their budget.

Working for Publicity

You also will occasionally find yourself considering whether to give your work away in return for publicity or exposure. Most of the time, this isn't worth it. Proceed with caution.

For the most part, if you would work as you normally do, yet receive nothing but publicity or exposure in the end, it probably isn't worth it. (As you might have noticed from the previous chapter, getting exposure or publicity isn't that expensive!) Similar to asking for a discount on your standard rate, this person or organization probably doesn't value what you do. Providing advice or making an appearance free of charge is perfectly acceptable in many circumstances. Doing the actual work free of charge, in exchange for publicity, rarely is.

> **caution**
>
> Run, don't walk, away if someone approaches you implying that she is a regular prospective client, yet at the last minute mentions that the pay is exposure or publicity only. (She not only doesn't value your work, but she's been deceptive as well.)

Speaking in front of a group and talking about what you do (or some related topic) is the most promising example of giving your work away for publicity or exposure. The key questions to ask yourself are, "Are the people I'm talking to truly likely to become my clients or to refer a lot of clients? And, are they in the appropriate venue to receive the information?" If the answer to both questions is anything but "yes," decline the offer. In other words, if you are asked to speak about your accounting practice (or an accounting topic) at a Rotary meeting, it's probably a good opportunity. If, however, the Rotary wants you to provide free advice at the annual fun fair, the venue isn't appropriate to what you're offering. (On the other hand, if you offer massage services, the fun fair might be a better venue than the meeting.) And, as with volunteering your work, the more you can limit the scope or time frame, the better the opportunity.

Bartering Your Services

At some point, you also might consider whether to do a "trade." Bartering for goods or services you need or want is fine. The key part of that sentence is "for goods or services *you need or want.*" Unless you are truly in the market for what is being offered, decline. Otherwise, you're throwing away your money before it's ever earned.

Forget about losing business or making the other person unhappy. If she offered you a strange credit card—one you'd never seen before—you would decline it, wouldn't you? You aren't saying what she does doesn't have value. You're just saying that you cannot readily use the currency she's offering.

If you do go through with a trade, however, it is very important to clarify the terms of the trade. Say that you charge $75 per hour, but your bartering client only charges $45 per hour. Is the exchange based on an even number of hours or an even dollar amount? In most instances, the dollar amount is the better way to go—

both of you have already established these standards, which have been applied to (and supported by) your clients.

You'll also want to talk to your accountant or tax preparer regarding the appropriate records to keep in such a situation. Work you do should be invoiced just as you would for a customer paying money directly. Work you receive should be recorded as payment. And of course, the entire agreement should be put in writing, no matter how well you know the person.

Building Value into Your Pricing Structure

I highly recommend that you build value in to your pricing structure. What do I mean by building value? It means that your pricing structure reflects the fact that your services are valuable. So, in addition to an hourly rate or standard rate, you also set charges for missed appointments or no-shows, travel charges for anything beyond a specified mileage or area, and a surcharge for rush jobs. As a service provider, your time is your biggest asset, yet it's easily wasted or abused. Setting up prices that reflect the value of your time tells prospective clients they should value that time, too.

Maintaining Scope

Scope is the granddaddy of client disputes. For our purposes, "scope" is the set of parameters limiting a project or service. No matter what service you offer, you can't do everything for everybody, and providing the scope of a service or project helps your client understand your limits. For example, a carpet cleaner provides a quote to clean your carpets. He stipulates a four-hour arrival window, and also states that furniture over 50 pounds will not be moved. He will do area rugs, but for an extra fee. All work will be done in one visit, with no return visits included in the price. He is providing the scope of the services he provides.

Most people in technical fields, or who have worked for large corporations, are familiar with the term "scope creep." This is what happens when a project starts out well-defined, but other items are added to it, bit by bit, expanding the work to be done. The result is a goal that is always missed because the definition of the goal is always expanding.

As a home business owner, you really want to avoid this at all costs. Here's how:

- **Get the scope of the project in writing.** If you are working informally, this might just be an email to the client spelling out your terms. If the project is larger, include the scope of how you work in the contract. Either way, make it clear that any work outside these parameters is going to cost the client at your standard hourly rate, or won't be performed.

A MINIMUM PRICING POLICY

If you provide a service, no matter who your client is, there are certain minimum activities you will have to do. You will probably have at least one meeting that is not billable time, where you market your services. You will have to take time to create a contract (or write an email or work order confirming the service), send an invoice or bill, and track payment. You will have to respond to emails and voicemails. You will have to explain the process and answer questions. At some point, doing all these things isn't worth it. You need to figure out what that price point is for you, and address it in your pricing structure. So you either

- **Set a minimum price.** Let's say that any work requested below $100 simply isn't worth it. And yes, a client who orders $100 of work can ask just as many questions—and often more—than a client ordering $1,000 or $10,000 worth of work. In fact, clients on the lower end of your pricing structure are more likely to be hiring someone in your profession for the first time and therefore more likely to need additional hand-holding. Err on the side of setting your minimum price a little high. You can always make an exception or lower it if you come across a knowledgeable client who will take up less of your time than the average person.

- **Define a very specific, strict scope for certain low-end projects, no matter who the client is.** The client, in return, gets a service she needs at a reasonable price. Let's say, as a graphic artist, that business cards are a key moneymaker for your business, but they fall well below your minimum price of $100. So you "retailize" this service by stipulating that clients can have their first run of business cards for $75, but *only if* they a) have no logo or artwork on the card, b) have all information emailed to you, and the information is correct as sent, with no changes, and c) agree that cards can be printed on a specific type of card stock (only)—they don't get to choose. The printer has limited the customer's choices, but has served a definite need. These small pieces of income might keep the printer going through dry spells, and some of the initial "retail" customers might turn into full-service customers who order other, more expensive work. The key for "retailizing" your services is a very, very strong set of parameters, which are stated up front—and always, always, prepayment in full.

- **Spell out the obvious.** Take the time to make sure that you and your client have some common ground rules. For instance, with my writing clients, it is crucial that any drafts be reviewed and responded to in a timely manner. So, in the contract, clients are expected to respond to requests for comments within a set time frame, depending on the length and size of the project. Now to most of us, it seems obvious that if the client wants a project done by her stated deadline, she needs to respond to a draft in a timely fashion. But telling the client up front that either a) additional charges might be incurred or b) the deadline might not be met if no response is received makes it crystal clear—and doesn't allow the client to make any other assumptions. It is worthwhile to sit down and ask yourself, "How do I expect a client to act?" Then be sure those parameters are considered and included when you enter into a contract or confirm business by email. You don't want the wording to sound belittling or condescending—just a businesslike representation of how things will work.

- **Be polite, but assertive, with your client.** If someone doesn't show, there's no need to be rude. Just merely mention that you missed her today (or yesterday) at the scheduled appointment/meeting, and mention the no-show charge. Keep your approach matter-of-fact. The client made a choice to incur additional charges (as per your contract), and you are merely confirming that the charge has been incurred. Don't avoid the subject, but don't be nasty, either. And be sure that you communicate in writing.

- **Be detailed.** If you offer services for a flat fee, your scope must be very detailed and must always include when the process ends. Even if an apparent end of the project is obvious (for example, a tax preparer, whose work will clearly end when the tax return is submitted), you need to clarify what services the client receives for the flat fee. Otherwise, clients will continue to use your services ad infinitum. In the case of the tax preparer, the flat fee might cover the draft of the return, and once approved, double checking the return for mistakes in calculations or the application of the tax code. If the client suddenly unearths a pile of receipts after the draft is presented, however, the return will be redone at the preparer's hourly rate. This tells the client that, although you are sensitive to her budget (because you're offering a flat rate), you won't allow the process (or your time) to be abused. It shows that you value both your client and yourself.

> **tip** Even your quotes or estimates should set forth the scope of the project. Be sure that you include them as "assumptions" on which your pricing is based. And, be sure that the quote or estimate itself has an expiration date (say, 30 days). You will raise prices and get busier or slower, and your assumptions about a project will change. So your quote should have an end date.

Making Sure That You Get Paid for Your Work

You probably enjoy what you do, and you enjoy working from home, setting your own schedule, and being a part of your own community.

But let's face it. You also have to get paid. And not getting paid is a big deal. Here's how to make sure that happens:

- **Screen your clients.** Everything in this chapter applies. You want to work for nice, ethical people you enjoy being around.

- **State up front (in the contract or confirmation of service) how much you will be paid and when.** Ask for a deposit. Tie the remainder of what you are owed to either stages of the project or service provided by the end of the month—whichever is shorter. Avoid doing work for more than 30 days without sending an invoice or receiving payment. The longer you wait to invoice, the more likely a client will take your work for granted.

- **Set limits, in your contract and restated on your invoice, for the time frame for payments.** Again, keep this tight, and ask for payment within 15–30 days from the date of the invoice.

If there is no payment after the set time frame, particularly if this is the first time you have worked with the client, you need to contact the client to determine when the payment will arrive.

Start out as politely as possible, but also make it clear that you expect payment. If there's no payment forthcoming, you'll get less friendly later on, but for now, assume that the client merely made a clerical error or became overwhelmed by other commitments and simply forgot. For clients who have done business with you before, inquire as soon as their pattern changes. For example, a client might consistently pay you in six weeks (instead of the usual four), but she does so month after month. You know that, and come to expect it, so don't bug her after four weeks if everything else is fine and the relationship works. But if, after six weeks, no payment is received, contact her and use these guidelines:

- **Don't accept silence.** Follow up with another email or phone call, a little less friendly, if there is no response to your payment inquiry within two weeks. Give her another two weeks to respond.

- **A final letter (not email or fax), sent certified and receipt requested, is the last notice if there is no payment and/or no response.** The last notice isn't very friendly and lets the client know what you will do if you don't hear from them or receive payment within a set time frame. (Two weeks is recommended.) Your options might include: Reporting to the BBB or professional organizations, turning the matter over to a collection agency, or suing them in small claims court. If you don't hear anything from a nonpaying client, and you said that you might take additional action, do whatever you said you were going to do. Don't make empty threats.

tip

After the first contact, if there is no response (or promises but no check), be sure that you mention that you will consider a payment plan. A client might feel embarrassed by her current financial situation, and offering her a payment plan option shows that you, too, can be flexible, and understand these things happen.

If you must send that final "pay or else" letter, don't worry about making the recipient angry. She isn't paying you! Your concerns are paying clients, not scoundrels who don't meet their commitments. Don't worry about threats or promises of additional work, either, that come only at this stage. She hasn't paid you—and that isn't the kind of work you're seeking! Don't be surprised if such a "client" raises quite a ruckus—but don't be swayed by it.

Above all, don't continue working for a client who is more than 30 days in arrears (unless the client is well established and their payment schedule is too). You might not be paid, and continuing to do work would be risking more money than you already have. (Make that clear in your communications, too.) Good paying clients who want your service are out there. You need to be focusing on them.

After the relationship is terminated (or the confusion is cleared up, or the client has paid), ask yourself what you might have done differently to prevent or limit the extent of the situation. Take that answer, and rework your pricing, marketing, and contracts accordingly.

Maintaining Good Communication

A good pricing structure and a solid contract are meaningless unless the client knows about them. A lack of communication can foil a business that is well-run in every other respect. As a business owner, communicating with your clients is one of the most important things you do. Stellar work might be perceived negatively if the client has questions or concerns, and you aren't addressing them.

Following a few simple communication guidelines will keep your business on the right track:

- **Communicate any special circumstances.** Let's say that a client calls up and asks you to perform work. You're thrilled. But you are heading off for a vacation toward the end of the anticipated project deadline. Accept the work on the condition the client can provide you with what you need to perform the work and complete it early. If you're squeamish about discussing the fact that you'll be away, you can be a bit more vague: "I have another commitment starting …", or "I won't be able to work on it the week of …" are perfectly acceptable alternatives.

- **Ask the client how she wants to proceed.** And listen carefully. You will hear a lot of her assumptions about how you work and how soon she needs what she needs. In other words, you're getting her to state the obvious (which is obvious to her, but not necessarily to you). Always ask if the client has any questions, and invite her to contact you if she thinks of questions.

- **After you've negotiated contracts with clients, communicate, verbally and nonverbally, in a way that shows you want them to be your clients for a long time.** Keep your clients happy. Provide updates. Err on the side of too many updates rather than too few (until the client tells you to send fewer of them). Go the extra mile. Give the client the benefit of the doubt. Arrive at meetings on time. Return phone calls punctually. It's cheaper to treat good clients well than it is to always be on the lookout for new ones.

> **tip**
>
> If your work is due on a specific date, be sure that you are clear what time on the given day. One of the worst nightmares for any service provider is to think they have until 5 p.m on the day of the deadline—and the customer thinks she will have what she wants by the start of business at 8 a.m. If your work is being used in part of a larger project, get a sense of the deadlines your client is working under.

- **If you make a mistake, say so.** And don't lie about it. (In fact, don't lie about anything.)

Above all, make time to communicate. Don't overlook time to send emails, return phone calls, and otherwise keep in touch with clients. Try to return voicemail and emails alike within 24 hours during the business week, or the next business day on holidays and weekends.

> **caution** *Watch Out*
>
> If you are in a particularly foul mood, and it can wait, don't speak with clients or prospective clients. Try to communicate when you are alert and in a fairly positive mood.

Creating a "How I Work" Document to Set Policies for Good Practices

You might have noticed that each of these four areas—pricing, communication, scope, and payment—are best handled by regularly using standard procedures, regardless of who the client is or what the circumstances are.

But you have a lot on your mind as a home business owner, so you might not remember each of these standards when you meet with a client. In fact, you might be so excited at the prospect of having the client hire you that you forget about them altogether! But that is practically guaranteeing disaster.

What you need to do is start another document. I refer to this document as "How I Work," but it is much more than that. This document

1. Is your ready reference for doing things correctly. As you think about how you will handle pricing, communication, payment, and scope issues in your own business, write out the ground rules in this document.

2. Is not your business plan. Your business plan gives the overall picture of what you are doing and how you manage finances, with your business budget fleshing out the financial picture. This document, initially, is more personal in that it needs to remind you of everything you should be doing—terms and conditions you should include in a contract (and mention to a client beforehand), major hours of operation, your policy on late payments or early payments, and so on.

3. Will serve as a series of checklists for your business. What do you tell a client about pricing and payment? And when do you tell him?

4. Should you decide to expand your business, this document serves as your policy manual.

5. Is a living document—it changes as your business changes. However, particularly after your first year in business, you should not be changing the policies after each client interaction. Be sure that changes are made because you have realized a policy or process improvement, **not** because you are trying to bend your business in to something it isn't.

6. Is a way of setting boundaries. By having minimum price limits, work hours, and a discount policy written out, you are more likely to consistently adhere to these policies and, therefore, balance your life more easily. And, on those occasions when making an exception makes excellent economic and business sense, you might have some added leverage for charging additional fees because you are making an exception (which of course, is communicated, professionally, to your client). Even if you forego the additional charges, stated correctly, you will generate additional goodwill from your client, who is now aware that you are bending the rules *just for him, in his special circumstances.*

Be careful about making exceptions, however. By having a standard set of rules, making exceptions might also be seen as discrimination, or other unethical or illegal activity. Review the ethics guidelines within your profession to be sure when and if exceptions are allowed. You might also want to record exceptions made, with the business and economic reasons, so that any questions as to the propriety of such an exception can be readily explained.

So how do you start writing this document? Your initial table of contents should look something like this:

Chapter 1: Work Hours

Days

Times

Chapter 2: Pricing

Standard Rates (subsections for each service offered or each rate)

Minimum Pricing

Discount Policy

Chapter 3: Free Work

Criteria for free work (that is, what must exist for the free work to be worthwhile?)

Criteria for free speaking engagements (publicizing your business)

Criteria for free articles (publicizing your business)

Chapter 4: Payment

Deposits (when and if required, how much—amount or percentage, how often required—first time customers only, or everyone every time?)

Payment Terms

Late Payment (What do you do if someone doesn't pay? Do you send a letter or call? When? What is next?)

Chapter 5: Communication

Questions to ask potential clients

(Flyer or brochure to provide potential clients—so they know what to expect)

Questions to ask clients at the beginning of a project

(Flyer or brochure to give to clients at the beginning of a project—so they know what to expect)

List of guarantees to provide to clients (if any)

Your business' own communication strategy—how often do you update clients and in what way

Chapter 6: Scope

Defining Deadlines

Defining services you provide

Services you do not provide—particularly services that clients might confuse with your business (if you do printing, do you also do graphic design? Can you mail it for me?)

Services you provide indirectly (for example, subcontract)

Chapter 7: Your Work Process

This is a general work flow description. If you offer several types of services, include a work process for each service (for example, separate work flow descriptions for, say, writing and tutoring). What happens from the moment a client signs a contract until he pays you?

Chapter 8: Required and Important Training

What training must you attend (for example, to maintain licensing)? What makes a conference or training worthwhile (beyond any apparent marketing value)? What topics would be most helpful?

Don't gasp as you see this outline. Chapter 1 is most important. As you have read this chapter, you should have a pretty good idea of Chapters 2, 3, and 4. Chapters 5, 6, 7, and 8 may wait until the early days of your business operation.

You might also change, add, or delete certain areas, depending on your specific type of business.

The important thing to realize is that the outline isn't as daunting as it might seem. You already have much of this information in your head, and it has probably popped up while you were in the shower, driving the kids to school, or at other odd times. But you need to get this out of your head and on to paper, so you remember to communicate your policies to clients, and implement them evenly.

Summary

Any business can fall prey to expensive mistakes if the business owner doesn't plan to avoid them.

You can begin this planning process by having a fully fleshed out forecast in mind, so you know how much money you hope to make and whether you can take on additional work, how much work you can take on, and whether other commitments might conflict with it.

As you learned in this chapter, you next need to ensure that you avoid taking on business that can cause you financial, legal, and administrative headaches down the road. Here, you learned to carefully define and protect your status as an independent contractor and to avoid taking on clients who might want to treat you as W-2 workers, or who might be rude, difficult to manage, and reluctant to pay for your services.

Good clients should be cherished, valued, even downright spoiled. But don't let bad clients spoil your business. By making clear your services, your pricing, and your expectations, you are telling the world how clients will treat you, as well as how you treat them.

How you treat a client determines whether your business succeeds. After the prospective client contacts you (or you contact him), your professional behavior tells the client that you are professional. Regular communications about the project are provided to the client after a clear contract (with a set scope) is signed. Pricing is straightforward, clear, and easily understandable.

Not only do these practices make good business sense, but also a balanced approach to managing clients helps you balance your own life. In the next chapter, we'll talk about maintaining a balance between your work and home life and managing the resources most likely to get out of balance—money, time, and health.

Conserving Your Resources: Time, Money, and Health

A t this point in the book, you might have realized that much of running your home business is a balancing act, as illustrated in Figure 9.1. As a self-employed, home-based entrepreneur, life will be an ongoing series of balancing acts. You have plenty of free time (if you want it), but you don't want to just goof off, or the bills won't get paid. On the other hand, you don't want to work all the time either. You will enjoy the flexible schedule self-employment brings, but you don't want a schedule so flexible that you never get any work done. You want to be safety conscious and aware of your surroundings, but not paranoid and suspicious. You will be subjected to a constant learning process, long-term, but the work still needs to get done today. You want to invest in your business, but you don't want to bankrupt yourself with too many business expenses, either. This section of the book is dedicated to keeping your business (and you) in balance, so your endeavors are as successful as possible.

9

In this chapter:

* Learn important tips for setting and maintaining a work schedule, prioritizing tasks, and avoiding common time traps

* Learn important guidelines for getting—and staying—healthy, so your business can be healthy, too

* Adopt some basic practices for staying within the business budget you created in your business plan

FIGURE 9.1

The balancing act of home business owners.

Free Time	Don't Miss An Opportunity
Flexible Schedule	Meet Commitments
Open To Everyone	Need To Be Protective
Need to Connect	Need To Get Work Done
Take Time To Learn	Work Has To Get Out
Look At Big Picture	Study Details

To do list

❑ Establish optimum hours for your business

❑ Prioritize tasks and estimate how long they'll take to perform

❑ Review time usage and eliminate waste

Managing Your Time

Of all the resources you have to manage, time can seem the most difficult. Nothing is due today, but something is due tomorrow. Do you work ahead? Visit a prospective client? Is there time to drop by your child's school or pick up the birthday gift? Then again, you'd give anything for a nice, hot bath, and the house is quiet, so no one is going to be pounding at the door every five seconds. Your head is spinning. You have four hours this afternoon, just four hours, and the seconds are slipping away as you debate their best use…it was so simple before, wasn't it? You were Jane, worker bee from 8 a.m. to 5 p.m. (or whenever you left the office), and then you came home and were Mom and Honey; then you left for aerobics and were Jane the dieter.

You'll need list

❑ Business plan

❑ Calendar

❑ Business journal

Perhaps the best way to manage this new time frame is to look to the past. About 150 years ago, most of the United States lived in a household with a major home business—the family farm. No bosses. No set hours. No one worried whether it was "okay" to bring the kids to work—they were already there. The key was to do what needed to get done, with "what needed to get done" varying from getting in the harvest to fixing a scrape on a child's knee to meal preparation to sitting on the porch and visiting with a neighbor. No one's lives were compartmentalized, and no one suffered solely because they chose what tasks to do when.

In other words, setting your own schedule—as home-based business owners do— is normal, natural, and, until the late nineteenth century, the standard. Unfortunately, in the last 100-plus years, we have gone so far away from that way of life that setting our own schedules in this manner feels weird to many of us.

Don't worry. You know how to do it. When you get the hang of it, you'll actually enjoy it much more than the compartmentalized life you led before.

Knowing what to do when comes down to two key tasks:

1. Setting priorities (that is, what is most important at this moment)
2. Knowing how long a given task might take

In the sections that follow, you learn about these tasks. First, however, you learn about setting the schedule for your working day. The following sections also discuss how to manage your schedule and ways to avoid time conflicts, so you get the most from your working day.

Setting Your Working Hours and Hours of Availability

Set general work hours and general hours of availability. Although you will mix business, personal, and pleasure when it makes sense, there should be general hours when, for the most part, you are working. You will also need to set general hours of availability. Remember these guidelines:

- **Your work hours are the hours you actually work.** These will be longer than your hours of availability and might be Monday through Friday, 6 a.m. to 6 p.m., with Saturday mornings thrown in as needed.

- **Your hours of availability are when your clients know you are working and they can generally reach you.** These hours, for many of us, are 8 a.m. to 5 p.m., Monday through Friday.

Why two sets of hours? You need time to bill clients, return calls, check email, forecast future income, check your PO box, and perform other duties without interruption. You might also need some time to work on client projects undisturbed. The additional hours also act as "overflow" time to help balance your schedule and keep you from being overwhelmed with work.

tip As you become comfortable with setting priorities and managing your time, these hours can become more flexible to suit your particular business and lifestyle. But you will always need some "quiet time" to work uninterrupted, and you need to be sure that you do not schedule every available hour on behalf of a client.

Prioritizing Tasks

Let's start with setting priorities. If you are in a business with deadlines, those deadlines pretty much tell you whether something is a priority. If your project is due tomorrow, it isn't as much of a priority as something that is due today.

The other side, however, is knowing how long a given task is going to take. Let's say your project due tomorrow actually needed to be started last week to give you sufficient time to complete it. If you know that, and start it when you should, the day before you might be able to fit in something fun (such as that long, hot bath), or work ahead, or work on some marketing.

Most of the tasks for your business will fall into one of the following categories:

- **Deadlines.** You have to get client work done by a certain time. You have to file taxes by a certain time.

- **Important, but no deadline.** A prospective client wants to meet with you. There is no deadline, but if you constantly put him off, you risk losing any business.

- **Timely, but no deadline.** You meant to send out postcards today, but didn't get to it. You can do it tomorrow, even two months from now if you like. But the longer you put it off, the more your business might suffer.

- **Lowest priority, but will make your life easier.** Is it okay to bring your accountant that pile of receipts, or should you do some filing? Probably the latter. Getting labels on client files and filing the current work will make projects easier to find.

- **Emergencies.** No set schedule. They just happen, and everything else will take a back seat. If you have a firm grasp on the first four priorities, these are the exception, not the rule.

Estimating Time

Although setting the priorities is relatively easy, trying to figure out how much time something will take is more difficult. Not only are you inexperienced in gauging your time in this way, but you are also on a steep "efficiency curve."

What is an "efficiency curve"? That is the learning curve you experience in starting and running your business, as you become increasingly efficient in performing many tasks. The first time you do your financial forecasting, it will take much longer than the second time you do it. And one year from now, you will be much more efficient at forecasting than you were when you started.

This efficiency curve affects almost every task you do in your business, including the very service you offer. You might find, for example, that when you initially started your business as a consultant, you could write a 10-page report for a client in 10 hours. One year later, that might only take you 8 hours, and three years after you start your business, you might have it down to 7 hours. Or, it still takes 10 hours, but the report you submit after three years is much, much better, and garners higher praise.

So right now, most tasks will seem to take forever, and you might even be wondering whether you can really run a business profitably while working fewer than 18 hours a day because *everything takes so much time.*

Relax. Focus on what you are doing, and perform the task as well as you can. As time goes by, you will automatically become faster.

Managing Your Schedule

Between the newness of your business and the efficiency curve, setting a realistic and workable schedule is tricky. What starts out as a busy but manageable week on Monday afternoon can become an unforeseen time crunch by Wednesday morning. So keep these tips in mind as you create your home business and deal with time issues:

- **Get and keep a calendar.** Whether paper or electronic, this calendar should be the very first thing you look at every morning. (See the discussion in Chapter 6, "Getting Technology You Really Need (and Only What You Need)," regarding PDAs and electronic calendars, too.) Look at today's schedule first—but don't overlook tomorrow, next week, and later in the month. What is due today? What is coming up tomorrow? What do you need to start today to finish satisfactorily?

- **For the first year of your business, schedule everything.** If you mentally think, "Oh, Friday afternoon will be a good time to get caught up on the filing," schedule that for Friday afternoon. You're free to change it later, should a higher priority arise, of course. But in the meantime, you've given yourself a concrete picture of what you plan to do each day. If it will take more than five minutes, schedule it, no matter how mundane.

- **Don't overlook common activities that will need time, including planning for a meeting, traveling (even locally), errands, and paying bills.** These take more than five minutes most of the time, so you should schedule them accordingly.

By being this meticulous, you give yourself power over your schedule. Let's get back to Friday afternoon. Your good friend calls and wants to know if you can meet her for drinks at 4 p.m. Your child says her soccer game starts at 2 p.m. Now, if you leave the house at 1:30 p.m. to head to that soccer game, and then meet a friend for drinks—there goes your filing time. Unless you have an avalanche of filing, you would probably be okay. But by documenting every activity, you are in full control of making that decision rather than sitting on the bar stool with a second margarita in your hand and realizing you really meant to be doing something else because it was a higher priority. It gives you the opportunity to make a conscious decision about what to do with your time and when.

> **tip**
> Don't be afraid to mix personal, business, and pleasure activities within your schedule. If, after you see a client, the store that carries your husband's favorite birthday gift is nearby, take advantage of it. While shopping with your family, if a good prospective client is the store across the street, drop in (assuming, of course, that the kids aren't out of control and you aren't wearing your oldest sweats). There are plenty of demands on your time as it is—you don't need to keep abiding by the old rules of compartmentalization.

Avoiding Common Time Problems

As this new way of scheduling your life (and thinking about time) becomes comfortable, there are several common problems you might need to address:

- **No set wake-up time.** When you first launch your business, continue waking at the time you woke up for your prior job, and start work no later than the time you normally left the house for work. As you become more comfortable with scheduling your time, you can adjust this as necessary. But avoid the trap of sleeping the morning away (unless you work well into the night). Even if you are a "night owl," and want to radically change your schedule to fit your body clock, be sure that you have a set time to be awake—and stick to it.

- **Inappropriate interruptions.** Even though you are fully in command of your new schedule, you will probably need to work at least eight hours a day, five days a week. Whatever regular hours you need to work, however, you can be sure that someone will find out you are home and consider it an invitation to call or drop in for a social visit (unannounced, of course). Don't let this behavior happen, and if it is already happening, put a stop to it. How? See the "Business Owner at Work" sidebar.

BUSINESS OWNER AT WORK

How to put a stop to those inappropriate interruptions? Here are a few suggestions:

* Don't answer the door unless it is a delivery or a client you are expecting. (If this is a relative with a key, by all means, change the locks!)

* Don't answer your home phone when you're working.

* If someone calls on your work line with a social call, time the call and make sure that it lasts no more than five minutes. Before the time is up, interrupt (if you must) and tell her you're working and have to end the call. Give a quick and friendly "good-bye," and hang up.

* Use caller ID to your advantage. If it isn't a business call, let it go to voicemail.

* **Doing nonbusiness work during business hours.** This occurs when you do more housework than business work, when your kitchen is spotless but your marketing is nonexistent. Dusting the living room while a 100-page opus prints in your office might not be such a bad thing. Dusting the living room when you should be in your office working toward a deadline is a problem. If you tend to focus on domestic responsibilities and ignore your business, you will need to be less flexible with yourself and not do any home-related activities during your normal work hours.

  When you find yourself doing tasks during business hours, ask yourself, "Am I doing what is most important?" If the answer is no, change direction. Don't be afraid to close the door to your home office so that you can't see the rest of the house.

* **Doing business work during nonbusiness hours.** This occurs when you are working during "off" hours, or working too many hours with no urgent goal in mind. There are times, such as when you are working toward a large project or first become unusually busy, that work will be more of a priority. But if you are always missing family outings (and they weren't last minute suggestions on a Tuesday afternoon), or spend an inordinate amount of time over the weekend on work, you need to reassess priorities. Ask yourself, "Must this work be done right at this moment? If Monday comes, and the work isn't done, what will happen?"

As a business owner, there will be plenty of times when working during nonworking hours is fully justified. Don't add to it by thinking that you must *always* be working.

Likewise, let your schedule work for you instead of against you. Don't schedule every waking hour you have. Prospective clients will contact you all the time—evenings, weekends, early mornings, whenever. When your hours of availability are over, turn off the phone's ringer and allow calls to be picked up by voicemail. Take at least one weekend day when you do not check email.

tip

Don't forget to involve your family. If you attended a soccer game during the work week, went to the doctor, did the grocery shopping on Tuesday because it's easier, and met one of your spouse's relatives, you've put in some considerable personal time during your normal work hours. Be sure your family is aware that, when you later spend most of Saturday in your office, you aren't short-changing them—but merely making sure that your business gets the deserved attention. Likewise, your significant other and children need to understand that you can arrange your schedule as you see fit—but they must tell you about things in advance, so you can get the activity on to your schedule.

The Gradual Transition to a Flexible Schedule

If it sounds as if we've been bouncing back and forth between setting and eliminating boundaries, you're right.

You need time and practice to get used to an open schedule. Set standards, practice being a little bit flexible, see how you do, and make any needed adjustments. This process will be repeated over and over again as you build your business.

How flexible your schedule is also depends on your personality. Some people simply cannot handle even a small amount of variation—if they're allowed to run one personal errand, the entire day will be shot. The more you need to stick to a set schedule and the more likely you are to be distracted, the less flexible you should be.

To do list

- ☐ Plan and maintain a healthy diet
- ☐ Follow good health-maintenance routines
- ☐ Schedule time for regular exercise

WASTING TIME

There are plenty of ways we waste time. We play a game of solitaire while a project is printing out instead of making a phone call or completing some small activity. Walking back from the post office, we see something in a store window and become distracted. This sounds like no big deal, but let little time wasters add up, and the next thing you know, you have no time for your business or your personal life. Stay on top of it, and learn to recognize when you're wasting time.

After you have been in business two to three months, keep a log for a week of how you spend your time. What do you do that could be eliminated?

Sometimes, time wasters come to us in unexpected packages. Be on the look-out for the prospective client who is all (time wasting) talk and no action, the home business neighbor who keeps dropping in uninvited, or the unnecessary trip to the grocery store.

Maintaining Your Health

As the central figure of this home business, maintaining an excellent diet is the best way to ensure you are ready for whatever challenges you face.

But let's be absolutely clear: Maintaining your health isn't just a nice idea. From a pure business perspective, scheduling regular office visits to the doctor, dentist, and eye doctor is just as important as maintaining your computers and printers. Even if you feel healthy, neglecting regular checkups is a bad idea. (Refer to Chapters 3, "Creating Your Business Plan, Part 1: What, Where, When, and How," and 4, "Creating Your Business Plan, Part 2: The Money Pages," if you need tips on health and disability insurance.) You need down time for checkups and maintenance, too, just like your copier or web server.

In fact, ignoring your health is ignoring a key component of your business. Remember back in Chapters 1, "Exposing Myths of Self-Employment," and 2, "Assessing Your Home-Business Readiness," when we talked about it all being up to you? Well, if you aren't up to handling the business, it will go downhill very fast. Although your business can handle some sick time here and there (as we'll discuss in the next chapter), a longer illness could be devastating.

You'll need list

- ❑ Your daily calendar
- ❑ Access to home gym or workout equipment

The Home Business Diet

Most of the dieting talked about in this book is financial; however, now that you are working from home, the close proximity of your refrigerator (and the lack of other people watching how much you eat) might cause you to put on weight. Working from home will probably involve decreased activity—and an ever growing emphasis on being in your chair, in your home office, and getting work done will significantly increase the chances of your waistline expanding. Even if you had a desk job before, weight gain is quite likely unless you watch your diet carefully and get plenty of exercise. (Remember all the calories you burned off while commuting—not to mention walking back and forth among your colleagues' cubicles and your own? You might not realize how many calories can be burned off while "paper-pushing" in a downtown office until you begin working from home!)

As much as possible, step out for some fresh air. Walk to see clients and run local errands, if you can. Keep exercise equipment handy, too. As a home-based entrepreneur who is just starting out, your hours might find you wanting to work off some adrenaline—but at four o'clock in the morning, you might not feel like going to the gym.

Schedule your regular workouts just as you would schedule a client's appointment. Not only are you more likely to stick to your exercise regimen, but this also helps you schedule time accurately.

For the first year, I'd also recommend keeping candy, cookies, chips, and any other easily eaten junk food out of the house. The temptation (particularly while under stress) to nibble throughout the day will be greater than you realize.

Illness and Stress

Amazingly, even though we know we are humans, we tend not to plan for either one of these events.

See Tool 1, "When Your Business Is Well—But You Aren't," for information on how to keep your business running smoothly, even during an illness that incapacitates you. Shorter illnesses—such as when you wake up feeling lousy and know a day in bed would knock it out of your system—are a bit easier to manage. If your schedule allows, take it easy on such days. But, what if your schedule doesn't allow it? Perhaps meetings can be converted to phone conferences. (It doesn't take as much energy to talk on the phone as it does to get dressed up and try to look "well" when you're not.) Think of other ways to take care of yourself and give yourself an "easy day."

When seeking to reduce stress, the proverbial ounce of prevention is important. Follow these guidelines:

tip

Like an unexpected (but brief) illness, stress can sort of surprise us. Don't be afraid to get up from your desk and take a walk around the block. Give yourself a 15-minute vacation. And most of all, avoid making big decisions or communicating with clients when you're in a stress-induced funk.

- **Get enough sleep.** If a project requires you to burn the midnight oil, make up for it the next day.

- **Schedule some "down time"** the day after a particularly large project, so you don't feel like you don't have time to feel grounded again.

- **Don't schedule every possible minute.** Prospective clients can be persistent, but you don't have to explain every waking moment to them. Simply say that you aren't available until "x." (See Tool 5, "Keeping Up When You Have Too Much Work," for tips on handling too much work.)

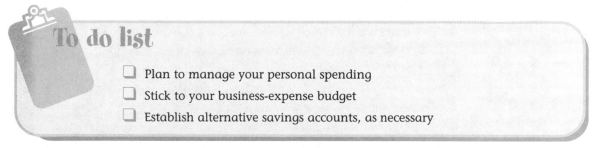

To do list

- ☐ Plan to manage your personal spending
- ☐ Stick to your business-expense budget
- ☐ Establish alternative savings accounts, as necessary

Conserving and Managing Your Money

We've talked about money quite a bit already. Why does it need to appear here?

Like your other resources—namely, your health and your time—money can be misused, and spending can get out of whack.

This is one of the shorter sections in this chapter, but don't mistake brevity for a lack of importance. Ignore these admonitions, and any amount of money will seem like "not enough." You should be well aware that people go bankrupt on hundreds of thousands of dollars, and even millions of dollars, every year. Barring catastrophic illness or other emergencies, these folks didn't go bankrupt because they didn't have enough money; they went bankrupt because no amount of money was ever "enough."

You'll need list

- [ ] Your business plan
- [ ] Ongoing expense records

Personal Spending

Particularly for the first several years in business, personal spending needs to be on a "need to spend" basis. Here are some guidelines for managing personal spending while you're launching a home business:

- Remember that it isn't always about denying yourself something you want to buy or do; often, you simply must buy or do the right thing. Can you take a vacation? Sure. But you might want to go camping instead of staying at a luxury resort. Or, if the luxury resort is a true vacation as nothing else is, you might want to stay 5 days instead of 10.

- Some personal spending will probably go up as a result of your new business. You need to be sure that this is balanced by cuts in other areas of your personal budget. For example, you might have a cleaning service come in and clean your home—yet only a portion of that is a business expense. Or, you might send out your laundry in order to minimize the amount of time it takes when you are not working.

  You might want to revisit Chapter 1, when you considered the costs of both employee and business owner. Review Chapter 4, the budgeting chapter, too.

- If you tend to spend money you have, set up a savings account in a separate bank (preferably in a different state from your own, and with little to no Internet access, so it is more out of reach). The idea here is to make it difficult to get the money out once you make a deposit. Once a month, send money (in an amount based on your income for that month) to this account. So, if you brought in considerably more than your basic expenses, send more to this account. If you barely broke even, send a smaller amount. (But never skip a month—send something, even if it is just five dollars. Stay in the habit.) This is your "unexpected necessity" fund. Spend it only on a wise personal investment, such as a home, or unexpected expenses, such as a medical emergency not fully covered by insurance.

Business Spending

Business spending is not an excuse for spending money however you like. Just because you can deduct business expenses doesn't mean that a particular purchase is always a good idea. There is still a finite amount of money, and you need to be sure that you spend it so that you gain the maximum benefit.

Investing in your business is good, and there will always be equipment, software, or other large ticket items you could be purchasing. As a business owner, however, you must wait until your business is earning sufficient money to justify the investment and plan your expenditures, stretching them out over the course of a year if need be (see "Planning for Budget Items As Outlined in the Business Plan Form," in Chapter 4). Follow these guidelines:

- Do not spend money on whatever you want and then try to justify it later as a "business expense."

- Do not assume that it is okay to spend money simply because it is for your business. Scrutinize your business purchases as closely as your personal purchases. Either way, money is going out the door. Not only does this attitude court trouble with the IRS, but also your family could become resentful that you are spending money so freely on your business while asking them to stick to a budget.

Finally, watch where your money goes. In the first year of business, you will probably be trying out many ways of marketing yourself and pursuing business. After the first year, you need to make sure that your expenditures are justified. Did that type of marketing bring in customers? Then repeat it. Was it a dud? Don't spend money on it again. What did you get out of your membership in that organization? If the answer is "little" or "nothing," don't renew your membership automatically.

Summary

Life is about balance, and (perhaps for the first time ever) the ability to balance your life in a meaningful way is entirely under your control. But with this potential comes the need for a lot of discipline, and like the driver on the freeway, a never ending mode of watchfulness and making adjustments. Make your decisions wisely so you don't crash.

In the Small Business Troubleshooting Toolkit, we'll talk about how to handle some of the more common problems in running a business—things that occur no matter how well you manage your time, your money, and your health.

10

"What I Did": Five Home-Based Entrepreneurs Talk About Their Most Important Decisions and Dilemmas

Learning how other home business owners operate helps you better determine how to run your own business. You can learn from their mistakes, listen to their tips, and weigh their decisions—without impacting your own business unless and until you decide to implement what you have gleaned. Knowing that a particular home business owner is successful only adds to the credibility of his or her advice and insights.

The stories of these home business owners make the information in this book more three-dimensional. In addition, the advice you read here comes directly from these home business owners—these are the words they stake their businesses on, the advice they give because of their own personal experiences. Although some have been in business more than a decade, whereas others have been in business a matter of months, all of them are successful.

But this chapter isn't just about feeling good and knowing that you're in good company. At the end of each section is a short self-assessment exercise, consisting of questions about each profile and how the information you learned there applies to your own home business. Answering these questions is important, as it provides you with a chance to learn from others' experiences and change your business plan or budget accordingly.

The Two-Business Couple—an Engineer and an Educational Consultant

Hans Bockenkamp, *Engineering and Manufacturing Consultant*
Vickie Bockenkamp, *Owner, Power Tools for Learning*

Can each person in a couple run his or her own successful business *and* maintain their relationship? The answer appears to be yes—though, as this case study illustrates, running two businesses from the same home office isn't always a good fit for either entrepreneur.

Vickie and Hans Bockenkamp are husband and wife. Both are also business owners—and for a time, both were home business owners. Today, Hans maintains his engineering and manufacturing consultancy at his home office, whereas Vickie's educational consulting practice is located in a nearby office building. "We still have two desks in the office," she explains. "But if I take a day to do filing or taxes, it gets really hard, working back to back, particularly because the office is small. I distract him; he distracts me."

When Vickie started her business in 1994, Hans' business, started in 1988, was well under way. Initially, having two home businesses seemed like a good idea. It quickly became clear, however, that although Vickie and Hans got along fine, their two distinctly different businesses weren't necessarily compatible.

As an educational consultant, a good portion of Vickie's clients are children. A child's naturally rambunctious behavior is a wonderful thing—but it's not really suitable for the workplace of an engineering and manufacturing consultant. "There was one kid in particular…" Vickie recalls. More mischievous than most, this child often did things that were annoying, such as jumping up and down, trying to see over the fence and into their home when he showed up at the wrong time for an appointment. "That kid really brought home to me that my type of business needs to be in an office somewhere else," Vickie says.

But even without impish children, Vickie concluded that she would still do better in an outside office. "Hans visits customers at their locations. His office is used for phone, computer work, bookkeeping, and paperwork. He doesn't see clients regularly at his office, but I do," she explains. "I also had trouble ending the day. I couldn't pull myself away when I worked at home. If the work was there, it was too hard to walk away. I'd be sitting there at 3 a.m., working on stuff. Hans isn't like that. He can walk away at the end of the day, water the flowers, and start barbecuing."

Although Hans can walk away at the *end* of the day, he is definitely there for his clients for hours and hours before that. As an engineering and manufacturing consultant with decades of experience, Hans' know-how is highly valued. "What I see on this side of it is his discipline," Vickie explains. "You will *never* see him using working from home as an excuse to not work." As we talk on a late spring morning, it is 8 a.m., but Hans is already halfway through his workday. By 8:30 a.m., a call comes in he has to take.

Although he only averages about five clients at any given time, the work is intense, and many, such as Rolls Royce, are household names. Dealing with drawings, specifications, and precise measurements, his clients need his expert input when they call. "It's very important for me to be available and to return calls the same day. Immediate contact, an open line all day long, is crucial," Hans says. And, Hans is quick to point out that availability allows him down time. "I'm available about 10–12 hours per day, six days a week. Being that available allows me to turn off my phone on evenings and weekends."

A lifelong student of engineering, Hans had his own business outside the home until 1986, when he decided to sell the business and retire. "I decided to go back, so I started another business. I wasn't really ready to fully retire. So, I made a few phone calls and said, 'Hey I'm available again.'"

Hans says the highly specialized nature of his business leads to some unusual quirks. "I don't have business cards," he explains. "I don't need them. I get clients through the contacts I've made during my 46-year career in engineering." As he describes his business, he's uncertain whether he even wants his business information published. "It's a niche market, so I'm not sure that would be useful," he explains. In other words, although Hans provides a service that has a very specialized market, he has captured a good portion of that market.

Although not everybody has that level of expertise, some things are the same for every business owner. To new home business owners, Hans says, "People come to you for your knowledge, your experience, and your integrity. All three are equally important" He also adds that the joy of what he does and who he works with is very important. "I enjoy what I do, and all of my customers—we like each other; we enjoy doing business together. That's important."

In addition to providing more enjoyment, Hans appreciates the tax advantages of owning a home business. "I could get a job working for someone else. I even tried it. But you have no tax breaks, no real tax advantages as an employed person." Hans also says that being self-employed provides easy motivation, too. "As a self-employed person, you're better motivated, because you *have* to perform, or you lose your customers."

When Hans and Vickie are asked about a couple who each wants to start their own home business, Vickie says, "Don't start your businesses at the same time." Hans agrees. "Phase it in. Have one start a business, and then another," he adds. Dealing with the insecurities and financial fluctuations of a new business is difficult for one member of a couple. If both income sources are struggling to establish themselves, the strain can be brutal.

"It would be rare if a couple could hold up under that kind of stress," Vickie notes.

But neither one would trade what they are doing now. "There's value in what we both do," Vickie says. "Both of us have niche markets. For both of us, what we do is unique. That helps."

To apply the insights you've learned here to your own home-business situation, take a moment to answer the following questions. Review Hans' and Vickie's story as needed:

1. Compare and contrast Vickie's and Hans' businesses. How are their businesses alike? How are they different?

2. Is your business more like Vickie's or Hans'? Why?

3. What challenges might you face if you and your spouse/partner were starting home businesses at the same time? What businesses would best complement your own?

4. What issues of availability and work hours come up in this profile of Vickie and Hans? How does this compare with your own style—do you tend to always or never be available? How well does that style fit your business? Why?

5. Both Hans' and Vickie's businesses are "niche" markets. Would you describe your market as a niche market? Why or why not? Approximately how many potential customers can you think of for your own business? (If you can't think of exact numbers, can you list professions or situations in which someone might be in need of your services?) What percentage would you need to serve in order to be successful?

6. Based on the information you've learned from Vickie's and Hans' story, have you determined that you should make any changes in the way you run your business? If so, modify your business plan and/or budget accordingly.

The Printer/Graphic Designer

Ken Loyd, *Owner, Keness*

Ken Loyd's printing and graphic design business, Keness, has taken many twists and turns since he started it in 2000. But don't call any of them surprises. The changes his business has experienced have been the direct result of his careful, unflinching analysis.

Before Ken started his business in 2000, he worked in Japan for Yamaha, doing Japanese English translation and teaching. Although he enjoyed the work, he had other dreams he wanted to pursue. "It wasn't that I disliked my job," he explains, "but it was more of a desire to do my own thing."

Ken had already been involved with graphic design before going to Japan. "I wanted to continue where I left off in graphic design," he explains. "I wanted to not have to answer to anyone but the client."

Returning to the United States in 1999, Ken took a job in San Francisco that provided him with additional graphic design and printing experience. With his feet on the ground, literally and figuratively, he began taking on freelance graphic design projects to supplement his income. In 2000, this grew in to his own home business. Although the business started primarily as a graphic design business, Ken began to research digital printing equipment, and was soon able to offer select printing services as well.

By being able to offer both printing and graphic design, Ken's business boomed. Clients could come to him with some ideas and copy, and take away a full-color brochure days later. He kept his business home-based (sort of) by also renting the apartment next door and using that as his base of operations. "It worked out well, because I had more division between work and home, so there was some balance—but I could come to work any time I wanted to as well," he explains. For example, he was able to start a print project, and then return next door (home) while the machines worked. For very important, rush projects, he could even set his alarm every few hours to check on the machines and reload paper during the evening. This gave him the ability to keep up with his ever-increasing client list.

What allowed for this arrangement is Ken's neighborhood and his landlord. "My landlord has been very flexible, and I live in a very urban—you could even say industrial—neighborhood. I think a lot of very urban locations, like this one, are going to be much more flexible than suburban locations. Living in this very urban environment has really made a big difference."

Ken's business continued to grow, and Ken continued to look for ways to expand his offerings. After adding printing to his graphic design business, he also expanded his print offerings. "I've done a lot of different types of projects," he explains. Those projects range from postcards to books, from glossy brochures to black-and-white copies. "Being able to offer a wide range of options to my clients is really important. I want to give them what they want, and I don't want them to feel like I'm forcing something on them they don't really want or need."

Eventually, however, even his "expanded" home-based arrangement couldn't accommodate the business. In early 2002, he moved into a bona fide office that could handle all of his printing equipment.

But the outside office didn't work out as well as he had hoped. "I missed the ease of going right from home to office in a matter of seconds," he explains. "It's too easy to say, 'Well, I don't really have to go into the office today' if the office is 10 minutes away rather than 10 seconds away." Meanwhile, as Ken reviewed newer printers coming out, he realized that advances in most printers had streamlined the technology, making it possible to offer the same high-quality services with fewer, newer, smaller, and streamlined printers. "After I saw that, I realized returning to a home-based business would be more productive." The headache of ending the office lease and moving again were minimal compared to the pleasure he felt in being able to (again) work from home. "The actual office required so much additional red tape," he explains, "including an extra set of utilities, lease requirements, and a jump to 'commercial' prices for a lot of things. I really appreciated how efficient it was to work from a home office, and was really happy to do so again."

So, in late 2003, Ken returned to being a home business owner. And he will be the first to tell you that it was a wise move. "I know I'm more productive, and my clients are better served." Ken also realized that, although having a separate office had looked more official, it was further out of the way for most clients. Now that he has returned to working from home, his central location gives him an added advantage when competing with other printers. "I'm in a more central location than I could possibly afford as a separate office, so clients don't have to travel out of the way to see me," he notes.

Because printing equipment is so important to what he does, Ken keeps an eye on the latest models being offered. "I'm always looking to improve my business, of course." But purchases are generally spread out. "I don't finance purchases. I'll see something that I think is right for the business, and then figure out what I need to do to afford it. "I like to invest in my business, and by avoiding financing, new equipment is a paid-in-full asset right from day one, rather than a liability. Not having monthly payments also makes it easier to weather lean times."

The biggest piece of advice Ken gives to other new home business owners (or would-be home business owners): "Make sure you have plenty of money, and can weather the first year." Ken was able to ease in to the financial aspects of running his own home business thanks to the freelance work that was readily available while he was still employed.

Today, Ken's business continues to thrive. "What continues to surprise me is how much I enjoy doing what I do for my clients," he says. "And I enjoy doing it at my own speed, having my own way of working. As long as I meet my clients' deadlines, I have that freedom. And so far, it has really worked out well. I'm always amazed at how happy it makes me."

Answer the following questions for your own business. Review Ken's story as needed:

1. What did Ken do to ensure that he had enough money to start his own business?

2. Why did Ken's business grow? Did he increase customers, increase services offered, or both? Could your business grow in a similar fashion? Why or why not?

3. What mistake did Ken make? At what point did he realize that he had made a mistake? How did he fix the mistake?

4. What does Ken do to run a business successfully? Can you list at least five things Ken does that are discussed earlier in this book?

5. Based on Ken's story, would you run your business any differently? If so, adjust your business plan and/or budget as needed.

The Coach

Lisa Betts-LaCroix, *Partner, Paragon Strategies*

When asked how she decided to base her new business in her home, Lisa Betts-Lacroix has no trouble answering. "I hadn't necessarily thought of my business as a home business. I decided to do what I wanted, and it made sense for it to be a home business," she explains, referring to her coaching services for small business owners. "I first made the decision to do the kind of work I was doing, and it didn't make financial sense to have a separate office."

Prior to starting her coaching business, Lisa and her husband ran a traditional business together, complete with a separate office. But neither one of them felt fulfilled by the lifestyle. "We closed the business and decided to make some radical changes."

Their initial plan was to buy a trailer, traveling the United States and working and living out of the trailer. Lisa wanted to move into coaching, while her husband made plans to start another business.

But soon, the traveling seemed superfluous. They never left San Francisco, although they did leave the trailer, moving first into a loft and then a house. Along the way, the outer trappings of their business have been steadily shaped by their inner vision. "We've basically been following our vision of what our professional lives should be, and the office has evolved around that."

While growing her list of clients, primarily owners of small and midsized businesses, Lisa realized that she wanted the business to grow in breadth as well as numbers. With two business colleagues, she formed Paragon Strategies, a training and meeting facilitation company, in 2003. "We have a small office, but I work from home frequently," she explains. "I rarely use the separate office," she says, noting that maintaining her home office helps her balance family responsibilities as well— most notably, sharing responsibility for caring for the couple's young son.

Lisa says that having a home business and raising kids at the same time, "definitely has specific requirements. A separate office space is really useful. You can say, 'Okay, this is hands-off.'"

But Lisa is careful to use that tactic. "It's a double-edged sword to do that because it's really valuable to have kids see what you do. On the other hand, you don't want your kids writing on your paperwork." Although she would like to integrate caring for her son and working seamlessly, Lisa admits that is very tough to do. "The pressure of taking care of my son while I'm working doesn't work well for me because I don't focus my attention on either one very well."

That is a challenge she struggles with to this day, particularly with memories of her own childhood in mind. "My parents ran a photography business," she explains. "I worked there in the summer. And recently, I was reflecting on how great it was that I could just show up. I was pretty much welcome to be there. It was like, 'Okay, here are my kids.' We were embraced in the situation. We weren't considered an inappropriate addition to the scene."

And her own son might very well feel that way about both of his parents' businesses—perhaps once he is older. "It depends on a kid's age, too, of course," Lisa adds. "But by working at a business and hanging out, I got a good idea of what's involved. By the time I started my own business, I knew a lot about running a business that I didn't know I knew."

That might also explain why Lisa has never been an employee. "I've never had a regular job. My example, growing up, was that you're in charge of your work life. You create your own work environment the way you want to."

But Lisa sees wider implications than those for herself and her family. "I have the belief that we've built a situation in our society, where family and home is very separated from work and business. That creates a lot of gender polarization, especially for heterosexual couples with children. That big split between business and domesticity is unhealthy for everyone involved." She believes that home businesses and family businesses might be the solution to the unspoken problem. "I see a quiet crisis happening. There's a real integration needed. Family businesses and home businesses provide an opportunity for that integration."

But she also sees some drawbacks. "The danger, of course, is that work becomes everything. And it's important, with kids, to draw clear distinctions, and in general, to have clear responsibilities—to know who's responsible for what."

Whether a home business owner has kids or not, however, Lisa says breaking the isolation is key. "One thing that's really critical is to get out of the house. Do some professional development; do some networking. Get out there and interact with people. When you're working at home, by yourself, you can get extremely insular." Lisa has made it her goal to attend one networking event and one professional development or professional association meeting each week. "It's about building resources you don't have," she explains.

After reviewing Lisa's story, answer the following questions:

1. How does Lisa approach owning her own business? Does she see it as risky, normal, or somewhere in between? How does her attitude toward owning a business versus being an employee compare with yours? Would you say that your attitude toward owning a home business helps you or hurts you? Why or why not?

2. If you have children, how does your plan for their care compare with Lisa's? Do you anticipate having your children help you in any way? Can you imagine your children "just hanging out," as Lisa did in her youth? How do you think your children's involvement (or lack of involvement) in your business will change as they get older? How might it change as your business grows? What skills will your children gain as a result of your home business?

3. Did you decide to own a home business and then choose what to do, or did you choose what to do and then decide to make it a home business? Why?

4. What professional or networking events could you attend each week to prevent being too isolated? What else might you do to avoid isolation and insular thinking?

5. Based on Lisa's story, would you run your business any differently? If so, adjust your business plan and/or budget as needed.

The QuickBooks Consultant

Jody Linick, *Owner, Linick Consulting*

At the time of our interview, Jody Linick had been in business for fewer than seven months. But don't mistake a new business owner for a struggling one—particularly in her case.

"The first year so far has actually been pretty good. I'm paying my bills, which was my goal," she says, pleased. In fact, business has picked up so much recently that her total working hours each week have greatly increased. "I'm working a lot more weekends and late nights. It's getting to where there's more than one person can handle," she explains. However, the newness of her business makes her reluctant to expand beyond her home office. "I'm not really ready to handle employees, either," she adds.

This success is a welcome surprise to Jody, who grew tired of the all-too-common frequency of layoffs. When she was laid off from her high-tech job, just one year ago, she decided that it was time to do something else. "This was the second layoff for me, and the second time that I had been laid off after being with a company for seven or more years," she explains. "I started thinking, 'I don't want to do this a third time. I don't want to be laid off again.'"

From the beginning, Jody found friends and colleagues who could act as a sounding board and provide additional insight and encouragement when she had to make decisions. "I had QuickBooks knowledge, and talked to friends about whether I could make a go of it." Building on her knowledge of QuickBooks, Jody studied for, and became, a certified QuickBooks ProAdvisor.

note See www.intuit.com, or Appendix A, "References and Resources," to contact Jody or find a QuickBooks ProAdvisor in your area.

Resources · Must See

Laid off in August, Jody received her business license in October, and by December had her website up and running. "That timing worked out okay," she says, "because January is the start of the tax season." She had opened for business just as many customers began thinking about taxes—and also began asking for help.

There have been a few challenges along the way, but Jody has successfully met them. Keeping a focus on business, and preventing distractions, was key. "In the beginning, it's hard to have the discipline, to not be distracted by laundry or yard work." Friends and family members would also disrupt the work day. "They would call up because they knew I was at home. And initially, people think you're not doing anything because you're not 'in the office.'" The solution, she found, was quite simple. "They almost always asked if I could talk. Sometimes, I'd say 'yes.' Other times, I'd say, 'No. I'll have to call you back after 5 o'clock.'"

DEALING WITH EARLY-STAGE GROWTH

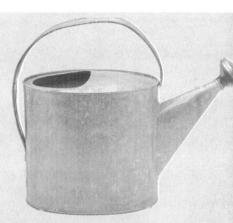

As Jody indicates, dealing with growth in the early stages of your business can be exhilarating—and perplexing.

The exhilaration comes when you realize that you are meeting or exceeding your wildest dreams—not only surviving, but thriving, and all in a very short time.

That excitement begins to fade, however, when you wonder how to handle all the extra work. After all, expanding while your business is still very new is a bit like discovering a beautiful (but unanticipated) plant in your garden. You now want it to grow, you're excited—but what will it really require? In the case of the plant, you aren't really sure what caused it to grow so well—was it the sunshine? The unusually heavy rain? Shade from other plants? All three? Could it have grown more without any of these factors—that is, are these conditions contributing to or impeding growth? And how much more will it really be able to grow, anyway? Is this as tall as it will get?

So it is with your new business. You are growing. You know that you're successful, and that's good. But will your business handle the growth? Is this a momentary "blip" because your particular service is hot for the moment, thanks to some 15-second trend? Is this a normally busy season you weren't aware of? Does the potential for readily available, additional growth exist—or will you have to invest heavily to expand the business further? With less than a year in business, it's hard to answer those questions. You don't really have the hard data that even 3 or 5 years in business would provide.

So how do you handle the busy times without overextending yourself or your business? Outsourcing and outside contractors can do wonders—both are flexible enough to give you what you want when you want it. Of course, additional efficiency might be gained, too, eliminating some of the busy-ness. And you need to be sure that you're not only **busy**, but also **profitable**. (The two might or might not go hand in hand, although most of us are quick to assume the latter when we experience the former.)

For more ideas on how to handle early-stage growth, see Chapter 14, "Keeping Up When You Have Too Much Work," particularly the section "Alternatives to Expansion." Many of those suggestions are meant to tide you over until you are certain that expanding in a "big" way—for example, hiring employees and maybe moving outside of your home office—is truly justified by your long-term business revenues.

Keeping Internet time in check was another challenge. "In the beginning, particularly, I'd get lost on the Internet. I'd start looking for clients. Then I'd notice something else, and something else, and another thing. The next thing I would know, I've spent three hours pointing and clicking. It's very interesting to spend all day doing that, but you also feel you haven't gotten anything done."

As business increased, Jody found she had less time to do that, so the surfing diminished. But she also found that talking to other home business and small business owners helped, too. "To keep from doing that [spending all day on the Internet], I talked to others with small businesses. One person told me to go out and make some flyers. She said, 'Building contractors don't have time to do their books. Go make some flyers and put them on every truck you see in the parking lot at the hardware store.'" The tactic didn't garner any clients, but it got Jody to think beyond the Internet and connect with potential clients more directly. However, Jody says tracking your marketing efforts is important. "I do track marketing. Right now, ads I put on craigslist [.org, an online bulletin board] have generated the most business for me. But I track the success of everything I do."

Jody's network of other small business and home business owners has helped her immensely as she has launched her business—and not just with marketing. "I have two other small business owners who are mentors. One is a woman I knew through karate class. She runs her business and takes it seriously, but also has free time. That's what I aspire to. Eventually, I'd like to be able to take off and have others continue the business activity. I have a QuickBooks mentor, too."

But in spite of her solid resources and success, she is cautious about expanding. Her business is not even a year old, and she is keenly aware that business can cycle further upward—or downward. "I also want to think it through," she says. "I don't want to hire an employee, and then end up making it up as I go."

As with the start of her business, Jody envisions a methodical, logical approach to expansion, beginning with a set of policies. "I've been reading the Ivan Misner books," she explains, noting that the ability to franchise a business—to standardize each detail—has inspired her. "And I already do this. I've got a list of interview questions I ask people when they initially call and ask for my help. I also have a list of things to do the first time I visit a client."

note Ivan Misner is the founder of BNI, Business Network International. Visit www.bni.com for more information, or see Appendix A.

This approach not only helps Jody remember what to cover at each visit, but boosts clients' opinions of her as well. "It lends an air of legitimacy and makes me look more professional," she says. She's noticed other details that can have that effect, too, such as carrying a briefcase instead of a canvas bag. "It's a simple thing. Who would have thought?" she muses.

Additional advice to new home business owners emphasizes that professional image as well. "You definitely need a website even if customers aren't finding you that way.

It lends legitimacy to your business. And get business cards. I had someone design a logo that I could also use on my website, so they matched."

Behind the image, however, Jody says that there are some things a home business owner should do to make things easier for themselves. "Get a post office box. When I filed my Fictitious Business Name statement, I got a flood of mail, and you really don't want that coming to your home address necessarily." She also pared down finances as she started her business. "I was laid off, I have a home, and I have no one else to help me pay for that," she notes. "I got a housemate to help cut costs, and that has worked out very well. It relieved some of the financial pressure. I also cut some things, such as Netflix, and found a cheaper gym package."

Once her business was up and running, she found that professional organizations helped her save additional money. "I joined the American Association of Professional Bookkeepers, and was able to get better rates on liability insurance through them," she adds, noting that the organization offers both networking and cost savings at the same time.

After reviewing Jody's story, answer the following questions:

1. What did Jody do to ensure that she had enough money to start her own business? What did Jody do differently from Ken Loyd, the owner of Keness (you read about him in "The Printer/Graphic Designer," earlier in this chapter)? For your business, what might you do to put yourself on a firmer financial footing?

2. By putting flyers on construction contractor's trucks, Jody met her customers where they were—at the hardware store during the work day. Where could you meet your customers? Could you write up a likely schedule for your target customer? How might you get their attention, other than through email, phone calls, or regular mail?

3. The Internet can be a good thing—and sometimes, there can be too much of a good thing. What other activities, although seemingly productive, might turn into a waste of time? How can you recognize when an activity has ceased being productive?

4. Jody has a support system. What other small business owners or home business owners do you know? Who might be your support system? Do you see one or more of these individuals as possible mentors? If so, talk to them about mentoring you as you begin your business.

5. Do you have written procedures for your business? What questions will you ask potential customers? What must you do the first time you visit or work for a client? If you haven't already done so, prepare these checklists for your business.

GLEANING INFORMATION FROM OTHER HOME BUSINESS OWNERS

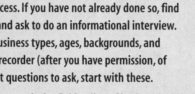

A lot can be learned by interviewing other home business owners—regardless of their level of success. If you have not already done so, find 5–10 home business owners and ask to do an informational interview. Try to find a wide variety of business types, ages, backgrounds, and business styles. Set up a tape recorder (after you have permission, of course). If you are unsure what questions to ask, start with these.

1. Why did you choose your particular field or line of business? Did you consider others? If so, what made you choose this one over others?

2. What events or factors made you decide to become a home business owner?

3. What has surprised you the most about owning your home business? What are your greatest joys in running your home business? Your greatest challenges?

4. What do you wish someone had told you before you started your home business?

5. Can you give any advice on how to balance work and personal life? How do you handle interruptions by family, friends, or neighbors?

6. What did you do to organize your business in a way that made sense? What tips for setting up a business, logistically speaking, can you provide?

7. How do you market your business? What marketing advice would you give to home business owners? Which of the following general categories have been most successful for you, and why?

   Categories: a) Networking; b) Mailings; c) Flyers; d) Display advertising (newspaper/magazine); e) Internet advertising; f) Networking via the Internet; g) Professional groups; h) Family and friends; i) Other clients; j) Cold calling or knocking on doors

8. Can you give any advice on how to manage money or how to minimize the impact of startup costs when beginning a home business?

9. Have you ever had an angry or upset client? How did you deal with it? What would you say that you learned from the experience?

10. Where do you see your business in 5 years? In 10 years? What do you think will happen to your home business eventually? Do you plan to retire? Pass the business on to children? Move the business out of the home?

6. Jody obtained her QuickBooks Professional Advisor certification. Are there professional certifications or enhancements you could obtain that would make you and your business more marketable?

7. Based on Jody's story, would you run your business any differently? If so, revise your business plan and/or business budget accordingly.

Summary

Because a home business is intrinsically enmeshed in who you are as a person, and your own experiences, no two home business owners will ever have the same story. But by sharing our stories and gleaning important information from them, we can help each other avoid mistakes, work more efficiently, and enjoy more successful home businesses.

And in a sense, this chapter (and this book) are not yet complete—they are waiting for you to add your story, your experience.

This is the point at which you are taking the leap. You aren't really jumping off a cliff—that implies a lack of preparation, a lack of knowledge that the cliff exists and the drop is steep, and a lack of recognition that gravity applies to you. Rather, you are writing a new chapter in your life—you, home business owner: prepared, informed, and ready to succeed.

Part III

Appendix

References and Resources

Chances are, while reading this book, you have said, "Great. I know that's what I need—but where do I find it?" The answer, to some extent, is, "Here, in the appendix."

But don't think of this appendix as your only resource; rather, it is a jumping-off point. As you set up and operate your business, you will develop your own resources (both long-distance and local) that provide you with the help you need to succeed.

Forms and Templates

Here are some extra copies of the most important forms and templates used in this book. Whether you want to review the form in its entirety (outside of the text) or simply start with a fresh, blank form, these tools will help you structure your home business.

Business Plan Format

This form, as originally introduced in Chapter 3, "Creating Your Business Plan, Part 1: What, Where, When, and How," provides the framework of your business. Before you buy office supplies—or even create a budget, as you do in Chapter 4, "Creating Your Business Plan, Part 2: The Money Pages"—you need to figure out the who, what, where, when, and how of your home business. This business plan format helps you do just that.

Whether you are filling out the form for the first, fifth, or twentieth time, however, be sure that you read Chapter 3 as you fill it out. The form provides the structure, but Chapter 3 provides additional information that will help you flesh out your business accurately.

1. **Introduction/Overview**

   This is written last, and it is a summary of the rest of the business plan. Return to the introduction and write it *only* after you have completed the rest of the business plan.

2. **The Basics**

   A. What is the business name? Is it a sole proprietorship, partnership, or corporation? If it's a corporation, what type (for example, S-Corp, C-Corp, LLC)?

   B. Where will the business be located? (Presumably, you have answered this, and the answer is in your home.) Is there a Post Office Box?

   C. Will the business have a web presence? What is the domain name(s)?

   D. Who is the proprietor(s)? What is it about the proprietor(s) that makes him/her/them the right person(s) to run this business?

   E. What needs or wants of customers are being met? (Give a brief overview of who you are serving and why.)

3. **Business Overview**

   A. What does the business do or provide?

   B. To whom or what does the business provide these service(s)/product(s)? Are there specific industries or geographic locations services are provided to, or are they offered to the public? Is the entity Business to Business, Business to Consumer, or both?

4. **Marketing**

   A. How does the business reach customers? What need or desire is being fulfilled?

   B. What are the unique features this business offers that competitors do not?

   C. How will the business interact with and retain customers?

   D. How is pricing structured in your line of work? What is the going rate for the service you provide?

5. **Logistics**

   A. Where is the business located? How much space is rented/allocated?

   B. What equipment is purchased/needs to be purchased?

C. What arrangements have been/need to be made with other businesses in order to provide the product(s) and/or service(s) offered by the business?

6. **Financials**

(This section is discussed in detail in Chapter 4.)

A. How much money do you need to start this business (day 1)?

B. How much money do you need, monthly, to operate the business?

C. How much money do you need, monthly, to live on, regardless of what the business brings in? Will this come from savings, partner's/spouse's income, part-time job, or other source?

D. How much money can you reasonably expect to make from the business initially? (Take the going rates from the Marketing section of your business plan and expand them here.) What variables exist in pricing? What is the maximum income you can generate?

E. What can you reasonably expect to earn from the business during the first year? Second? Third? Fourth, Fifth? Years Six through Ten?

7. **Assumptions, Expansion, and Exits**

A. What assumptions have you made in order for your financial projections to work? What happens if those assumptions are incorrect?

B. What assumptions have you made in your marketing and logistics? What happens if those assumptions are incorrect?

C. At what point would it be impractical to run the business? At what point financially? Logistically?

D. At what point would it be impractical to run the business from your home? At what point financially? Logistically?

Budget Templates

In Chapter 4, you learn how to create a budget. These additional budget templates can be used to either correct your initial budget or revise your budget after your business is up and running for awhile.

As with the preceding business plan format, the budget templates work best in conjunction with the text in Chapter 4. So be sure to reread the chapter, if necessary, to complete future budgets.

Startup Analysis

Item Description	Startup Deductible	Ongoing Deductible	Startup Not Deductible	Ongoing Not Deductible

Ongoing Business Expense and Income Tracking

Because Chapter 4 discusses setting up your accounts based on the headings and divisions used in Schedule C, be sure to check that form when preparing your own expense and income tracking documents. Always be sure to use the appropriate form when filing your taxes—you can do this by checking the IRS website, www.irs.gov, for the most recent forms and publications.

Here is the expense format, based on Schedule C. This spreadsheet example provides a column for the date, as well as a description of the income or expense. After you input the date and description, you will enter the amount of each expense or income item in the appropriate column. Note that the numbers in the column headings correspond to the line number on Schedule C. For additional information, refer to Chapter 4.

Date	Desc.	Cost of Goods Sold	$	8-Adv.	11- Comms	15- Ins.	17 - Legal/Pro	18- Ofc	22-Sup.

23- Taxes/Lic.	24a-Trav.	TOT Meals/ent.	24b 50% of Meals/Ent.	25-Utilities	27- Other	TOT Home exp. total	30- % Home exp	TOTALS

Sample Invoice

Use the sample invoice on the following page as a reference when creating your own. Put your invoice on your company letterhead, so your business name and contact information are prominently located.

In this example, explanations of some sections of the invoice appear in brackets []; this text wouldn't appear, of course, on an actual invoice.

Sample Press Release Format

The example below displays a suggested format for a press release you could use to announce the opening of your business, business expansion, or the acquisition of major contracts that might be of local interest. Bracketed text explains each element in this example.

Press Contact: [Person's name]

[Person's title]

(415) 123-4567 [Email address is okay here, too, but a
phone number is still a "must."]

[PRESS RELEASE TITLE—MAKE IT CATCHY!]

SAN FRANCISCO, March 31, 2005 [Note the city is in all caps, followed by the date in lowercase. If your city of origin is not a major metropolitan location, put both city and state. For example: "CHICAGO" is fine, but "PEORIA, ILLINOIS."]—
[Introductory paragraph goes here. Paragraph should grab an editor's attention. Tell them something that will keep them from throwing it into the garbage. And hurry—you don't have many words to do that. If it doesn't seem worthwhile within the first one or two lines, it's in the trash.]

Second and remaining paragraphs: Go in to more detail about what was introduced in the first paragraph. Note that the body of the press release is double-spaced.

About XXX: At the end of the release, give a brief biography or history about you/your company.

# # #

[Three marks show the end of the release, and they are always centered. The entire press release should be no longer than three pages.]

November 1, 2004   #1234
[always use date sent]   [number invoices sequentially]

[Put this invoice on your company letterhead, so your business name and contact information are prominently located.]

George's Graphic Design, Inc.
1122 Better Way Park, Greenland, MD 00044
777-555-1212

INVOICE

[This needs to be clearly noted; you might want to make this print larger or otherwise more noticeable.]

To: ABC123 Company
Attn: Violet Smith
           1234 Ivy Way
           Myrtle, CA 94150
Via Email: violets@abccompany.com

[Always note whether an invoice has been sent via email or special courier—anything other than standard mail; this makes it easier to track payment efforts, if needed]

Amount	Description	Rate	Total
10.0 hours	Graphic design services for new brochure; October 2004	$75/hour	$750.00
5.0 hours	Graphic design services; rework business card, October 2004	$75/hour	325.00
	Credit—Deposit 10/4/04		(400.00)
	TOTAL DUE		**$675.00**

[If the client requires additional detail, add it here; remind your clients of your payment terms, and be sure to thank them, as shown next.]

Please make checks payable to: George's Graphic Design, Inc.

If you have any questions concerning this invoice, please call me at (510) 123-4567. Invoices are payable immediately, and due within 30 days of the date of this invoice, unless other arrangements have been made in writing. Invoices are payable by check, money order/bank check, or by debit/credit card. A $35 (U.S. dollars) handling fee will be added to the total amount due for any returned checks or refused credit cards.

THANK YOU FOR YOUR BUSINESS!

Helpful Resources

These are the names, addresses, and websites that form the beginning of your list of resources. Look here if you need a specific referral to a person or organization to help you, from tax and legal advice to organizational help to therapists and related consultants to cope with the changes resulting from starting your own home business.

Financial, Tax, Insurance, and Legal Matters

Financial, tax, insurance, and legal matters scare a lot of people. They shouldn't. Granted, there is a lot to know in these areas, but a trusted professional will guide you through seemingly treacherous legalese so that you run your business in a legitimate, financially sound manner.

Financial and Taxes

American Institute of Certified Public Accountants (AICPA), www.aicpa.org/yellow/ypascpa.htm—This is the national body of CPAs. Its website lists state-affiliated organizations, which can provide referrals to a CPA near you.

Enterprise Zones, www.ezec.gov—Areas where incentives can be provided if you set up a business or hire employees, these can be found by contacting your state or local government offices. Learn more about Rural Enterprise Zones, a similar type of zoning, at www.ezec.gov.

Internal Revenue Service (IRS), www.irs.gov—Whether you were raised to pay your taxes up front or avoid them at any cost, the IRS website is a must (and an ideal starting place in your research). Get current and previous year tax forms, publications that specifically address business issues, and more. Be sure to check out the special page for small/home-based businesses and self-employed individuals.

Intuit ProAdvisors, www1.intuitmarketplace.com/fsg/ReferralDB/ReferralDataBaseMemberSearch.AS—The makers of Quicken bookkeeping software offer a database of its certified ProAdvisors who can help you with your Quicken bookkeeping. This includes Jodie Linick, who is interviewed in Chapter 10, "'What I Did': Five Home-Based Entrepreneurs Talk About Their Most Important Decisions and Dilemmas."

Small Business Administration (SBA), www.sba.gov—For possible funding sources beyond your local bank, check with your local Small Business Administration office (or go online).

Insurance

In addition to the following resources, check professional organizations and organizations geared toward small business and self-employed individuals. (See the section "Organizations Helpful to Self-Employed and Small Business in General," later in the appendix, for contact information.)

COBRA Information, www.dol.gov/dol/topic/health-plans/cobra.htm and **www.dol.gov/ebsa/faqs/faq_consumer_cobra.html**—These sites offer information about COBRA (Consolidated Omnibus Budget Reconciliation Act), including whether you qualify to continue your employer's health insurance, even after you leave that employment.

Independent Insurance Agents and Brokers of America, www.iiaa.org—This listing of insurance agents provides you with referrals to agents who are not affiliated with a particular company. Because they can offer products from one or more organization, these agents are likely to search for a product that best suits your needs and budget.

Medicaid, www.cms.gov—This is the government health program for low-income individuals.

National Association of Professional Insurance Agents, www.pianet.com—Another website of professional insurance agents, this group also consists of agents who are not solely affiliated with only one insurance company.

Online Insurance information, www.insureme.com and **www.equote.com**—These are just two of a number of consolidated, one-stop shopping sites that offer health insurance. Check any site's privacy policy, so you're comfortable providing information for a quote. You'll also want to check out the company providing the insurance, so you know they're legitimate before sending any premiums.

Poroy, Maria, Health insurance consultant, 415-986-7726 or visit **www.accessbenefitsgroup.com.**—My recommendation is Maria Poroy, Access Business Services, Inc. Based in California, she is licensed in some other states as well. Maria has been invaluable to me when assessing health insurance options.

Roger Duke Insurance Agency, 510-614-0100, rduke@farmersagent.com—This is another insurance recommendation. Roger has been a huge help when it comes to homeowners and other insurance products that are right for home business owners.

Social Security Disability Coverage, www.ssa.gov/notices/ supplemental-security-income/—See this site for information about Social Security Disability coverage, including a screening tool that allows you to put in possible scenarios based on your own personal circumstances.

State disability insurance programs, www.edd.ca.gov—Rhode Island, New Jersey, New York, Hawaii, California, and Puerto Rico offer state disability insurance programs. California has an elective program for self-employed individuals (see www.edd.ca.gov/direp/difaq9.htm#Elective_Coverage).

Legal

Although none of these sites are intended to take the place of an attorney, they do provide helpful information and good background so that you sound intelligent when you meet with your attorney (and don't run up unnecessary billing). You'll want to review what these sites have to say about contracts, business formation, intellectual property, and other business issues.

American Bar Association, www.abanet.org—This is the national professional association for attorneys. This website provides helpful information about what to consider when hiring an attorney, as well as referral links. Because attorneys are licensed to practice on a state-by-state basis, you might want to check your state or local Bar Association referral service first. Most states and larger cities have online Bar Association information.

Online legal information www.FindLaw.com and **www.AllLaw.com**—The two most commonly used sites for all-purpose legal information sites, these sites also offer a combination of current events, basic information, and referral sources.

Patent and Trademark Office, www.uspto.gov—A visit to this website will not only provide information about the trademark process, but also help you make a decision whether you need the help of a lawyer. (For websites, you'll also want to check for existing domain names on an Internet registration site, such as www.Register.com.)

Technical Resources

Where do you get computers? Software? Other technical items? This section takes you straight to the "horse's mouth," so to speak—that is, right to the software and hardware manufacturers themselves.

Hardware Vendors

Apple, **www.apple.com**

HP, **www.hp.com**

IBM, **www.ibm.com**

Software Vendors

ACT! www.act.com—Contact management software.

FileMaker, www.filemaker.com—A very helpful, powerful database program.

Microsoft, www.microsoft.com—In addition to visiting this site for information about the Microsoft Office suite, be sure to check out special offerings, including Visio—drawing software bought by Microsoft several years ago—and Entourage, Microsoft's latest calendaring and contact management software.

Quicken, www.intuit.com—Bookkeeping software

Web Hosting and Design

Domain name registration, www.register.com, www.valueweb.com, and **www.netsol.com**—These sites also allow you to build your own website through a database of templates, colors, graphics, and typestyles, with many additional features.

Hurricane Electric, www.he.com—Web hosting/web support services.

InSite Web Services, www.iswebservices.com—For web development, particularly when mixing membership or other databases with the Internet, I recommend this company.

WSI MagicWeb, www.wsimagicweb.com—In addition to web hosting/web support services, this company offers web development, hosting, e-commerce, and many other related services.

Marketing and Networking Resources

See also the organizations of general help to self-employed and small business owners later in the appendix. Many professional and business organizations are also a great source of networking and marketing contacts.

Business Network International (BNI), www.bni.com—One of the most far-flung and effective networking groups around, this organization probably has a chapter near you. The website offers philosophy of its founder, background in the organization, and allows you to find chapter meetings in your own area. Check out a local meeting, and join if you can. This is a great way to buck the isolation blues and generate business at the same time.

Direct Marketing Association, www.the-dma.org—Offers resources, guidelines, and other help for anyone dealing directly with potential clients, either on the phone or by mail or email. Does the "Do Not Call" list affect you? What are your obligations when someone asks to be taken off your mailing list? This is where to find out.

Federal Trade Commission's Do Not Call website, www.ftc.gov/ donotcall/—Check here before conducting a mass cold-calling campaign to private households.

Keness Company, www.keness.com, 415-462-1738—For printing and graphic design help, contact Ken Loyd (profiled in Chapter 15).

Paragon Strategies, www.paragonstrategies.com—This company (cofounded by Lisa Betts-LaCroix, profiled in Chapter 15) provides many types of training, including communication, management, and sales skills.

PressRelease.com, www.pressrelease.com—This is a great do-it-yourself tool for those seeking a lot of exposure. Send press releases and manage the flow of information about your company—all online.

U.S. Postal Service website, www.usps.gov—Order stamps, check regulations regarding mail size, find current postal rates, and more at this helpful site. It has a special section dedicated to small business that is definitely worth checking out.

Personal Development Resources (Organization, Learning Disabilities, and More)

This might sound like an odd category, but if a part of you is "broken," it will show up in your business operations, too. So improving yourself is going to show improvement in your business.

American Association for Marriage and Family Therapy (AAMFT), www.aamft.org—This professional organization provides referrals to licensed therapists in your area.

International Coach Federation, www.coachfederation.org—Visit this site to find a certified coach in your local area. Coaches specialize, so you should be able to find one who is experienced in the area you want to work on, too—whether it is business, personal, financial, a combination, or some other area.

Nonviolent communication skills training: If you would like to communicate so as to minimize tension, visit the **Center for Nonviolent Communication (CNVC) website at www.cnvc.org**. Another website, **www.nonviolentcommunication.com**, offers books on the subject, and other helpful information from CNVC and its founder, Marshall Rosenberg.

Consumer Credit Counseling, www.nfcc.org—If you are struggling with being honest about your financial situation, or if your bills are substantial, do not hesitate to visit this site to find the location nearest you, or check your phone book for CCCS (Consumer Credit Counseling Services). If you go with a different firm, be sure that it is both a) a member of the Better Business Bureau, and b) nonprofit. Scam artists lurk in every industry, and this also includes credit counseling.

National Association of Professional Organizers, www.napo.net—If you need help with organization—if your office is a sea of confusing paper—consider hiring a professional organizer.

Power Tools for Learning, www.toolsforlearning.com, 510-337-9838—Struggles that seem to be about procrastination on the surface, organization, and reading comprehension might have more to do with a learning disability—or simply understanding how you absorb information. This company, run by Vickie Bockenkamp (profiled in Chapter 15), offers testing and remediation for both children and adults.

Helpful to Self-Employed and Small Business in General

These resources don't fall into the preceding categories because most of them offer something in *every* category (or many of them). They act as one-stop shops for many or most of the things you need and want to know as you start your home business, from financing options to insurance resources to networking contacts in your local area.

Association of Small Business Development Centers (ASBDC), www.asbdc-us.org—This organization offer business plan information and free one-on-one counseling, as well as resources on a wide variety of subjects.

Better Business Bureau, www.bbb.org—Offers information to help you check the reputation of potential clients (if they are also businesses). Membership in the organization is also recommended—it provides you with added credibility, and services, such as informative quarterly newsletters and client conflict resolution services, are well worth the price. The BBB has chapters in most major metropolitan areas.

National Association for the Self Employed, www.nase.org—This membership-based organization offers political advocacy and member benefits such as health and financial programs.

Bureau of Labor Statistics, www.bls.gov—Occupational and labor related data, as well as statistics on economics and related areas, can be found here. A great source of information if you want to know whether your particular business has any "staying power," what the government recommends/considers normal in terms of education for a particular line of work, and so on.

Census Bureau information, www.census.gov/acsd/www/sub_c.htm—This link provides you with an index of Census Bureau information by subject, so you can find just what you need whether you are researching a particular customer base, industry trends, or cost of living.

Dun & Bradstreet, www.dnb.com—Offers member-based services that allow you to verify a client's ability to pay.

FEMA (Federal Emergency Management Agency), www.fema.gov—This is an excellent website that covers disaster preparedness and some security issues. See the many publications the agency offers, including, "Emergency Management Guide for Business & Industry," written by the Federal Emergency Management Agency with the help of the American Red Cross, Building Managers and Owners Association (BOMA), and others. Available at www.fema.gov/library/bizindex.htm.

Hoover's Online, www.hoovers.com—Whether you go the "free" or "subscription" route on this website, you will definitely get quite a bit of information. Subscribers get more in-depth information, and this might be a wise investment for some businesses that need the information. Use it to research companies that might be good potential clients.

HowStuffWorks.com—This website can be useful while doing marketing research—a great way to help you decide whether a need truly exists. It can also help you understand the technology that now surrounds you, as you rely on computers, faxes, printers, phones, copiers, and PDAs more than ever.

SCORE (Senior Core of Retired Executives), www.score.org—This volunteer organization is composed of retired executives who assist existing and startup small businesses. These services are free.

note Both the ASBDC and SCORE are nonprofit organizations, but they are partners of the SBA (Small Business Administration).

Small Business Administration, www.sba.gov—This government agency is charged with supporting smaller businesses, from starting a business to financing. Their programs range from seminars to encourage small businesses to bid on government contracts, to special loans, to providing resources businesses can use throughout their life cycle. Visit your local SBA (Small Business Administration) office, or find it on the Web. State, county, and local development offices might also offer some additional assistance.

For additional help, check the many free publications available from the Small Business Administration. Much of the information can be downloaded from the website, **www.sba.gov/library/pubs.html**. Booklets and other informational pieces include a home business overview, how to determine if you are ready for business, and a wide variety of general and specific business plans. If you do not have Internet access, look up the nearest Small Business Administration (SBA) office in your phone book under the blue pages/government listings section.

State Department, www.state.gov—You might only think of this government department as being important when the United States is at war (or when the U.S. government tells you what countries are unsafe), but it also offers extensive online information about business in foreign countries.

Further Reading

Although this book shows you how to set up your home business in no time, other books might help you with related subjects you'd like to explore in greater depth. From a deep-seated fear of doing what you love to someone who feels forced into business ownership, these books will provide that additional dimension to help you succeed.

Do What You Love, The Money Will Follow: Discovering Your Right Livelihood, by Marsha Sinetar. If you're worried that the title is too "New-Age-y," buy it anyway—and open your mind to the possibilities that are waiting to be realized. (Available on Amazon.com or from your local bookseller.)

The Accidental Entrepreneur: Practical Wisdom for People Who Never Expected to Work for Themselves, by Susan Urquhart-Brown. If you "fell in to" owning your own home business, or felt forced in to it by downsizing, pick up this book by Urquhart-Brown, a career coach and former *San Francisco Chronicle* columnist. It's the perfect read for anyone who read this book *after* they were forced in to (or fell in to) business, and wonder if they did the right thing. (Available from careersteps123.com.)

tip

Don't forget to visit the Que Publishing website (www.quepublishing.com), where you can find many books on technical topics. Learn how to master Excel, divine the secrets of your favorite database program, or produce Word documents faster than ever.

Index

B

S

J-L

journals. *See* **business planning journals**

keeping business records, 106-109

Keness Company Web site, 224

laptops, required mobile technology, 114

lawyers, IP (intellectual property), 52

lead times

accessing readiness, 18

considering, 90

learning curves (heavy workloads), PDF:54-56

legal issues, clearing up (business plans), 38-39

legal resources, 222

legal services, Schedule C, 78

liability insurance, 53, 77

licenses, Schedule C, 80

licensing, accessing readiness, 21

life insurance, 77

Limited Liability Company (LLC), 54

Linux, purchasing, 116

LLC (Limited Liability Company), 54

loans, 93-94

locations, business (business plan), 55-56

logistics assumptions, defining (business plan), 63-64

Logistics section (business plan)

allocated space, 60

budgeting, 73-75

equipment needs, 60-61

geographic areas, 60

vendor relationships, 61

logs, phone, 98-100

long-term illness handling, PDF:5-6

long-term storage, required technology, 114

lost clients calculating costs, PDF:28-29

M

Macintosh, purchasing, 116

mail. *See* **voicemail**

maintaining health, 188-191

maintenance, Schedule C, 80

managing operations (hardware failures), PDF:15, PDF:18

managing money, 191-193

managing time, 182

avoiding conflicts, 186, 189

estimating, 184-185

prioritizing tasks, 184

schedules, managing, 185-186

setting hours, 183-184

transitioning schedules, 188-189

manuals, policy, PDF:27

Maria Poroy (benefits specialist), 40, 221

Rather than having you read through a lot of text, Easy lets you learn visually. Users are introduced to topics of technology, hardware, software, and computers in a friendly, yet motivating, manner.

See it done

Do it yourself

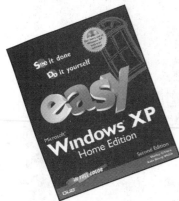

Easy Microsoft Windows XP, Home Edition

Shelley O'Hara, Kate Shoup Welsh
ISBN: 0-7897-3036-7
$19.99 USA/$29.99 CAN

Easy Microsoft Money 2004

Gina Carrillo
ISBN: 0-7897-3070-7
$14.99 USA/$21.99 CAN

Easy Quicken 2004

Sherry Kinkoph
ISBN: 0-7897-3073-1
$14.99 USA/$21.99 CAN

Easy Microsoft Office PowerPoint 2003

Sherry Kinkoph
ISBN: 0-7897-2964-4
$14.99 USA/$21.99 CAN

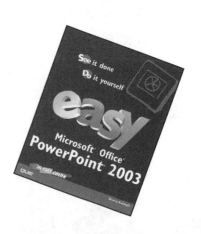

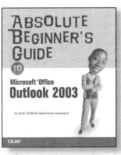

Do Even More
...In No Time

Get ready to cross off those items on your to-do list! *In No Time* helps you tackle the projects that you don't think you have time to finish. With shopping lists and step-by-step instructions, these books get you working toward accomplishing your goals.

Check out these other *In No Time* books, coming soon!

Organize Your Personal Finances In No Time
ISBN: 0-7897-3179-7
$16.95
August 2004

Plan a Fabulous Party In No Time
ISBN: 0-7897-3221-1
$16.95
September 2004

Speak Basic Spanish In No Time
ISBN: 0-7897-3223-8
$16.95
September 2004

Organize Your Garage In No Time
ISBN: 0-7897-3219-X
$16.95
October 2004

Quick Family Meals In No Time
ISBN: 0-7897-3299-8
$16.95
October 2004

Organize Your Family's Schedule In No Time
ISBN: 0-7897-3220-3
$16.95
October 2004